HEIGHTS OF
MADNESS

HEIGHTS OF MADNESS

IN 92 DAYS I WALKED AND CYCLED 5,000 MILES
AND CLIMBED THE HIGHEST PEAK OF EVERY COUNTY IN
THE UK... WHAT WAS I THINKING?

JONNY MUIR

metro

Published by Metro,
an imprint of John Blake Publishing Ltd,
3 Bramber Court, 2 Bramber Road,
London W14 9PB, England

www.johnblakepublishing.co.uk

First published in paperback in 2009

ISBN: 978 1 84454 664 0

British Library Cataloguing-in-Publication Data:

A catalogue record for this book is available from
the British Library.

Design by www.envydesign.co.uk

Printed in Great Britain by CPI Bookmarque, Croydon CR0 4TD

1 3 5 7 9 10 8 6 4 2

Papers used by John Blake Publishing are natural, recyclable products
made from wood grown in sustainable forests. The manufacturing processes
conform to the environmental regulations of the country of origin.

CONTENTS

Four

Five

Six

Seven

Eight

Nine

Ten

Eleven

Twelve

INTRODUCTION

CARN EIGE

The world seemed about to end. Nature was wreaking her revenge. A shrieking storm laced with daggers of icy shrapnel. Ghastly drum beats of thunder as if mountains were cleaving and tumbling. Shadows were moving in, growing darker by the moment. A captive in a mist-obscured prison, my universe had shrunk to no more than five metres in any direction. The sky had succumbed. The valley had vanished. Life on Earth was no more. I was the only one left, a desperate stumbling soul.

An hour earlier, I had been sheltering in the sanctuary of the stone cairn on the 1,183-metre summit of remote Carn Eige, the highest point in the old Scottish county of Ross and Cromarty and the 12th tallest mountain in the UK. Now I was wandering aimlessly east across rock and ridge, willing the devilish furore to hoist me from this perilous perch and end the misery. I was lost, and with every step – if such a thing were possible – becoming ever more lost. The right way led to the west, first over Mam Sodhail, and then down a bealach which would return me to Glen Affric. If it still existed.

Instead, I was ghosting towards oblivion, time passing in a blur. It was five hours, maybe six, since I had left my bicycle on the midge-cursed shores of Loch Affric. They had been dreadful hours, the omens ill from the off. My last human contact had come with a thick-set Scot marshalling a quad bike along a path, which had been flooded by a swollen stream. I stood aside, watching the vehicle approach through the gloom and slanting rain. Hoisted on the rear of the quad bike was an adult stag, slain that day by a stalker's bullet, blood still dripping from its gaping mouth. Gazing into the beast's black eyes, I had shuddered as a wave of anxiety swept over me. It was little wonder nature sought revenge.

Quelling doubts and fears, up the mountain I had gone, in search of the pot of gold – the summit. It didn't matter how, just get there. Sloshing through pools of green slime and brown sludge, fumbling across rolling scree and ankle-jarring rocks, staggering over grassy tussocks and wading through surging streams. Small steps, never pausing, eyes fixed on the ground. Heavy heart, heavy legs.

As I zigzagged up a thin track to the high ridge attaching Ciste Dhubh and Mam Sodhail, the wind lulled for a moment. During this peaceful calm the only sounds were the drip-drip-drip of raindrops on the hood of my waterproof and the distant pounding water of Allt Coire Leachavie. As I stepped on to the exposed ridge, the wind returned, a frantic, furious swirl, hurling icy pins that pricked exposed cheeks and forehead. From that moment till now, the storm had refused to leave. Relentless winds eddied, gyrated and twisted across Mam Sodhail and Carn Eige, at times forcing me to crawl on all fours, clinging to the mountain's bare rock for dear life.

The concentration, the effort, the endurance: I felt I could bear it no longer. Before this interminable struggle, I had already tortured my hollow legs by pedalling 55 miles from Invergordon to Loch Affric. That was on top of the 4,200 miles I had cycled, from Cornwall to Shetland, and the 500 miles I had walked, all in the previous 90 days. The mountains, of course, had no sympathy. To them I was nothing but a 25-year-old scrap of skin and bone daring to breach their defences, millions of years old.

I was so tired, so very tired. Hands and feet were chilled until there was no feeling. My head was light and as thoughts relaxed, my stride became careless and clumsy. The roar of the wind bothered me less. I was calm. I plodded on. My legs were good at that. Just keep going, up or down, round and round, on a hill, on the flat, it didn't matter. Just keep going. But I was lost and losing it, and mountain madness was slowly gripping me. I was howling like a dog, swearing at the sky, jabbering nonsense. Repeating the words of the National Anthem in my head, over and over again, faster and faster, unable to stop, I knew I was in trouble. I had to get off this mountain.

ONE

**A ONE-WAY TICKET TO BODMIN – MY SANLUCAR DE
BARRAMEDA – CLIMBING BROWN WILLY – AN
ALTERCATION WITH A COW – MR TWIT – GIVING UP –
ROAD-KILL – A SWISS SEDUCER – THE MAGICAL 1,000-
FOOT MARK – A BACK GARDEN IN KENT**

DAY 1 – BODMIN TO OKEHAMPTON: 56 MILES
Brown Willy (Cornwall): 420m

Every journey has to start somewhere. Ferdinand
Magellan's circumnavigation of the Earth set sail from
the Spanish port of Sanlucar de Barrameda. South Pole-
bound Roald Amundsen went forth from the Norwegian
capital Oslo. Neil Armstrong's mission to the Moon
blasted off from the Kennedy Space Center.

Somehow Bodmin on a grey and blustery morning in
May lacked that soul-stirring quality. I was on the starting
line in Cornwall, the jagged foot of England that dips a
toe into the Atlantic Ocean. Sitting on the town hall steps,
I looked around for inspiration – something to frame the
moment or simply remind me this wasn't just another
unremarkable happening in infinite time. Wind-blown
chip wrappers tumbled across the road and a pair of
seagulls pecked at the remains. An inquisitive mongrel
sniffing at my bicycle's front wheel was mid-cock when I

shooed him away. Peering through a steamed-up café window, I envied the hungry eaters devouring bacon, egg and beans. Behind them, on a TV in the corner, a weather forecaster pointed animatedly at a black cloud and three blobs of rain parked over the West Country. This was my Sanlucar de Barrameda.

I emptied the meagre contents of my rucksack onto the steps. I had embraced the thinking of the French writer Antoine de Saint-Exupéry, who once declared: 'He who would travel happily must travel light.' In went the essentials: a change of clothes, bar of soap and toothbrush, camera, road map, journal, a well-thumbed copy of Apsley Cherry-Garrard's *The Worst Journey in the World* and a cheese sandwich. What more did I need? Unlike Amundsen, Armstrong and Magellan, I'd be able to nip into the Co-op if I'd forgotten anything.

It was time. There were no cheering crowds or rousing speeches – only one anonymous spandex-clad cyclist setting off on a long journey. Tingling with trepidation and my heart thumping with freedom, I pushed off. Before long, Bodmin was gone in a blur and I was zipping merrily along high-hedged Cornish lanes towards Camelford. Next stop Shetland, the 60th parallel.

It had to be a bicycle journey. How else? I had exhausted the alternatives. Car – too easy. Train – too complicated. Bus – too unpredictable. Helicopter – too expensive. Walking – too long. A bicycle fitted the bill. Here was a mode of transport fast enough to cover a respectable distance each day, but slow enough to absorb the changing sights, smells and sounds of the UK. When tarmac ran out, I would continue on foot. There would be no buses, no trains, no taxis and absolutely no lifts. The result? An entirely self-propelled journey between the highest point in each of the UK's historic counties – the first of its kind. There were 92 counties and 92 summits. It was logical therefore that my journey must take 92 days and no longer.

There was, however, a stick in my spokes. My quest meant I had to reach five islands: Arran, Ireland, Orkney, Hoy and Shetland. To claim a truly self-propelled journey, I would have to swim to each. When Charlie Campbell set a new record for the fastest self-propelled traverse of the 284 Munros – Scottish mountains higher than 914 metres – in 2000, he swam from the mainland to Mull and the Isle of Skye. Campbell completed his feat in 48 days and 12 hours, but his swimming amounted to little more than two miles in relatively sheltered waters. I was faced with a swim across the Irish Sea to Northern Ireland, the Firth of Clyde to Arran, the Pentland Firth to Orkney, across Scapa Flow to Hoy, and 50 miles of ocean between Orkney and Shetland, twice. Aware that the notion of swimming such distances was ludicrous, I accepted that ferries would be a necessary evil.

Today I was bound for Cornwall's highest lump of earth and rock, the saucily named Brown Willy. The hill lies at the lonesome heart of Bodmin Moor, a place famed for its beast and beastly weather. Measuring a meagre 10 miles across, Bodmin Moor's size is in inverse proportion to its sense of isolation and loneliness. Stroll for only a few minutes and you will feel lost in what seems like inescapable wilderness. Nevertheless, Brown Willy is easy to find – it is circled in every schoolboy's atlas. But if you are imagining a phallus-shaped peak, you will be disappointed, for Brown Willy comes from the word Bronewhella, simply but quite appropriately meaning highest hill.

A short way out of Camelford, I followed the whaleback rises of Rough Tor Road until tarmac gave way to moor. Faster than Superman can slip on his suit, I swapped my blue and yellow Argentina cycling jersey for a T-shirt and fleece, pulled trousers over Lycra shorts and trainers replaced cycling cleats. Cyclist to hiker in a seamless transition, and I didn't need a phone box.

To non-Cornish dwellers, Bodmin Moor is synonymous with the legendary Beast of Bodmin, a mysterious creature – a jaguar, lynx, puma or big cat – which allegedly mauls livestock when it's feeling peckish. However, despite massacred sheep, six-inch paw prints and video footage of a yard-long black animal, RAF reserve volunteers who scoured the moor one night in 1999 didn't turn up so much as a lost tabby. I kept an open mind, for Bodmin Moor had a queer air to it – an air that made me throw the odd cursory glance over my shoulder.

Treading a springy path to the granite summit of Rough Tor, I caught my first glimpse of Brown Willy a mile in the distance. In between these two elevated points the land dipped to the De Lank River, a ribbon of water that cuts a channel along the valley floor. Fewer feet trod the moor to the south of Rough Tor and the only other life was a herd of cows grazing lazily near the river. Head down, wading through gorse and balancing on wobbling boulders, I concentrated on keeping my feet. Then, something stole my attention in the distance. Perhaps it was a beast howling from the summit of Brown Willy, blood dripping from its fangs? But for a few seconds, I stopped looking where I was going and it was in those moments that I walked headlong into a cow.

Are cows happy or sad? I find it hard to tell. A cow might have won the lottery, but it would still wear the same doleful expression. That is why cows would make brilliant assassins. As the cow stared at me, I didn't know if it wanted to murder me or lick me. I glanced down. Udders. I took small comfort: at least it wasn't a bull. My thoughts flashed to the extreme survival book I had unwrapped on Christmas morning. How to survive a plane crash? Easy. What to do if Osama Bin Laden moves in next door? Not a problem. How to pacify a herd of cows? I flicked through the pages in my mind. No, I don't remember that one. I must write to the editors. How could they have overlooked it?

Daisy challenged me to a staring contest. First one to blink loses. I lost. Meanwhile, her pals had gathered around, seeking a piece of the action. I was for it. One slipped a knuckle-duster over her hoof, while another made a cut-throat gesture in my direction. Day one: trampled to death by a herd of cows on Bodmin Moor. It wasn't the kind of start I had hoped for. I could see the newspaper headlines: 'Man savaged by cow. Police hunting real beast of Bodmin.' After much foot-stamping, tail-swishing and sporadic urinating, the herd lost interest and resumed their cud chewing. Cautiously backing away to a safe distance, my foot slopped through a pile of steaming cowpat. I'm sure I heard the cows snigger as I scurried down to the river.

Marching up Brown Willy, I passed a sign with an ominous warning: 'The climate is susceptible to rapid change. Dense fog can descend quickly.' The forecast rain must have been held up over the Atlantic, for today the clouds were high in the sky and only a fine haze blocked the panorama to the north and south Cornish coasts. It isn't always this calm. The weather can be so extreme on Bodmin Moor that Brown Willy has a meteorological phenomenon named after it: the Brown Willy effect, which was blamed for the flash floods that wreaked havoc in Boscastle in August 2004.

I was on the summit of 420-metre Brown Willy, home to a stack of granite boulders and an Ordnance Survey triangulation pillar, one of more than 7,000 concrete obelisks built for the benefit of cartographers. All around was a wilderness, an endless vista of brown hillocks, grey granite and yellow and green gorse. Yes, it had been a less than glorious ascent, but I was standing on the roof of Cornwall, punching the air on my first county top.

An hour later, after skirting Crowdy Reservoir and dipping off the high moor, I was in Launceston, where Morris dancers leaped around the streets, flicking handkerchiefs and clanging bells. Clutching a Cornish pasty, I dived into a pub to indulge in an English tradition greater even than Morris dancing. It was FA Cup final day, Liverpool against West Ham.

Inside, it was standing room only and the drinks had been flowing long before 'Abide With Me' rang around the Millennium Stadium. Not being Cornish, I can only speculate that the good men and women of Kernow feel as little affinity with cockneys as they do scousers, yet today the majority of the crowd were cheering for the London club. When West Ham scored twice, pandemonium swept through the bar. A swaying fan – who looked like he'd been on a week-long bender followed by another 20 pints of lager this afternoon – led a constant 'Irons, Irons' chant. Liverpool scored and equalised, before West Ham swept into a 3-2 lead.

All this excitement was thirsty work and as the room became steadily more inebriated, the volume cranked up a notch. In the final minute, Liverpool's Steven Gerrard thumped the kind of goal every schoolboy imagines himself scoring in the playground – a 30-yard screamer into the top corner. The room erupted. The air was a sea of thrashing arms and pumping fists. Fickle Cornishmen who were roaring for West Ham moments earlier were dancing a conga around the room. A roly-poly fellow behind me discovered gymnastic skills he never knew he had, leaping on my shoulders, flinging the contents of his pint glass over my head. Another supporter jumped on the pool table, tugged down his trousers and underwear, and started frantically slapping his bare backside. Ah, the tranquil charms of Cornwall.

Across the Tamar, I swapped Cornwall for Devon and cycled 20 miles to Okehampton in a fine mist that had enveloped Dartmoor. Ten hours after leaving Bodmin, I laboured up the last slope to the town's youth hostel, an old railway building next to the train station. Dumping bicycle and bag, I set off into Okehampton in search of food. A fair was sprawled across Simmons Park, bringing with it a pack of cider-swigging teenagers, who jockeyed each other from across the Okement River and paired off to snog on a bench. Picking at fish and chips under the shelter of a bus stop, I pulled my mobile phone from a pocket and scrolled down to my girlfriend's number. Fi had been as supportive as any long-suffering partner could be. It had helped that I had broken the news of my impending trip on a drunken New Year's Eve. 'I'm going to cycle to the highest point in every county,' I had slurred in her ear.

'Of course you are,' Fi said with a knowing smile. She had heard it all before. Each year, as everyone promises to give up cigarettes and alcohol, I was coming up with some absurd adventure far beyond my means. This year I'll cycle across Mongolia. This year I'll go trekking in the Himalayas. This year I'll climb Mont Blanc. I never did. My enthusiasm tended to last as long as the hangover. But this year had been different. This year was going to be the year.

I had offered Fi the chance to wave me off from Bodmin. She stood me up. Instead, she wished me luck, gently pointed out that it wouldn't be terribly exciting for her, and fled to Scotland. Now her number was ringing. Embellished stories of fending off a heated herd of cows, of clambering across high moors and getting beer thrown over me in Launceston, were on the tip of my tongue. I wanted sympathy for my aching legs, congratulations for my first 56 miles and an ear to listen to my weather whimpers.

'I can't talk,' Fi whispered. 'I'm at the opera.' She hung up.

With the freedom of the open road came the loneliness of the long-distance traveller. Loneliness gave me too much time to think, to ponder, to dwell, and it was nourishing a nagging seed of doubt in my mind. Reality had come home to roost. Ahead were another 91 days and 4,950 miles of effort on my own. I was cyclist, walker, navigator, nutritionist, chef, mechanic, weatherman, motivator, psychologist and bed-booker all rolled into one. The first day had been tough and here I was at the end of it staring morosely at an Okehampton pavement, just thinking, thinking, thinking. It was always the same question. Why am I doing this?

My mental state wasn't helped by my exhausted physical condition. Pedalling uphill for 1,300 metres – just a few shy of Ben Nevis – had taken its toll. My legs were stiff and weary. Although today had been harder than I imagined, far more extreme days lay ahead. Days when it would hammer with rain, winds would fight my every move and thick mist on mountaintops would frighten me to half to death. On the first page of my journal I wrote: 'Totally emotionless. Void of any feelings'. Exultant is how I should have felt. This is what I had dreamed of, what I spent six months of my life obsessing about. Now the gremlin of self-doubt was murmuring in my ear, 'Give up.'

DAY 2 – OKEHAMPTON TO EXFORD: 44 MILES
High Willhays (Devon): 621m
Dunkery Beacon (Somerset): 519m

One of nature's most extraordinary gifts is her power to lift the human spirit, bringing peace to a tortured soul. As I stepped into the morning sunshine, golden rays threw a comforting, warm arm around my sagging shoulders. The shroud of mist that had hidden Dartmoor had vanished in the night, taking the darkness of my mood with it. The world grinned with perfection. The browns and greens of the rolling moor were sharp against the backdrop of a blue sky, and I couldn't wait to be standing on top of those hills looking down.

Dartmoor's 365 square miles of bog and granite were designated as a National Park in 1951, but much of it is used by the Ministry of Defence as a practice ground and firing zone. The 621-metre High Willhays, Devon's loftiest spot, lies in this swathe of land in the park's northwest and is marked as a 'danger area' on maps. Fortunately, it was Ten Tors weekend – an annual challenge involving 2,400 teenagers who carry everything they need to survive for two days and a night on the moor – and the MoD had suspended firing. My route followed a military road and a course through the boggy moor before rising to Yes Tor, a hill that misses out on the title of Devon's summit by a mere two metres. A quarter of a mile further on, I reached High Willhays, an unremarkable rocky outcrop that is the highest slab of land in Devon. Knowing I would not stand this high again in England until the Peak District, I savoured the moment.

A cyclist again, I rode north to Somerset. As Dartmoor vanished behind, Exmoor rose imperiously in front. In my mind, Somerset means Cheddar cheese, Roman baths and a day waiting for the sea to roll in at Weston-super-Mare. Ranges of hills don't spring to mind and Somerset, as seen from a car window on the M5, is frisbee-flat. Yet the county has six notable areas of high ground: Blackdown, Brendon, Mendip, Polden, Quantock and Exmoor, and it is the last of these, to the far west of Somerset, which boasts the highest heights. The tallest of them all, Dunkery Beacon, rises from Exmoor's central ridge.

With a gentle wind on my back, I pedalled along bluebell-decked lanes, following the trickling of the River Taw and then the River Mole. Happy wanderings through Devon lanes were brought to an abrupt halt by a two-mile, thigh-wrenching climb out of North Molton. My reward for struggling up Devon's answer to an alpine pass? I was sent plunging down into a valley, so in a few but glorious seconds, I was back at my original North Molton altitude. Such is the frustration of two-wheeled travel.

Fed up of riding – not a good sign since my journey was only two days old – I left my cycle in Exford and hiked the last four miles to the summit of Dunkery Beacon. A monotonous bridleway gave way to road before I picked up a path that weaved its way to the great cairn on top of the 519-metre beacon. But the views across the Bristol Channel and Porlock, as well as ancient summit cairns dating back 3,000 years, were lost on me. The ripple of adrenaline at the prospect of crossing my third county off the list was replaced by an overwhelming lethargy. I had misjudged the length of the walk, and the thought of the four-mile trudge back to Exford in near-darkness made my eyelids droop.

Famished and fatigued, I stomped into Exford's ivy-clad White Horse Inn, taking a seat opposite a fellow lone diner. What a man he was. With a frame like a wrestler and a grey nailbrush beard, he was half Giant Haystacks, half Father Christmas. Not that I fancied sitting on his knee. I named him Mr Twit.

Mr Twit was shovelling gammon, double-egg and chips into his cavernous mouth at an indigestion-inducing rate, and my appetite drained as I watched yellow yolk drip from his bristles. His plate was nearly empty when he stopped for a moment, initially to draw breath and then to cough. A gentle clearing of his throat this was not. It was a deep, guttural hacking from the depths of his barrel chest, the kind of mucus-rattling echo that makes you screw up your face and go 'eurgh'.

The veins on Mr Twit's face turned a dark shade of purple as he attempted to suppress another splutter. Just as his cheeks looked set to explode another cough lurched from his lips. And then he couldn't stop. The room fell silent. The silence only punctuated by cough after cough after cough. We were watching a man die, gurgling and choking on German gas in a First World War trench. His eyes rolled in their sockets as every breath grew more frantic and seemingly a last attempt to cling onto life. No one did a thing. We just watched, as if we were at the cinema, while Mr Twit clutched his pint of ale without spilling a drop. His fingers were turning white as he held on grimly. Maybe rigor mortis was setting in and he couldn't let go of the glass? Or he thought, If I'm going to die, sweet beer, you're coming to heaven.

Finally it stopped, and somehow he was still alive. Although dazed and puffing like a steam train, Mr Twit's brush with the grim reaper hadn't diminished his appetite. A waiter hovered near him. 'Have you finished, sir?' he asked, making to scoop up the plate. Glaring at the boy, Mr Twit polished off the gammon, used a last chip to mop up tomato ketchup and egg yolk, before draining his beer. With that he was off, spluttering into the Exmoor night.

As I pushed open the door to the hostel dormitory, I was confronted by a wide bottom, wearing a parachute-sized pair of suspiciously stained underpants. The bottom slowly turned around. It was Mr Twit. The room we were forced to share was tiny, with two bunk beds an arm's length apart. Mr Twit had settled on a bottom bunk on the right, while I positioned myself as far away as possible, on the top bunk on the left.

Having stayed in hostels, I had expected to share a room with a person I'd really rather not. However, I thought I had seen, heard and smelt it all: snorers, groaners, farters, tossers and turners, sleepwalkers and sleeptalkers, even the odd sexual shenanigan. Clearly I hadn't. As soon as I entered the room I noticed something about Mr Twit I hadn't in the pub. How can I put this kindly? Actually, I can't. He reeked. It was mouldy sprouts, rotten fish, raw sewage, a year of sweat, all congealed into one festering lump of a human being. How could fate have dealt me such a cruel blow?

Mr Twit peeled off his clothes and I nearly had a nosebleed. How could anyone or anything smell so terrible? The stench hung in the air like fog on a January morning, wafting up my nostrils. How would I survive the night? Lights out. Cue the wretched coughing, but it was a mere warm-up act to the main event – snoring. It was only 11 o'clock, with seven dreadful hours until dawn.

At midnight, my eyes were still wide open, while my

head was perched on the window sill where I could breath the clean Exmoor air and listen to the youthful gurgling of the River Exe. The room was a thunderstorm of body noises. Mr Twit was a human musical instrument, able to create a tune from every orifice. Tears of frustration came. I just wanted to sleep. Please let me sleep! But if I close my eyes, maybe I'll asphyxiate? I don't want to die. Please let me stay awake? At last, sheer tiredness from the day's exertion lulled me to slumber.

It wasn't long until I woke with a jolt. Something was different. The smell still hovered, but the room was silent, dead silent. I peered over the wooden slats of my bunk. There the sorry man lay, flat on his back, looking peaceful but motionless. He's dead, I thought. This time he really is dead. I lay paralysed in my bunk. What do I do? Kiss of life? I retched at the thought. Panic gripped me, but like all those people in the White Horse Inn a few hours earlier, I did nothing. A minute went past and still no sound. Then two, and three. Not a peep. Go and tell someone for pity's sake, I yelled to myself. As I lowered a leg to the floor, he stirred. I looked straight at him and as if in a horror movie, Mr Twit's piggy eyes flashed open for a moment. It would have been at this point in the blockbuster when I would have met a grisly end, but instead, something far worse happened. He let out a loud lingering mega-fart. Then, like an engine revving up, the snoring started again. I preferred him when he was dead.

DAY 3 – EXFORD TO LITTON CHENEY: 79 MILES
Lewesdon Hill (Dorset): 279m

It may sound gruesome, but only a cyclist can understand the devastating death toll on the nation's roads. As we pedal happily along, our eyes focused on the rising and falling tarmac ahead, the carnage of beheaded corpses, mutilated bodies and dismembered limbs surrounds us. Road-kill is alarmingly abundant on rural roads; few more so than the twisting 25-mile stretch between Exford and Tiverton, where little bodies littered the carriageway. To motorists, these are nothing but bumps in the road, a smear of grey and red blotting the black surface. But to cyclists who glimpse the bulging eyes and unravelled intestines, witness the final twitches and sniff the stench of rotting flesh, each death is a mini-tragedy, another wasted life.

But let's not get overly sentimental, because road-kill is a useful indicator of what creatures inhabit our island and in what numbers. Using the children's I-Spy spotter guides as a model, I devised my own points classification based on how unusual I deemed each sighting.

- Rabbit – 5 points. The very reason rabbits breed like rabbits. Their road-kill numbers are so high that in some parts of Somerset road surfaces are half-tarmac, half bunny.
- Squirrel – 10 points. Quick, but unfortunately, not always quick enough.
- Bird – 10 points. You could say it serves them right because they are normally feasting on road-kill. Still, as the saying goes, two wrongs don't make a right.

- Hedgehog – 15 points. Double points for a flattened one. Lack of pace lets them down.
- Fox – 20 points. For all their cunning, they really should know better.
- Badger – 25 points. Very smelly. On a par with Mr Twit.
- Stoat or weasel – 25 points. Double points if you can actually tell the difference.
- Deer – 50 points. Along with badgers, the saddest sight of all. Can cause serious damage to cars and occupants.
- Otter – 100 points. You would feel guilty if you killed an otter. Think of Tarka. It's probably one of his cousins.
- Wolf – 1,000 points. Rare, and in the UK, a miracle.
- Elephant – 1,000,000 points. Unlikely. Unless you are in Africa or India. Still unlikely. Car versus elephant – elephant would win, every time.

There is a Cornishman who holds road-kill in the regard most people would their local chip shop or curry house. 'Just popping out to get a bite to eat,' the peckish man tells his wife. Tearing down a country lane, headlights on full beam, he spots a dazzled victim. A thud. Daddy's bringing home the bacon.

OK, maybe he doesn't actually kill the animals himself, but should the practice of collecting road-kill to eat be seen as so peculiar? It's free. It's fresh. It's organic. And it's no different to early man having to hunt for his food, except for the messy slaughtering bit.

'What did you get?' his wife calls down the stairs.

'Well, I was on my way to Tesco when I saw....'

'Don't tell me. What have you found this time? A rattlesnake? A polar bear? A duckbilled platypus?'

'No, better than that. I've got some lovely weasel thighs. Thought I'd marinate them in a red squirrel sauce. Delicious.'

Galloping through Tiverton, Cullompton and Honiton, England's crinkles were slowly being ironed out, heralding an end to rollercoaster roads of punishing ups and breakneck downs. Not long after Axminster the rain stopped, only to be replaced by a pea-soup sea mist wafting northwards from the English Channel for the afternoon shift.

An inability to plan beyond the first 48 hours of my journey meant I reached Dorset with doubts over the identity of this county's summit. As this was the whole point of my coming here, it represented a significant spanner in the works. There were two contenders, Pilsdon Pen and Lewesdon Hill, neighbours overlooking Marshland Vale but separated by two miles of countryside. I'd have to climb both of these short stumpy hills to be sure I'd definitely reached the highest place in Dorset.

Under a blanket of heavy mist, I scaled Pilsdon Pen, the site of a Roman fort where four bewildered sheep stood sentry at the top. Ten minutes later, I was following the muddy trail of the Wessex Ridgeway as it climbed steadily through bluebell woods. The summit of Lewesdon Hill lay hidden among trees, marked only by a distinctive green National Trust sign. At 279 metres above sea level, I was standing on the roof of Dorset, two whole metres higher than Pilsdon Pen.

Wandering back down the slope to my bicycle, I mulled over the options for dinner that night. I could stop at a supermarket in Bridport, or – and here's an idea – I could follow the road back towards Pilsdon Pen where I had spied a road-kill fox earlier. Skin it, fry it, add garlic, onion and a sprig of parsley. Serve with chips and voila! A rustle from the undergrowth interrupted my thoughts. A golden Labrador, usually the most genial of God's creatures, pounced on me, doing its best Rottweiler impression. Why was the animal kingdom turning against me – first cows and now a dog? I picked up a stick and tossed it down the slope.

'Fetch,' I commanded rather meekly.

It watched in disgust as the twig disappeared into bushes before turning back to show me a mouthful of shiny pearlers.

'Listen up,' I barked. 'I'm hungry and I'm not afraid to kill. I'll have you for dinner if you're not careful.'

Muttley was thinking the same.

'Maisie!' came a cry from the woods. 'Maisie!'

As the dog's owner ambled towards us, Maisie turned into a loveable, fluffy, tail-wagging canine. Maisie? How could I be scared of anything called Maisie?

I decided against the fox and pedalled to shelter in Litton Cheney, a Dorset village six miles east of Bridport. Later, as muck from my legs turned the shower water brown, I mused on the day's events. Hours of rain: six. Hours of mist: two. Hours of sunshine: minus one. Asked if I was from Argentina: three occasions. KitKat Chunkies consumed: four. Encounters with savage beasts: one. Dead animal count: 467, plus several million rabbits. Distance covered: 78 miles, my longest day yet. In three days, I had travelled nearly 200 miles across four counties. There was still the small matter of 89 days to go. If I kept rushing at this hectic pace, I knew my legs would wilt long before I crossed the border into Scotland. With that in mind, I vowed to take it easy the next day.

DAY 4 – LITTON CHENEY TO SALISBURY: 60 MILES

And so I did. I took a day off from walking across hills and put on my tourist cap. Without wanting to blow the trumpet of Dorset's tourist board, the county was a vision of loveliness and deserved perusal.

After swooping down Wears Hill, every signpost goaded me towards Abbotsbury Swannery. Instead, I made a beeline for the seaside, a misty Chesil Bank. Here really is a wonder of nature: a 15-metre high, 15-mile long bulwark that is part of a 95-mile length of coastline, granted World Heritage status because of its complete record of Triassic, Jurassic and Cretaceous rocks. If I were a smuggler, I'd have been able to pinpoint precisely where I was on the beach just by the size of the pebbles. Where I stood – roughly at the centre of Chesil Bank – the rocks were smoothly rounded marbles. Go west, towards West Bay, and they become pea-sized gravel. Bear east to Portland Bill and they turn into tennis-ball-sized cobbles.

Dorset is famed for its two Thomas Hardys, the war-hero and the writer. From Portesham, I cycled up to Black Down, where the 22-metre Hardy's Monument stands proudly over Lyme Bay. It was erected as a memorial to Rear Admiral Sir Thomas Masterman Hardy, the flag-captain of HMS *Victory* at the Battle of Trafalgar in 1805.

It was to this man that a dying Lord Nelson uttered the immortal words: 'Kiss me, Hardy.'

After whiling away an hour in Dorchester waiting for a storm to blow itself out, I pedalled towards Higher Bockhampton, the home of the 19th-century author who created Wessex. It was in a cottage in the woods above the village that Thomas Hardy entered the world in 1840, penning *Far From the Madding Crowd* there 33 years later.

Half a dozen miles on, I was sheltering again, this time under a wooden bus stop in Tolpuddle. Workmen were digging up the road, but as thunder crashed overhead they downed tools and sat in a white van leafing through yesterday's tabloids. Were we in 1831, these work-shy slackers would have been sent to Dorchester and suitably punished. Tolpuddle is the home of the Tolpuddle Martyrs, 18th-century farm labourers who enraged their employer by having the nerve to ask for a pay rise. Their employer refused and the labourers were marched seven miles to Dorchester where they were sentenced to seven years transportation.

A day without a hill to climb is a suitable juncture for me to explain an essential aspect of my journey. On the eve of my trip, England, Scotland, Wales and Northern Ireland were divided into 162 administrative areas. The traditional notion of counties has long gone. Nowadays, our land is split into a confusing hotchpotch of unitary authorities, metropolitan counties and administrative districts. An expedition to the summit of each of these 162 areas would be a daunting, but largely meaningless venture. Such a journey would take the adventurer to the

11-metre roof of Kingston-upon-Hull and the giddy 30-metre summit of Warbreck Reservoir in Blackpool. They weren't enticing prospects. And the chances are that once you complete the list of 162, there will be a newly formed batch of 'counties', instantly making the original journey out of date. So I had decided to step back in time to a period when the UK's four nations were simply split into 91 counties, and for my own amusement, added a 92nd top – Hampstead Heath, the summit of London's 13 inner boroughs.

Many of these historic counties existed for centuries, from the Middle Ages to the age of Prime Minister James Callaghan, shaping the UK's cultural and geographical identity. In the 1970s, politicians trampled over nearly a millennium of tradition and tore up the map. They shifted boundaries, scrapped some counties and created new ones. It was a watershed moment and numerous changes followed and, unfortunately, continue to follow. However, the ancient counties were never formally abolished, so although their boundaries may no longer be marked on maps, they live on.

Without getting bogged down in the quagmire of local government changes, let me compare the 1974 map of the UK to that of 2006. In England, gone are the famous old counties of Cumberland, Westmorland and Huntingdonshire, while the Lakeland county of Cumbria has come into being. In between those years, Rutland disappeared and then returned, while Herefordshire and Worcestershire joined up before parting again. The central Welsh corridor of Brecknockshire, Montgomeryshire and Radnorshire is today Powys, while Caernarfonshire and

Merionethshire in the north are known as Gwynedd. In Scotland, the shires of Berwick, Peebles, Roxburgh and Selkirk are lumped into Borders. Meanwhile, Caithness and Sutherland in the far north have been joined to the expanses of Inverness-shire and Ross and Cromarty, plus Nairnshire in the east, to make up the vast Highland region. And the wonderful old names of Dumfriesshire, Kirkcudbrightshire and Wigtownshire have become one as part of Dumfries and Galloway.

All is not lost. Think of the 20 teams that play in English county cricket, the likes of Derbyshire, Essex, Lancashire, Somerset and Yorkshire. All those counties still exist with their boundaries more or less intact. In Wales, Anglesey, Cardiganshire, Carmarthenshire, Denbighshire (albeit it encroached by the new county of Wrexham), Flintshire and Pembrokeshire have survived. As for Scotland, the sprawling island communities of Shetland and Orkney have always proudly stood alone, while Aberdeenshire, Argyll, the three Lothians and Moray are familiar names from yesteryear. In Northern Ireland, 26 districts may have replaced the six traditional counties, but five of those old names – Antrim, Armagh, Derry, Down and Fermanagh – form some of today's districts.

Braving the wet, I vowed not to stop again, come hell or high water, until I reached the day's end in Salisbury. Water came at me from every direction. Face-stinging diagonal drops from the sky, a shower of oil and grime flung my way by overtaking cars and a constant spray up my back. Soaked to the skin, my toes and fingers were numb, while snot streamed from my nose like a tap. All the while, water seeped through every crevice in my bag, drenching my only dry clothes. As I spied the spire of Salisbury Cathedral, my phone rang. It was my mum.

'Are you having a good time?' she asked cheerfully.

DAY 5 – SALISBURY TO HOLMBURY ST MARY: 81 MILES
Blackdown Hill (Sussex): 280m

The West Country was now a fading memory. Ahead was suburbia, with London beyond. Cycling due east, counties disappeared behind me, first Wiltshire and then Hampshire, before I slipped across the Sussex border near Petersfield. My next county top was Blackdown Hill, a low plateau in the North Downs, midway between Haslemere and Fernhurst. Leaving my wheels in a car park close to Aldworth, the former home of the poet Sir Alfred Tennyson, I soon found the hill's low summit, a triangulation pillar at the centre of a dripping glade.

These were quieter times in the history of Blackdown, a place that became etched on the national psyche after an Iberia Airlines jet crashed on the hill's southern slopes on 4 November 1967. All 37 people on board the flight from Malaga died when the aircraft clipped treetops before skidding around 400 yards in the dirt. Following an air accident investigation, the only assumption that could reasonably be drawn was that the plane must have been flying too low, possibly because a reading on an altimeter had been incorrectly noted. There had been only light drizzle in the air and the jet was on the correct flight path for Heathrow.

That evening I cruised along lush Surrey lanes, more Scottish than suburban, and a rutted track led me to a hostel on the outskirts of Holmbury St Mary. Inside the building, a group of around 25 Swiss men, none of them older than 21, were slouched in front of a TV watching Arsenal versus Barcelona in the Champions League final. The hostel warden informed me the party were trainee architects from Bern and were here in soggy Surrey to study building design. I laughed to myself. If the next generation of Swiss architects modelled their ideas on London's commuter belt, I felt sorry for the Alps.

At full time, with Arsenal beaten, the group trooped outside and lit up cigarettes. It was raining hard and the sky was inky black, even though we were so close to the bright lights of London. After I'd stepped into the open myself – for a breath of fresh air – one of the Swiss introduced himself. Otto had bleached blond hair and a 1980s England scarf wrapped tightly around his neck. I'd noticed him staring at me from time to time during the game, seemingly trying to catch my attention before looking away nervously.

'So, you are bicycling, ja?' he asked.

I explained my trip to the confused Swiss.

'But, zese hills, zey are so small.'

I could see his point. The English revere their little hills, but to an Swiss who has grown up with an Alp in his backyard, they must seem like insignificant pimples.

'You know ze bicycle is vewy vewy good in Svitzerland. Zere are lots of hills to vide your bike.'

24

He moved closer, just an inch or two, but too close for comfort. Near enough for me to smell the cigarette smoke on his breath and the aftershave he had splashed on that morning.

'You know,' he continued. 'You should come to Bern. You phone me, ja? I vill give you my number. Ve vill have lots of fun.'

He winked at me.

Nein danke. I did not like this amorous Swiss' idea of fun.

DAY 6 – HOLMBURY ST MARY TO CAMBERWELL: 54 MILES
Leith Hill (Surrey): 294m
Betsom's Hill (Kent): 251m

Lewesdon Hill and Blackdown Hill are off the beaten track, places people haven't heard off. They are left alone, because apart from being the highest point in their respective counties, they are quite indistinguishable from any other hillock in the south of England. Not so Surrey's county top, Leith Hill. This landmark is the highest point in southeast England (unless pernickety people want to count Walbury Hill in Berkshire) and is topped by a spectacular Gothic tower.

A short way north of Holmbury St Mary, I locked my cycle to a wooden post in Starveall Corner car park, where a sign pointing to Leith Hill indicated 'easy path'. The hill had become an unlikely venue for all-night raves and Surrey police had plastered warning signs around the muddy parking area. Some 1,150 years earlier, long before moshing, pill popping and other unseemly happenings at raves, Leith Hill summit had been the scene of a fierce battle when the Anglo Saxons, led by Ethelwulf, vanquished the invading Danes. Thousands of men fought on each side and 'rivers of blood' were to said to have run down the hill. And we kick up a fuss about the odd rave?

Leith Hill is 294 metres or 965 feet high. The fact that it was 35 feet shy of the magical 1,000-foot mark got right up the nose of Richard Hull, an 18th-century squire who lived at nearby Leith Hill Place. And then it came to him, his eureka moment. Why not build a tower on its summit that would raise the height above 1,000 feet? By 1765, his grand ambition had been fulfilled in the shape of a 60-foot tower, with a view from the top that extended to the English Channel, St Paul's Cathedral and across 13 southern counties. Hull was so taken with his creation that he demanded to be buried beneath it when he died. Legend says he was interned head facing down, so when Judgement Day arrived and the world was turned upside down, Hull would meet his Maker the right way up.

A turret was added in 1864 so people could access the top of the tower, but with Hull gone, it fell into disrepair and rubble blocked the entrance. It wasn't until the 1980s, when the National Trust stepped in, that the building was properly restored.

I raced around the perimeter of London, through the Surrey towns of Dorking, Reigate and Oxted, before reaching Kent, the so-called Garden of England. Kent's top lies between Westerham and Biggin Hill, on the county's western reaches. Under the M25 I went and churned up Betsom's Hill, darting right at the brow onto the North Downs Way. Then, on foot, I followed a steep muddy path around the edge of a large garden, but the track soon levelled off and led onto a road named Chestnut Avenue. I was clearly lost.

Ideally, I would have carried a map of every hill or mountain on my list, but I had deemed this too heavy and too expensive. Instead my research had extended to one panicked afternoon in my hometown library in Bromsgrove, photocopying bits of map that I thought might help me on my way. Some maps were out on loan and when the photocopier jammed I lost my temper and called off the trip for the umpteenth time. When the red mist had settled I told myself navigation was the least of my worries. After all, I just had to head to the highest point. What could be simpler?

It was, with a benefit of hindsight, a foolhardy assumption. Where was the sign saying 'easy path' now? The land to my right sloped upwards but a high fence blocked my progress. With little option, I continued along Chestnut Avenue until I reached a garden centre. Convinced Kent's highest point must be in its grounds, I walked purposefully through rows of shrubs and conifers. Again a fence halted my progress. I poured out my troubles to an assistant, who stared at me with wide eyes.

'You're off your rocker mate,' he said slowly. 'You won't find it here. Now if you don't mind,' he added, nodding towards the exit.

Growing ever more frustrated, I slunk along the grass verge of the A233 to a house named Westerham Heights.

Perhaps this was it? Not convinced, I left the road and dived into a wood. After wading through an abandoned Christmas tree plantation, I passed a battered horsebox and clumps of stinging nettles before dragging myself through a hedge and onto a nameless lane. On the verge of admitting defeat, I knocked on the door of the first house I came to and watched through the frosted glass as a figure scurried to open up.

A man with white hair and a red face now peered at me. 'Yes?'

As a journalist, I was used to knocking on the doors of strangers and asking questions they didn't want to answer. 'I know this might sound like a strange thing to say, but I'm looking for the highest point in Kent. I've been walking around for ages and I know I must be close, but...'

He cut me off mid-ramble. 'I'll show you. Let me get my coat.'

John led me down his driveway, up a little bank and past a row of stables into his back garden. Barely 50 steps from his front door, he stopped and pointed. 'Just there,' he said. 'Between those two conifers. That's the highest point in Kent.'

It was an unassuming spot. The summit of the ancient Kingdom of Kent, England's gateway county of white cliffs, castles and cathedrals, was a humble patch of grass between two trees. A few yards away chickens clucked in a cage. A Union flag hoisted on a pole flapped madly in the breeze. In the distance, an aeroplane circled Gatwick Airport. The soundtrack to all this was the incessant hum of the M25. What was I expecting? Some Leith Tower-style monument screaming, 'You're at the top of Kent'? John sensed my disappointment.

'Sorry it's not more interesting.'

'No, it's great,' I enthused. 'Not what I expected, but great.'

My guide pointed a finger to the southeast, where we could make out the silhouette of another hill rising through the mist.

'That's Ide Hill,' he explained. 'People say it's higher than here. Sometimes it even looks like it is, but it's not.'

The land between Betsom's Hill and Ide Hill offered a snapshot of history, reminding me of the words regularly trotted out by a geography teacher: 'A picture paints a thousand words.' Not far from our feet was the Pilgrim's Way, a track dating back to 500BC and the supposed route taken by pilgrims to the shrine of Thomas Becket in Canterbury. Centuries had passed and wars had been fought, but this corner of Kent remained green and pleasant. Then the motor car was invented. The A25 follows many of the early dirt roads dating back to the 18th century, but as the car became king, something bigger and better was needed. So, in the 1980s, along came the M25. What would the pilgrims have made of this monstrosity?

Turning back to the conifers, John said: 'I think I might have the most interesting garden in Kent. If it's not walkers, it's history buffs. There was a fort here once, one of a dozen that stretched across the Surrey Hills to protect against French invasion in the 1860s. The fort is long gone, but people come up here now and again looking for buried treasure I suppose. Other than that, it's you walkers that seem to turn up. Most of them are lost, mind you, and are searching for the North Downs Way. A Christian group asked if they could come here one Easter. I said it was fine, but I never saw them again.'

I didn't feel disappointed any more. Kent's county top was all the better for keeping itself to itself. I felt exhilarated to step where few have trodden and, when challenged, to have not given up. For the first time I realised it wasn't what I found, but how I came to the find. That, I decided, was the true wonder of travelling through the UK. In six days, I had reached the roof of seven English counties and pedalled 375 miles. London was upon me, the symbolic end to the first leg of my journey.

TWO

A NEEDLESS VISIT – ESCAPING LONDON – THE
WETTEST MAY FOR 27 YEARS – THE MYSTERY OF
DESERTED DUNSTABLE – PUNCTURES AND POWER
STATIONS – A GUARDIAN BRUMMIE – FLYING OVER THE
HANDLEBARS – ALIENS IN WILTSHIRE – YET MORE
RAIN – LOSING MY TEMPER

DAY 7 – CAMBERWELL TO CHISWICK: 36 MILES
Magpie Hall Road (Middlesex): 151m

Isn't the British obsession with weather curious? Our
sheltered shores escape the brunt of hurricanes,
monsoons, storm surges and tsunamis, and unless you
happen to live on top of a mountain, there are rarely
enough flakes to roll a snowball. A cold snap and the
occasional sunny afternoon are about as much
excitement as Britons can expect. Real weather only
happens in faraway lands: searing droughts that spark
forest fires, tremendous hurricanes that lash coasts and
flood entire cities, days of incessant rain that trigger
devastating mudslides... That is what you call weather –
moments when nature flashes her teeth in a show of
force. Moments like that just don't happen in
Basingstoke. So why the obsession with non-weather?

Two centuries ago, Dr Johnson commented that 'when
two Englishmen meet, their first talk is of the weather.'

31

Since he uttered those words, the Industrial Revolution has been and gone, and the aeroplane has replaced the horse and cart, but when it comes to the weather, nothing has changed. Our weather is meek and mild, yet it is so wonderfully temperamental that it seems always to take us by surprise, and every time we get some, it sends us spinning into a good old British panic. Rivers burst their banks after a day of rain. A flicker of sunshine brings a hose pipe ban. An inch of snow leads to chaos on the roads. A tornado that causes a chimney pot or two to tumble makes front-page headlines for a week. A warm October means the ice caps are melting and we're all doomed. Who needs a hurricane when it's bit blowy?

I'm afraid to say my personal obsession with the weather centred around rather selfish motives, for what came from the sky had the power to make my journey either merry or misery. A life in the open air left me at the mercy of the elements. When it rained I got wet. When the sun shone I would burn. When the wind blew the going got tough. Suddenly my ear was glued to a radio waiting for the forecast. I was comparing wind speeds in different newspapers and religiously scrutinising the outlook for the days ahead. Each morning, before flinging open the curtains, I would repeat a silent prayer: Let the sun shine. Keep the rain away. Let the wind be light. But as sure as it will rain on August Bank Holiday, you can never trust the beast that is the UK's weather.

I was now in London, Camberwell to be precise. My clothes were spinning in the washing machine, getting their first and urgently needed clean. *Big Brother* was on TV with another collection of oddities: Pete the Tourette's

Syndrome sufferer, Shabaz the gay Glaswegian and Imogen the Welsh beauty queen. It was my first night away from a hostel and I was staying with Tom, a friend from my time at university in Preston. In those intoxicating days of freedom, we would bunk off lectures and drive to the Lake District or Pennines. A walk up Scafell Pike would turn into a run up Scafell Pike, before escalating into a full-scale night time assault on the mountain. As the bar was raised, we were cycling over 2,500-metre alpine passes, running a marathon in Paris and scrambling to the rim of Mount Etna. Staying in a house was dangerous: creature comforts on tap, the lure of the remote control and the reassurance of the biscuit tin. I knew I had to leave before I settled, so in the early morning drizzle I was off, embroiled in London's traffic on the north bank of the Thames.

The highest point in Middlesex is in the north London suburb of Bushey Heath, within earshot of the M1 and not far from Watford. HG Wells liked Bushey Heath so much that in *The War of the Worlds* he made the town the fourth target of ten missiles that hit Earth. A glance at a London A to Z revealed the very top of Middlesex lay in an ominously empty white oblong, and it was that oblong I made for.

The fume and dust-filled air of the English capital was the least of my worries, for to cycle in London is to dice with death. Cars, cabs, lorries, buses, motorcycles and bicycles, even pedestrians with a death wish were competing for the same inch of road space, each believing their claim was superior. And cyclists? We are at the bottom of the food chain, the amoeba of the road.

In Kensington Road, a man in a black 4x4 Chelsea tractor swung across my path. I could have been a class of school pupils, a sisterhood of nuns, his wife and children. It didn't matter who blocked his road. He wasn't stopping for anyone. I launched a furious tirade of obscenities, which involved placing his bull bars somewhere other than the front of his tank. He didn't bat an eyelid. Nonchalantly, he waved me out of the way and drove on.

There is no secret to riding a bicycle in London. They – insert motorised modes of transport as applicable – either haven't seen you, meaning you will definitely die, or they have seen you, meaning you will probably die. As you can gather, I didn't like London cycling much. Harlesden, Willesden and Neasden merged into one confusing urban jungle. Red traffic lights meant constant stop-starts and a wrong turn nearly sent me pedalling up the M1 slip road to oblivion.

Surviving the labyrinth, I arrived at the supposedly empty white oblong, only to discover the area was not as vacant as I imagined. The oblong was ringed by a high metal fence with warning signs barking, 'private property'. The land belonged to Three Valleys Water, the largest water-only supplier in the UK. I stood outside the company's metal gates for some time, plucking up the courage to press the intercom.

'Can I help you?' a voice crackled.

'This might sound a little unusual,' I explained. 'But I am trying to visit the highest point in every county, and I think the highest point in Middlesex... well, I'm pretty sure it is... on your land.'

Silence. She was probably alerting security. There's a madman outside the gates. Unleash the dogs.

Another crackle: 'OK, what do you expect us to do? I'm not sure if you'll be able to come on to the site. I'll have to check it with my manager.'

A longer silence.

'Someone will come out to meet you.'

A buzz and the barriers clanked open. A manager greeted me with a firm handshake and sceptical smile, but with a little coaxing he was soon escorting me to the top reservoir. 'I've never heard anything like it,' he said, shaking his head. 'No photos though. Security reasons.'

It had already been a wet May, but Three Valleys Water had just enforced a hosepipe ban on their customers.

'I know what everyone is saying,' he said, as we strolled through the complex. 'But it would take six months of constant rain to fill London's aquifers. They're empty.'

We walked up a flight of concrete steps and emerged onto the dead-flat surface of a covered reservoir. 'Not much to see I'm afraid,' he said.

'That's true,' I agreed. 'At least I've been here. That's what counts.'

Or perhaps not. I had made an error. The reservoir couldn't possibly be the highest point in Middlesex – because it's not actually in Middlesex. Bushey Heath is a Hertfordshire town, and the water company's campus lies wholly within that county. Long before baffling Three Valleys Water, I had inadvertently reached the highest point of Middlesex in cycling along Magpie Hall Road, a street that straddles the county border on the southern fringe of Bushey Heath.

I cycled back towards London, this time to Chiswick in the west, where I was staying with Rich and Kate, two friends from my school days. Rich had graduated from one of London's top drama academies, but was still waiting for his big break. Like many actors, working at a restaurant paid the bills. We reminisced for an hour before Rich glanced at his watch and realised it was time he was catching the underground to Greenwich. There he was performing in a play where the cast outnumbered the audience. And there were only six in the cast.

Kate came home to find me camped on her sofa, flicking through a million TV channels, mug of tea in one hand, chocolate digestive in the other. After I'd hauled myself off the sofa, we relocated to the pub. Surrounded by air-kissing city workers boasting about their latest skiing trip to Val d'Isère, I sensed I stuck out like a sore thumb. It was hardly surprising. With a limited wardrobe, I had taken on a demeanour grubbier than a flasher in a trench coat, complemented by a distinct part-soap, part-sheep-turd whiff. Still, I wouldn't have swapped places with any of them.

DAY 8 – CHISWICK TO SAFFRON WALDEN: 76 MILES
Hampstead Heath (London): 134m
Great Chishill (Cambridgeshire): 146m
Chrishall Common (Essex): 147m

The morning skies were leaden. Looking up at rain-heavy clouds, I felt they were counting down to the moment I emerged into the open air before turning on the taps.

Over breakfast, Kate enthused about my trip. How exciting that I was spending the summer travelling across the UK by bicycle, a free spirit with a new horizon unravelling before my eyes each day. What an intrepid explorer I was! And didn't Kate wish she could pack it all in and set off on her own adventure. I forced a smile, but the prospect of cycling 70-odd miles in pursuit of a miserable hilltop made me want to weep. Couldn't I just stay in your lovely London flat and keep the sofa warm? As I slipped away from Chiswick, the clouds hurled a consignment of hail at me.

A flagpole on Spaniards Road as it crosses Hampstead Heath near enough marks the 134-metre summit of London's inner boroughs. It was the only county top I chose not to linger on, simply riding straight past, such was my desperation to escape London's endless urban sprawl. A hideous two hours followed. Wrong turns. Dead ends. Traffic lights. Speed bumps. Potholes. Diversions. Roundabouts. Bendy buses. Another dual carriageway. I passed through Highgate, Tottenham, Higham Hill, Walthamstow and Woodford, until I didn't know where I was any more.

'You're in Chigwell, my darlin',' cackled an old woman, when I asked the question. 'This is Essex.'

My intention was to cycle across Essex until I reached landlocked Cambridgeshire, a county that shares its border with eight others. I'd been told many times that Cambridgeshire's highest point must be the Gog Magog Hills, a series of bumps that provide the backdrop to Cambridge.

'No, it's not,' I'd say.

'Are you sure?' they'd retort with a puzzled expression.
'Quite sure. The highest point is Great Chishill.'
'Where?'
'Great Chishill.'
'Never heard of it.'

Granted, it is easy to miss Great Chishill. Perched on Cambridgeshire's southern lip and lying five miles east of Royston, the village is just another name on a map. It was part of Essex until 1895 when the boundaries were redrawn, with Great Chishill moving to its present county, even though the village uses the postcode for Stevenage, a Hertfordshire town. On the southern edge of Great Chishill, a rutted track off the main road leads along the perimeter of a farmer's field to another fenced-off covered reservoir, coincidentally operated by Three Valleys Water. There was no mistake this time, for it was here that I found Cambridgeshire's giddy 146-metre summit.

My brief encounter with Cambridgeshire ended as I pedalled back across the Essex border. Only a mile due south of Great Chishill, I left my bicycle next to a clutch of cottages in a tiny place named Building End and walked for 20 minutes through fields of gloopy mud. Standing a solitary metre higher than Cambridgeshire, the highest point in Essex doesn't appear to have a name so for argument's sake let's christen it Chrishall Common, after an area of grassland close by. Like Kent, Essex doesn't jump up and down about its county top. All I found was an unmarked summit in a field of calf-tickling grass.

DAY 9 – SAFFRON WALDEN TO JORDANS: 87 MILES
Dunstable Downs (Bedfordshire): 243m
Pavis Wood (Hertfordshire): 244m
Haddington Hill (Buckinghamshire): 267m

As I rolled over the Hertfordshire border – an invisible line midway between Starlings Green and Brent Pelham – the heavens opened. Stevenage, Hitchin and Luton drifted past in a rain-soaked blur before I reached deserted Dunstable, where my mileometer ticked over to 500 miles. The main street was empty, the shops were shut and only the occasional swoosh of a car on wet road broke the silence. Eventually I tracked everyone down. They were sheltering in Asda, tucking into sausage sandwiches.

After five trance-like minutes under a hand-drier, I emerged from the gents and ordered the obligatory sausage sandwich and mug of tea, then took a seat in the café to question my sanity. It didn't seem to matter if I was heading north, south, east or west, up or down – I could feel the desire to continue my journey seep from me with every drop of rain and every breath of wind. Why was I putting myself through such misery when I had a choice not to? For the moment, I tossed the doubts to the back of my mind and got back in the saddle.

The Dunstable Downs mark the northeastern reach of the Chiltern Hills, a line of low-lying lumps which stretch diagonally across the Home Counties. The roof of Bedfordshire lay half a dozen steps from the road over the Downs to Whipsnade. This was my 12th county top and already I had a well-rehearsed routine of taking a photograph – a memento of sorts – at each summit. I would look through the viewfinder and position the camera before setting the countdown timer. Then I would scurry into shot and perfect the faraway look. Wait. Has it taken yet? Step forward. Flash. Damn. Moved too soon. Check the picture. The top of my head is cut off and I'm wearing a perplexed expression. Try again. This time I'm blinking. Again.

Like all my belongings, my camera was damp, meaning it took an eternity to switch on. After ten minutes of button pressing until my finger ached, the blasted thing finally sprung into life. Positioning it carefully on the triangulation pillar, I set the timer and retreated several yards while it counted down. Four, three, two... whoosh. A gust of wind swept the camera off its perch, depositing it in the dripping grass below, where it switched itself off. After another five minutes of furious pressing, I managed to get the camera working again. Holding it at arm's length, I took a snap of my cross face. I was blinking.

That accomplished, I cycled downhill to the National Trust visitor centre, where even on the soggiest of afternoons the car park was lined with vehicles. Behind steamy windows people slept off roast beef and Yorkshire pudding and scanned the Sunday papers. Occasionally a brave soul emerged from a car and dashed to the café for another round of coffees. The hardiest pulled on waterproofs and dragged out a reluctant dog for a five-minute stretch of the legs.

'You've come on a bad day,' the woman in the visitor centre told me. 'On a clear day you can see for 40 miles across the Vale of Aylesbury.' But mist had descended and I couldn't see the other side of the car park.

On the road to Ivinghoe, the wind came at me in fantastic gusts, threatening to blow me clean me off my mount. Cursing every moment, I rode on grimly. Mother Nature was angry and she was having a tantrum. Although it seemed a black cloud was hovering permanently overhead, much of Britain was being buffeted by bizarre May weather. The Scottish Highlands were shivering in near-freezing temperatures, rain was deluging the Chelsea Flower Show and twice the monthly average was falling in East Anglia and Wales. It was rotten fortune that I was cycling through the wettest May in my lifetime.

I kept the chalk hills of the Chilterns on my left shoulder until I reached Tring, where I turned to face them. A flooded country lane wandered from the outskirts of the town and petered out into a muddy path. I began up the track, which was akin to climbing a slide slathered in grease. Horses hooves had churned up the surface and with every step my shoes disappeared into oozing sludge. Slop, slop, slop up the track I trod, making slow but sure progress. Just as the land began to level out and I could see the defined track of The Ridgeway tantalisingly ahead, I skidded, flailing a desperate arm at a tree branch. I missed. Hopelessly. Down I went with a splatter, face first into the mud.

The 87-mile Ridgeway, running between Overton Hill and Ivinghoe Beacon, is Britain's oldest road. Used since the days of prehistoric man, it is now a hotchpotch of metalled road, bridleway and footpath.

True to its random form, a path of mud and puddles soon emerged on to a hedge-lined rural lane, where the tarmac turned at a right angle. To the left, the road dipped under the A41 to Tring. To the right, the road meandered to the Hertfordshire village of Cholesbury. This patch of asphalt and gravel looked like any other anonymous bend in England's road network, but it also marked the highest point in Hertfordshire. Never had I travelled so far – four hours and 60 rainy miles – for something so disappointing.

Buckinghamshire's summit and the highest chalk in the Chilterns lay two miles to the west. The Ridgeway took me deep into Wendover Woods, a flat plateau scattered with picnic tables, where a stone monument marked the pinnacle. Under darkening skies I sped through Chesham and Amersham, until only the mile-long, dead-straight road over Gore Hill remained. It was a painful end to almost 90 miles of cycling and, heavy-legged at the crest of the hill, I freewheeled to sanctuary in Jordans.

Being a Quaker village, Jordans isn't the best place to drown your sorrows. I searched for a pub, eventually realising that there wouldn't be much call for one here. The village is, however, a tourist attraction for American visitors who come to pay homage at the burial place of William Penn, founder of the province of Pennsylvania. Or maybe they come hoping to catch a glimpse of Ozzy and Sharon Osbourne, whose mansion is close by.

DAY 10 – JORDANS TO WANTAGE: 49 MILES
Bald Hill (Oxfordshire): 257m

I was roused from sleep in the hostel by rain tapping the windows. As I ate breakfast it cascaded off the roof like a waterfall. When it was time to leave Jordans, heavy drops still fell from the sky. I'd have to build an ark soon. I pulled on sodden shoes and socks and cycled eight thoroughly depressing miles to High Wycombe, where I stayed until mid-afternoon, willing the downpours to ease.

Bald Hill lies at the meeting place of Oxfordshire and Buckinghamshire, to the west of the M40 between junctions five and six. A grand setting if ever there was one. I crossed six lanes of motorway traffic north of Stokenchurch and followed the curve of the road to a sprawling car park. With a name like bald, I expected the hill to have been scoured bare by foresting, grazing or quarrying. Instead, its slopes were smothered in thick woods and a glorious carpet of bluebells. Following the route of a sculpture trail, it wasn't long before I reached a clearing where electricity pylons dissected the woods. I could go no higher in Oxfordshire.

The descent to Watlington was on a badly pitted road, bouncing my eyeballs in their sockets and jangling my nether regions. Talking of nether regions, I had other pressing concerns. With no open shop in Jordans, all I had managed to scrounge in the hostel was four slices of brown bread, a can of baked beans and some high-fibre muesli. So it was roughage for supper and roughage for breakfast. The result? My rear end was trumpeting violently at such regular intervals I felt sure I was contributing to global warming. The sudden explosions of methane must have been causing ice caps to melt and slip into the ocean at that very moment.

Soulless bypasses dragged me around Wallingford and Didcot. The rain fell heavier. The wind blew harder. I was cycling at a snail's pace, a queue of impatient motorists strung out behind me, waiting for their turn to overtake. Rivers of water ran down the road throwing spray up my back. This was not how I'd imagined life when I sat daydreaming about this journey at work. I had envisaged long, hazy days of cycling under clear skies, and stopping in a quaint village to become immersed in conversation with a friendly local. Before I'd know it, I'd be introduced to the family and sitting down for a slap-up supper. Up to the pub we'd stroll, sink a pint of the local brew and I would be regaled by fascinating stories of yesteryear. Sleeping soundly in the spare room, I would wake to wafts of frying bacon. After breakfast, I'd be waved off like an old friend. We'd stay in touch, send Christmas cards each year and they would be godparents to my first born.

It wasn't working out like that. The smoking chimneys and water coolers of Didcot power station were looming over me, when all of a sudden there was a pop and a whistle of escaping air. It is the sound every cyclist dreads. A puncture. I groaned. Punctures never happen on warm sunny days when you have all the time in the world. They happen when the rain is falling diagonally and the best view you can hope for is of a power station.

Half an hour later, strange looks acknowledged my arrival in Wantage. To fix the puncture, I had to remove my front wheel, and the mud and grime caked on the rim was transferred to my hands, and subsequently to my face.

'Do you know where the hostel is?' I asked a woman wearing a Sandra name badge at the checkout in Waitrose.

Sandra shrugged. 'I'll ask Nicole. She'll know. Nicole… Nicole…'

Nicole finally looked up from her empty checkout and ambled over. No wonder Nicole didn't answer. The name on her badge was Helen.

'Where's the youth hostel, Nicole? I told this man you'd know,' Sandra said.

'You're going to the hostel?' exclaimed Nicole, or maybe it was Helen, with a gasp. It was as if I was lodging with Dracula. 'It's up on the Downs, three miles from here. The hill is a killer, though. It's like that,' she said, positioning her hand in an almost vertical position. 'I've never managed to cycle it without getting off. You'll have to push.' She took a closer look at my face. 'Do you know you've got oil on the end of your nose?'

Between securing my bicycle to a railing outside the supermarket and returning ten minutes later, my rear tyre had punctured. How could this be happening? I looked skywards and breathed the deepest of breaths. Fury raged within. I wanted to hurl the thing through the window of Waitrose. I wanted to scream and shout, turning Wantage's sedate air blue. Then I might have felt better. Instead, I balanced a shopping bag on each handlebar and cycled until the tyre could take no more. Nicole was right. Perhaps she had sabotaged my cycle when I wasn't looking? I got off and pushed – the ultimate ignominy. At the top of Wantage Down, I threw the punctured bicycle in a shed, secretly wishing it would be stolen overnight.

As I cooked sausages under the grill in the hostel kitchen, a middle-aged woman with curly blonde hair strolled in. 'Or roit?' she trilled, in a Birmingham drawl. My ears pricked up instantly. I may have grown up only 13 miles from Birmingham city centre, but I never picked up the accent that anyone who's not from Birmingham loves to hate. When university and work took me hundreds of miles from the city, the number of Brummies in my life dropped to virtually nil. So when I came across one, it was like meeting my brethren, a kindred soul. On these occasions, for some unfathomable reason, out of my mouth comes the voice of an archetypal Brummie. You would have thought I'd been dragged up in the back streets of Nechells, as I wax lyrical about groaty dick and the smell of the HP Sauce factory.

'Ooroyt. Yammorite?' I replied. 'Jawanna kipper tie?'

'Ta, bostin.'

I was still wearing a serious scowl, wondering where it had all gone wrong, and having to mend the latest puncture was still uppermost in my mind.

'Yow gorra feace lark a bulldog chewin' a wasp,' she said. 'S'up?'

A little taken aback, I explained about my boyk, my lung journey, the blastid rain and – because of all that – I had gorra cob on.

'Gerrout,' she laughed. 'Yow great tittybabbi.'

Brought bumping back to earth by a Brum.

DAY 11 – WANTAGE TO PEWSEY: 61 MILES
Pilot Hill (Hampshire): 286m
Walbury Hill (Berkshire): 297m
Milk Hill (Wiltshire): 295m

Perhaps she was my guardian Brummie. As I stepped out into the still morning air, Wantage Down was in the grip of a rare climatic phenomenon. A shining yellow sun had climbed high in the sky, warming the land. After a week of non-stop greyness and rain, it took my eyes some minutes to acclimatise to this unnatural light as I pedalled up and over the pleasant Berkshire Downs and past the not so pleasant Chieveley M4 services, en route to Hungerford. The weather had chosen the optimum moment to brighten because I had arranged to meet Fi in Bristol later that day, meaning I was faced with an 80-mile cycle and the little matter of three county summits before nightfall.

Walbury Hill rises four miles south of Hungerford and boasts a trio of monikers: Berkshire's county top, the highest summit in south-east England, and Britain's highest chalk hill. There are, however, precious few reminders that an Iron Age fort once sat atop the hill. In its heyday, Walbury Hill fort would have stood at the centre of a circle of defensive banks and ditches, but today it was sheep rather than soldiers who guarded the summit.

The hill overlooks Combe Gibbet, on the slopes of Combe Down, where the corpses of George Broomham and Dorothy Newman were draped in 1676. After Broomham's wife and son had caught the couple

47

canoodling, the lovers murdered them both, but their crime was witnessed by the village idiot Mad Thomas, who alerted the authorities. Broomham and Newman were tried and then hanged at the Winchester Assizes, and their bodies returned to Combe Gibbet. The original gibbet is long gone, but tradition dictates that a replacement should remain on the same spot.

Only a brief dip in the land – and a gap of around two miles – separated Walbury Hill from the roof of Hampshire, a county that stretches as far south as the English Channel. With a chorus of bleating sheep and clay pigeon shots ringing in my ears, I followed a footpath called the Wayfarer's Way until I reached the ramparts of Pilot Hill. No obvious route led to the top so I hopped over an electric fence and waded through long grass to a triangulation pillar, admiring the view across Newbury as I went.

Two down and on two wheels again, I roared down the slope towards Hungerford. Spying a fist-sized rock in the road, I swerved to avoid it. Never mind shards of glass or thorns – in my experience it was sharp stones that caused punctures. As I manoeuvred into the centre of the road, a car swept around the corner forcing a hasty re-positioning, a move that put me on a collision course with the rock. There was no avoiding it now and my front tyre hit the stone square on. As the tube exploded, I was sent flying through the air towards the prickly branches of a blackberry bush.

Lying on the grass verge, I quickly checked myself over. All anatomy was present and correct. Ego badly wounded but nothing broken. Black drops of blood dripped from both forearms, while the shock of the collision made me shake a little. Falling off is a minor catastrophe that happens to every cyclist at some time, whether the rider is a five-year-old with their stabilisers removed for the first time or Lance Armstrong charging through the Pyrenees. When elite cyclists know kissing concrete is imminent, they try to belly-flop to the ground, so instead of landing on hands or arms, their torso hits the deck first. In professional cycling, injured hands, wrists or fingers mean the end of a race. Curiously, it's much better to damage your upper body. That way you'll be patched up and back on the starting line for the next day of racing.

My reaction to being chucked off the saddle is always the same – blind panic. Falling off is a horrid experience when an innate survival mechanism takes over. Tumbling from a metre above the ground, at speed and on concrete is going to hurt. In the time it takes to hit the floor, I find the best thing to do is tightly shut my eyes and pray hard and fast. On a lucky day I will stand up unscathed. On an unlucky day I could die.

Visions of watching the Tour de France in 2003 frequently flashed through my mind. It was Bastille Day and the Spaniard Joseba Beloki was among the leading pack of riders who had just crested the Côte de la Rochette. Blistering heat was melting the tarmac. Beloki's lightweight bicycle skidded as if he were pedalling across ice and his rear tyre shredded. How could I forget the blood-curdling screams of pain as the poor man writhed on the floor? It was a career-wrecking fall, so severe that he broke his right femur in two places, along with an elbow and wrist.

After using two spares to replace the previous day's punctured tubes, my repair kit was bare. Bristol lay tantalisingly to the west but I had little option to head in the opposite direction to Newbury. As I pedalled gingerly through country lanes my deflated tyre rubbed against the brake pads, making a clip-clopping noise like a cantering pony. A frustrating hour later, I limped into Newbury, with my bicycle now sounding like a galloping shire horse, a noise which sent startled shoppers running for cover. Finding a repair shop, I threw myself on the mercy of a mechanic.

In the time it takes to consume a prawn mayonnaise sandwich, banana and a pint of milk, my cycle was fixed. Desperate to make up for lost time, I pedalled on the rivet to Hungerford, crossed the Wiltshire border and reached Marlborough an hour later. My third summit of the day, Milk Hill, which stands a single metre higher than its Wiltshire neighbour Tan Hill, has become synonymous as the location of the biggest crop circle ever recorded. On a summer's day in 2001, a microlight pilot flying over the hill spotted a vast pattern in the fields below. It contained 409 circles, covered five hectares and measured nearly 300 yards across. Crop-circle enthusiasts flocked to the area and many took to the skies for a better view, speculating whether it was a fake. Either way, it ruined £1,400 of corn belonging to a Stanton St Bernard farmer.

I stopped in Marlborough High Street, reputedly the widest in Britain, to consult the map.

'Where are you after, love?' a local enquired.

'Milk Hill. It's the highest point in Wiltshire.'

She studied the map for a few seconds. 'You know I've lived here all my life and I've never heard of it.'

Losing myself in leafy lanes, I crossed the lip of Wansdyke, a medieval defensive earthwork, before the green dome of Milk Hill loomed ahead. What I wanted was to take a stroll up to the summit – a UFO sighting would be a bonus, but not essential – before pedalling on to Bristol for a bath and bed. Why is it never that simple? Another puncture – I know, this is getting tedious, but imagine how I felt.

There was no explosion this time, just a slow but inevitable release of air. I looked closely at the tyre. It was torn. I now had enough spare tubes to kit out every rider in the Tour de France, but a spare tyre? Not one. Great lumps of hail powered by a wild wind now fell from the sky, forcing me to take shelter behind a parked car. And I'm ashamed to say I totally lost my cool.

Frustration had been bubbling up ever since I'd left London and it came to the boil on Milk Hill. It had been 300 miles of rain, wind, mud, falling off bicycles, chaotic traffic and punctures. Convinced the whole world was against me, I vented my fury on 12 kilograms of defenceless, blameless metal, plastic and rubber. 'You bastard, you absolute bastard!' I shouted at the bicycle. 'Why are you doing this to me?' Any semblance of common sense was gone. I snatched up the contraption by its frame, shaking it furiously. To achieve what I'll never know. Dropping it, I picked up my pump instead. 'You're to blame for all this,' I screamed, snapping it in two and hurling each piece across the car park.

I regretted my actions immediately. Not only had I

insinuated my bicycle was born of unmarried parents, I now had no way of repairing the puncture without a pump to blow the tube up. It was at that moment that Fi chose to ring me.

'What do you want?' I ranted like a lunatic. 'My bicycle's broken and I can't fix it. I'm not coming to Bristol. Just leave me alone will you?'

As I stomped up Milk Hill, tears came. Not of sadness, but of bitter frustration. It was after six o'clock. Every bicycle repair shop would be shut. For the first time in 11 days, I was beaten. I had to accept defeat. There was no way I could get to Bristol today.

Fi phoned back. 'There's a train station in Pewsey. Cycle there and you can get a train to Bristol.'

Swallowing my pride, I freewheeled the five miles to Pewsey and boarded the first train to Temple Meads.

THREE

DAYS 12 AND 13 – BRISTOL

After 16 years at the helm of a daily newspaper, my editor had heard every resignation speech going, from delirious tributes to diatribes of hate. I'd like to think my effort was unique, something she would remember. Not fondly, but remember nonetheless. When she had finished reading my notice – hastily typed on a square of paper five minutes beforehand – she asked where my new job was.

'Um... well... there is no new job,' I answered. And so, in a series of stuttered sentences, I explained. 'A 5,000-mile journey... to the summit of every county in the United Kingdom... there's 92 of them... seven times the height of Everest... it has never been done before... oh, and by bicycle.'

Maybe it was the word 'bicycle' that tipped her over the edge, for as I spoke her bewildered expression contorted into a look of disgust. She turned away, transferring her glare from the wretched reporter to some faraway point outside the window. Pausing momentarily for dramatic effect, she whirled around and spat a solitary word in my direction.

'Why?'

Damn. She had got me there.

In truth, she wasn't alone in asking that question. Long before I booked that one-way train ticket to Bodmin, friends, acquaintances, in fact anyone I came into contact with, admitted that they too were baffled. 'You're doing what?' was the standard response. Three months off and I was choosing to stay in Blighty? Madness. So I feel obliged to explain why.

This is what I think my editor meant when she uttered that word. When the world contains thousands of treasures – from Niagara Falls and the Pyramids, to the Taj Mahal and Table Mountain – why (oh why) would someone willingly choose to spend 92 days in the UK, cycling and walking in wind and rain, with only the prospect of a muddy hillside and a creaky bed to look forward to? It wasn't like I was picking the simple option. In our 21st-century world, travel has never been easier. Airports are everywhere, cheap flights are abundant. Globalism has created mind-boggling opportunities, opening our eyes and enriching our lives, but it's like having an affair. The grass is greener, so – impressionable creatures that we are – we go for it. But is it really greener?

Visiting the summit of every county was just an idea, a thought, one of trillions our fertile imaginations conjure up every day. Some ideas are silly, some are sexual and some are serious. Mine wasn't a lifetime aspiration. It wasn't for fame, fortune and glory. Nor was it a pilgrimage, or a charity stunt. And it certainly wasn't triggered by a Tony Hawks-style wager. They were rationalisations that irritated me. In our reason-obsessed society our every action demands an explanation, a defence. Can we no longer do something for the sake of doing it?

I rarely delved into why, largely because the impetus was so dull, leaving the questioner unfulfilled. What profound words did they expect me to utter? For world peace? To prove the Earth is flat? To discover the Scottish penguin? To find my inner self? For goodness sake, *must* there be a life-changing moment or a lightning bolt of inspiration? I just want to. Isn't that good enough? To borrow a phrase from Forrest Gump, 'I just felt like running.' Or, in my case, cycling and walking.

But for the record, I will explain how and where this particular idea – undoubtedly one from the silly category – sprung from. While walking in the snow-sprinkled Brecon Beacons, a companion remarked how Pen y Fan was the highest mountain in the old county of Brecknockshire. That night, I pulled out a map of Worcestershire and located the highest point in my home county. Over the next month, I found them all, from the obvious Ben Nevis, Scafell Pike and Snowdon, to the lesser known but wondrously sounding Bidean Nam Bian, Carn a'Ghille Chearr and Foel Cwmcerwyn. It was as simple as that: a seed of Famous Five-style curiosity that spawned a 92-day epic. Like a million other ideas, it could so easily have been cast on the rubbish dump of unaccomplished or forgotten thoughts. Only it wasn't.

That Jonny Muir, what conviction he has. If he wants something, he goes and gets it, irrespective of what others think. Really? John Bull, I'm sorry to say, but even I felt embarrassed – almost apologetic – when confessing to staying at home. When it comes to holidays, the notion of 'getting away from it all' means getting away from the UK, and fast. We're on the first plane out of here. A UK holiday – once the greatest institution of its time – has become something to be sneered and sniggered at. Why, I don't know. What is there to be embarrassed about?

The UK is beautiful and brilliant, challenging and chaotic. Let us be proud of our nation. Not by shaving our heads, swigging lager and stamping a 'Liz regina' tattoo on a left buttock. But by celebrating our eccentricities and peculiarities. Cornish cream teas. Cheese rolling. The shipping forecast. Weather chit-chat. Pigeons. Haggis. Red phone boxes. Tim Henman. Post Office queues. Sandals and socks. White cliffs. Fish and chips. Trainspotters. Cheese and onion crisps. Sunday drivers. Big Ben. Warm beer. If you would rather sizzle on the man-made dust of a Spanish beach by day and listen to the sound of vomiting Britons abroad by night, then that's your prerogative. You don't know what you're missing.

So, if there has to be a reason, let it be this. Written on a piece of paper I had 92 names and, to cure my curiosity, I thought I'd take a look at them. And on the way, I'd re-acquaint myself with our alien home. Why not? I say.

DAY 14 – PEWSEY TO CHELTENHAM: 56 MILES

The alarm sounded at seven o'clock, a blaring cacophony that shattered my dreams. Two easy days in Bristol had been spent mending a broken bicycle and patching up broken spirits. The bicycle had been easier to fix. I ran a finger down the spine of Fi's warm bare back. Scooping blonde hair off her shoulders, I nuzzled her neck. Outside, a lively wind whistled through trees, car horns honked and children shouted as the world sprung into life. It was time to go.

Two hours later, I was back on the station platform at Pewsey. The spring Bank Holiday was approaching and nature had responded with gales. A free spirit again, I wondered which way to turn: west to the high mountains of Wales, or north to the familiar territory of the Midlands. I flipped a coin. Heads. Wales it was.

It didn't take long to realise the folly of allowing a tossed penny to decide my direction of travel. I turned west into a furious headwind. Churning the pedals, I was barely moving as gust after gust swept over me. In a final act, the wind summoned all of its powers. The breeze accelerated across the Vale of Pewsey, plucking trees from the ground and sending sheep flipping through the air until it was upon me, like a seventh wave breaking over my head. 'OK, you win,' I bellowed at the sky, and turned back. Stupid coin. Now I had no choice but to go north.

From Purton, one of Swindon's outlying villages, there is a classically English view across the Cotswolds limestone belt, home to the highest point in Gloucestershire. Tumbling green wolds roll ever higher, reaching their zenith at Cleeve Common, before the land plunges over an escarpment and hurtles downwards to the Severn Vale. The Cotswolds are Britain's second largest Area of Outstanding Natural Beauty (behind Northumberland), and laid end to end its network of stone walls is said to be 4,000 yards long, equivalent to the Great Wall of China. Cirencester, the self-styled 'capital of the Cotswolds' – as opposed to Cheltenham which brands itself the 'gateway to the Cotswolds' – was Britain's second largest city during the Roman occupation, situated at the meeting points of three Roman roads, Akeman Street, Ermin Street and Fosse Way. Today's invading marauders are the rich and famous, including the likes of Kate Moss, Kate Winslet and Liz Hurley, whose castles are country piles.

I knew every twist and turn, pothole and manhole of the 17-mile stretch of the A435 between Cirencester and Cheltenham, having cycled or driven the route dozens of times. The road follows the route of the River Churn and noses through the villages Stratton, North Cerney, Rendcomb and Colesbourne, before rising gently to Seven Springs, where Cheltenham peeps through trees in the valley below. It didn't feel right being in Cheltenham, the regency, racecourse and spa town that up to a month ago had been my home and place of work. How could my journey have led back to the place I was so desperate to escape?

I knocked on the front door of my one-time rented terrace in St Paul's, where two ex-housemates, Laura and Jenny, still lived. No answer. I knocked again, harder, and pressed my ear to the door. They were in all right. The volume on the stereo was cranked up and I could hear the raucous laughter of half a dozen women. I rattled the letterbox and rapped the knocker again before Jenny finally flung open the door, greeting me with a boozy kiss on the cheek, while the gaggle of girls grinned at my oil and mud-stained legs.

'Drink?' Jenny suggested.

'Go on then. One won't hurt.'

Of course it depends what the 'one' is. She poured, and kept pouring vodka into a glass before throwing in a splash of orange juice.

The past two weeks had been a blur of concentrated effort, of gritted teeth and watching the sky. Life had been routine and rigid. Eat. Cycle. Eat. Walk. Eat. Cycle. Eat. Sleep. It had to be that way. Perhaps I shouldn't have set myself a 92-day deadline. If I had all the time in the world, I could say, 'I won't cycle today,' when it rained. But the target was set and I preferred it that way. Besides, my mode of transport demanded I look after myself. After all, it's hard to cycle 80 miles after ten pints of lager and a chicken vindaloo the night before. As dull as it may sound, food, sleep and hydration were the keys to keeping going.

However, even long-distance cyclists deserve a break. I sniffed at the orange concoction and knocked it back in one. Within moments I could feel a dizzying warmth trickle through my limbs.

'Another?' Jenny asked. I didn't hesitate this time and held out my glass. Tonight I'm getting drunk.

It didn't take much. A fortnight of cycling had sent my tolerance to alcohol plummeting. At 11 o'clock – a sensible bedtime for a sensible adventurer – we were stumbling along Cheltenham High Street, singing at the tops of our not-so-tuneful voices, 'I would walk 500 miles, and I would walk 500 more' – only in my drunken genius I substituted 'cycle' for 'walk'. The merriment ended three hours later, when I staggered away from the pounding music of a nightclub. As Chesney Hawkes told me he was the 'one and only', I was crouching over a kerb as a lurid orange vomit exploded out of my mouth.

DAY 15 – CHELTENHAM TO BROMSGROVE: 60 MILES
Cleeve Common (Gloucestershire): 330m
Worcestershire Beacon (Worcestershire): 425m

I woke up dribbling but feeling on top form, invincible even. I lay still, looking up at the ceiling. No hangover. Not even a headache. Glancing at the clock, I remembered I had arranged to meet Mike, a photographer and former colleague, in 20 minutes, and swung a leg out of bed. Hangovers are evil creatures. They lull their victims into a false sense of security. After a night on the tiles, I can wake up feeling as alive as the day I was born, but give it a few minutes and a hangover will be lodged in my brain, banging in nails.

A flat road escaped Cheltenham before beginning a relentless climb to the village of Cleeve Hill. I was already empty-legged and groggy, and a hangover – armed with a pneumatic drill and sledgehammer – duly arrived. Drunk in charge of a bicycle, I wobbled up the 10 per cent slope and was 15 minutes late when I greeted Mike with a vodka belch in the golf club car park. After a brief reminisce about the good, bad and awful times, with the obligatory 'Is so-and-so still there?' thrown in, we walked across a cattle grid and emerged onto the grassy slope of Cleeve Hill.

'OK, run up the path towards me,' Mike instructed in his familiar Kiwi tongue, while he snapped a series of practice shots.

'Run?' I queried. 'But I'm not running up these hills, I'm walking them.'

'It'll make a better picture,' he argued.

I did as I was told. Don't let the facts get in the way of a good story – or even picture. I had trotted up and down a stony path four times, when Mike called after me: 'Just once more.'

'Give me a moment,' I pleaded. I was in a bad way. The colour had drained from my face, while crippling cramps suggested that in my drunken state I must have swallowed a small animal, which was now trying to tunnel its way out of my stomach.

'I think that's the best we're going to manage,' Mike said after my last lethargic burst, and he showed me the images on the back of the camera. 'Pick one if you like.'

That was easier said than done. In each shot, I resembled a startled rabbit caught in a car's headlights. It looked as if Mike had jumped from behind a tree and shouted 'Boo!' before taking each photo.

'I look terrible, Mike,' I said gently, conscious of his professional pride.

'Don't blame the camera, mate. That's what you look like. Not very healthy. You need to do a bit of exercise.'

It wasn't long before I reached the top of Cleeve Hill, a 317-metre point that is often wrongly assumed to be the roof of Gloucestershire. The county's actual summit lies a further mile across Cleeve Common, albeit in a far less spectacular site under three soaring radio masts. Compared to the solitude of my previous hills, the common was a metropolis, heaving with activity. Even a blanket of fog had failed to deter walkers, mountain bikers, horse riders, cross-country runners and optimistic kite-flyers. Still, it was hard to imagine that a convoy of buses, caravans and trucks had once invaded the common and set itself up as a ramshackle community called Rainbow Village. Even in the 1980s the reaction to the 200-strong group, who were part of the Stonehenge Peace Convoy, was predictable. The good people of north Gloucestershire were appalled, convinced that rape and pillage would surely follow. The travellers did what they do best – cause a furore and then move on.

Cleeve Common's triumphant claim to fame is that if one were to head eastwards in a straight line, the next highest place would be thousands of miles away in Russia's Ural Mountains. Isn't that astonishing? I thought so, until I found out that Nottingham Hill, three miles to the north west of Cleeve Common, shares the same distinction. As does Bredon Hill, Clee Hill, Clent Hill, Lickey Hill, Turner's Hill, along with every single rise on the Malverns. Even West Bromwich Albion's football stadium does, for goodness sake. The only logical conclusion is that there can't be a lot of high land between the West Midlands and Russia. Since much of it is the

North Sea, Gulf of Finland and Baltic Sea, it's hardly surprising. So please, stop boasting about it.

The nine-mile chain of the Malvern Hills rises abruptly from the flood plains of the River Severn, so suddenly that it accentuates their splendour. The Malverns are at their most alluring at sunset, when the grassy humps are framed on the darkening sky. Inter-war Prime Minister and Worcestershire resident Stanley Baldwin was right. These hills – my local hills – are indeed the 'most beautiful silhouette in the world'. The Malverns are where Worcestershire meets Herefordshire, and two similar-sized beacons glare at each other across the border. It would be appropriate if both were their county tops, but only one is. Herefordshire Beacon is dwarfed by Black Mountain, close to the Welsh border, leaving Worcestershire Beacon to fly the flag for its county.

From Upper Wyche, the route to the summit of Worcestershire follows a tarmac track, meaning that even cars can make it. Like Cleeve Common, the beacon was a busy top. Children pored over the toposcope, built to mark Queen Victoria's Diamond Jubilee in 1897. Families lined up for a photograph and a group of mountain bikers lounged on the grass, eating sandwiches. Below the summit, I could make out where a log-built café, dating back to Victorian times, had existed until it burned down in 1989. The summit has a distinguished list of visitors. Edward VII was driven up in his Daimler. Sir Edmund Hillary, the first man to conquer Everest, presumably came on foot. And surely Baldwin must have paid a visit to the top of his favourite silhouette?

For the first 18 years of my life, home was the north

Worcestershire town of Bromsgrove. Despite a subsequent three years in Exeter, a year in Preston and two in Cheltenham, I always called this terribly ordinary town 'home'. That's not to do it down. I was there the day the town's minnow-size football club was two minutes away from reaching the fourth round of the FA Cup. (I still shudder when I hear the word Barnsley.) AE Housman, best known for his cycle of poems *A Shropshire Lad*, was born nearby in Fockbury, and today a bronze statue of the poet stands at the centre of Bromsgrove High Street. Meanwhile, the Avoncroft Museum of Buildings is home to the largest collection of telephone boxes in the UK. Exciting as this all may seem, Bromsgrove is still indisputably ordinary.

It may sound irrational, but as a young child I worried about growing up as ordinary as my surroundings. Our environs are what shapes and inspires us, setting the pattern for our lives. Take Reinhold Messner, for instance. The world's most successful climber was brought up in the South Tyrol in the Italian Alps. Messner was thrown up a mountain before he could crawl and by the time he was 20 he had conquered the hardest routes in the Dolomites and Western Alps. The bearded wonder went on to become the first person to climb each of the world's 8,000-metre mountains. But would Messner have been half the mountaineer he was if he'd been born in Walsall or Wolverhampton? I doubt it. In comparison, Bromsgrove's nearest high points are the Lickey Hills. No oxygen required for this climb. By the time I to was 20, I had scaled the 297-metre summit of Lickey and gazed down on the sprawling urban mass of Birmingham below.

I was never going to amount to Messner, but you can see why I feared for my future.

I turned left opposite Bromsgrove's running track – the scene of my finest athletic mediocrity – and onto the familiar tarmac of East Road. I was home. It had felt odd to be in Cheltenham, but positively wrong to be in Bromsgrove. Journeys of discovery aren't meant to lead you to your own front door. On his way to the South Pole, Captain Scott didn't have the option of popping home for a brew when he felt a little parched, nor did Christopher Columbus put off discovering America so he could have another custard cream.

DAY 16 – BROMSGROVE TO COALPORT: 48 MILES
Brown Clee Hill (Shropshire): 546m

Dogs don't like cyclists. I don't know why. Perhaps it's the Lycra? Or the shaved legs? Maybe they have signed a secret pact with motorists to root out cyclists one by one? I met my would-be assassin in Shropshire, a brute of a German shepherd. After two dreamy hours and 30 miles since leaving Bromsgrove, the road climbed through Stottesdon, where I raised a hand to acknowledge a girl standing at the roadside. A German shepherd lay idly at her feet, snapping at flies. With my back turned, the seemingly morose dog went in for the kill, clamping its jaws around my left calf. Turning around, I gave the girl my best 'Do something for God's sake!' look. Clearly an accomplice, she did nothing but smile sweetly. As I was still turning the pedals, the dog let go, only to renew his grip – a firmer one this time – on my left ankle. The animal and I were now playing tug-o-war with my leg. With no help on the way, drastic action was called for. Clenching a fist, I swung for the dog, catching him with a jab on the snout. At last the beast let go and scampered whining back to the girl, tail between his legs.

Stand on the summit of Brown Clee Hill – preferably on a clear day – and look around. Never mind the jagged heights of Snowdonia, the grey mass of the Peak District or Wolverhampton Wanderers' Molineux stadium, it is the sky-scraping air traffic control mast barely 20 yards away that draws the eye. Such towering obtrusions – I mean the mast of course, not Molineux – have a habit of shattering scenes of loveliness. Or perhaps it just marks another chapter in the busy history of Brown Clee Hill? Wind the clock back 4,000 years and I'd have found three Iron Age hill forts here. Leap forward two millennia and Brown Clee was Britain's highest coalfield; limestone and dhustone (a volcanic basalt) were also quarried on its slopes. Roll on the Second World War and the hill became a graveyard for aircraft: it is reputed to be the site of more wartime crashes than any other British hill. The crew of a German Junkers 88 were the first victims in 1941, and a total of 23 Allied and enemy airmen lost their lives on Brown Clee's slopes.

There are two faces to Shropshire. One is green, rural and as Mary Webb called it, 'the country that lies between the dimpled lands of England and the giant purple steps of Wales.' But it was this remote enclave of England that spawned the Industrial Revolution and an invention that changed the world. In 1709, Abraham Darby devised a way of producing cast iron by using coal instead of charcoal. Because Darby could now produce vast quantities of iron without having to chop down half a forest, Shropshire became the nation's industrial heart. It wasn't until 70 years later that Darby's grandson conquered the River Severn with the 30-yard long Ironbridge – the world's first metal bridge and the enduring symbol of the Industrial Revolution.

Turning back now and again to glance at Brown Clee – a sure sign this peak had me smitten – the road reached the pretty environs of Much Wenlock and soon afterwards I was freewheeling downhill to the banks of the frothy Severn. A mile downstream from Ironbridge, I came to Coalport, where I booked into a hostel that was once an 18th-century pottery factory.

Most nights followed a similar pattern. If I were staying in a hostel I'd bag the bottom bunk, shower, wash my socks and then head out in search of food. I would phone Fi and perhaps my parents to update them on my progress, before committing the day's events to paper – which today I was able to record as my first without rain. Sometimes I would wander up to the nearest pub, get chatting to fellow travellers or take a stroll to a local landmark. Occasionally a randy Swiss would try to seduce me.

As a rule, I didn't tend to fill my evenings with prostitution, drug smuggling or murder. I had never seen the film *Kiss of the Dragon*, and it became apparent that the families in the TV room at Coalport youth hostel hadn't either. It was ten o'clock on a half-term Sunday, meaning children were allowed to stay up long past their normal bedtimes. Families were still clustered around the room as *Kiss of the Dragon* rolled.

It's everything a good action film should be: drugs, sex, a good scrap and a spattering of death. After a relatively tame start, two prostitutes were soon peeling off their clothes. One of the prostitutes gyrated in front of a Chinese businessman while simultaneously snorting cocaine from a glass table. As she paraded around the room in black bra and knickers, I glanced at the family of four sitting immediately to my left. Dad shifted with unease, pretending to read the paper. Mum's cheeks had turned scarlet and she exchanged forced smiles with other mums. The son, who must have been around 12, sat agog, mouth open and drooling. The younger daughter had put her comic book to one side and was seemingly paralysed with fear. As the prostitute draped her near naked body over the businessman, she reached for a knife and stabbed him repeatedly. Just as Jet Li burst through the door, the dad coughed and announced it was time they were going to bed. On his cue, the room emptied as flustered parents took children by the hand as they asked, 'Mummy, what was that lady doing?'

DAY 17 – COALPORT TO CHESTER: 51 MILES

A dreary spell of sameness was shattered in Crudgington when a seemingly turbo-powered cyclist – a blur of multi-coloured Spandex and sweat – hurtled past my right ear. An instant later, a second rider followed in his slipstream, and together they accelerated up the A442 as if engines were attached to their rear wheels. These weren't your average Bank Holiday riders out for a spin around the block. Veins bulged from shaved calves and quadriceps of steel, powering featherweight machines costing more than a half-decent car. A handful of spectators had gathered on the verges to cheer on Shropshire's answer to Miguel Indurain and Greg Le Mond, and suitably intrigued, I pulled off the road to ask what all the fuss was about.

It was Anfield Bicycle Club's 105th annual 100-mile time trial, held traditionally on the Spring Bank Holiday, I was told by a bearded fellow from Whitchurch. He then launched into a potted history of the club. Formed in 1879, it took its name from the Anfield district of Liverpool, and its second president John Houlding had a hand in the evolution of a sports team with a degree more notoriety – Liverpool Football Club.

Back in the saddle, I glimpsed a racer ahead and set my sights on the fluorescent yellow number pinned on their jersey. Slowly, I reeled in my prey, before overtaking without a sideways glance on a gentle incline south of Peplow. My startled rival was a woman dressed from neck to ankle in black Lycra. My first scalp. Not that I was being competitive. Five minutes later, I overtook another competitor. Again it was a woman, who may not have been technically cycling at the time – she was fixing a puncture – nevertheless, scalp number two.

Peplow was where my overtaking form ended. In the three miles to Hodnet, half a dozen cyclists breezed past, with me resisting the urge to point out I'd cycled 800 miles in 17 days, which meant I had every right to be trundling at this conservative speed. The time trial winner, I later learned, put me to shame, sprinting around the 100-mile course in a scintillating three hours and 55 minutes, at an average speed of 25 miles per hour.

For me, there were another 30 lonely miles of cheerless skies and monotonous A roads to endure before Chester emerged through a hailstorm. Tonight I was staying in the canal side apartment of Fi's sister Catriona. Except Catriona wouldn't be there, which meant I would be sharing the apartment with her housemate – a woman I had never met. In the circumstances, Catriona thought it wise to introduce Siobhan and I first, before we had to make stranger small talk that evening. It didn't go terribly well. Don't get me wrong: I like my girlfriend's sister. Only she has a knack of being a little dramatic.

'This is Jonny,' Catriona said. 'He's not a rapist or a murderer or anything – or at least I don't think so – so you'll be fine. Right, must go. I'll leave you two to get to know each other.'

FOUR

CROESO I CYMRU – PURCHASING A YAK – CARBO-
LOADING – GORPHWYSFA – MOUNT SNOWDON –
THE HIGHEST SLUM IN WALES – NOT TIRED? CLIMB
A MOUNTAIN – FALLING OUT AND MAKING UP ON
ARAN FAWDDWY – A PAINFUL GOODBYE –
AN AXE MURDERER

DAY 18 – CHESTER TO BETWS-Y-COED: 52 MILES
Moel Famau (Flintshire): 554m

I was abroad. A place where the sun shone, the natives spoke in an unfamiliar tongue and the pace of life was a little less frantic. *Croeso I Cymru*. Reaching foreign soil gave me a sense of starting afresh. Shaking off the shackles of England, I shook hands with Wales.

Leaning against a post box in Mold, I was talking on my mobile phone to a journalist about my journey. After 10 minutes of questions and answers we were both keen to wrap up the interview.

'I'll finish on Ben Nevis in early August,' I concluded.

'Why Ben Nevis?'

'Because it's the highest point in the UK, so I thought it would be fitting to end the journey there.'

'And you'll need oxygen on Ben Nevis, won't you?'

'Oxygen? On Ben Nevis? You're joking, aren't you?'

'Um… no.'

'Mountaineers only need bottled oxygen on the tops of the very highest mountains in the world, where the air is so thin it makes it difficult to breath. Ben Nevis isn't high enough. In fact, it's not high enough by about... 6,000 metres.'

'Oh.'

How can a person of reasonable intelligence and common sense think oxygen was needed on Ben Nevis, a mountain that is climbed by 100,000 adventurous souls every year? Maybe it was a sign of the times. Many people are reluctant to climb the stairs, let alone a mountain. How would they know what it is like to stand at the top of one? To some, the mere word 'mountain' conjures up an image of an Everest-sized peak requiring several weeks, a herd of luggage-bearing yak and a dozen Sherpas to climb. With that daunting image, no wonder people can be reluctant to venture into the hills.

Nevertheless, like a Boy Scout I had to be prepared for every eventuality. After all, Welsh mountains are unpredictable creatures. Picture the scene:

'I'm looking for a yak,' I asked an assistant at a supermarket in Mold.

'Yak. Let me think,' she said. 'We've just had a reshuffle you see. I know. Third aisle. Between the eggs and the tinned peas. You can't miss them. Big, hairy fellows they are.'

A brown yak with his head in a cereal box caught my eye. With his shaggy hair and pointy horns he was an impressive beast, an ideal travelling companion. He could carry my luggage and would be the perfect deterrent against would-be bicycle thieves. We could chat late into the night about Tibetan politics, the exchange rate of the Nepalese rupee and debate the impact of commercialism on the Himalayas. I'd never be lonely again. We'd be like Dorothy and Toto, Michael Jackson and Bubbles, Winston Churchill and Rufus. Friends forever.

I came to my senses. 'Sorry, Mr Yak, it's just not practical,' I shrugged, throwing him one last mournful glance as I exited the third aisle.

'Not interested?' the assistant asked.

'Wrong colour,' I grunted, shaking my head.

Without a yak, I was still a little concerned about my level of preparedness for the long journey ahead. Erring on the side of caution, I slung a pair of crampons and an ice axe into my rucksack. On I cycled to Gwernymynydd, glancing over my shoulder now and again in case the Abominable Snowman was bearing down on me.

The Clwydian Range of hills straddles the border of Flintshire to the east and Denbighshire to the west. On top sits the honeypot summit of Moel Famau, the highest point in maritime Flintshire. Hill of the Mothers, as Moel Famau is known in the English tongue, is set in a 2,000-acre country park of heather moorland and forest overlooking Ruthin. To put its 554 metres in perspective, it is almost exactly the same height as the CN Tower in Canada, the tallest free-standing man-made structure on Earth. Moel Famau, however, is marginally less popular. From an expansive pay-and-display car park, rocky tracks dart up wooded slopes, all converging at the ruins of the Jubilee Tower at the summit. Built in 1810 to commemorate the Golden Jubilee of George III, the tower was ruined by a storm 52 years later. A family of scousers had got there before me, and the son was screaming into the wind: 'I can see Liverpool. Mam, I can see our 'ouse.'

My little scouse friend was nearly right. He'd have needed the eyes of an eagle to see his 'ouse, but there indeed was Liverpool, an urban jungle wrapped around the banks of the glinting Mersey. Sandwiching Liverpool was the unmistakable wedge of The Wirral and the dull grey mass of the Pennines. To the north of Moel Famau lay the coastal resorts of Prestatyn and Rhyl, the twinkling waters of Liverpool Bay lapping their sandy shores. Turning west, the land dipped into the Vale of Clywd, before rising violently and ending in the terrifying shark's teeth of Snowdonia. Fixing my eyes on these distant mountains, I trembled with excitement. It had taken 18 days of effort to get here, but this is what I had been waiting for. This was my reward for negotiating the roundabouts of Telford, surviving London's dual carriageways and resisting the urge to throttle Mr Twit.

With every turn of the pedals, Snowdonia's theatrical peaks, black and vast, loomed ever closer. I turned up my radio. It was The Automatic: 'What's that coming over the hill? Is it a monster? Is it a monster?' I shuddered. That's what the mountains of Snowdonia were – monsters. Fearful giants I was soon to do battle with.

DAY 19 – BETWS-Y-COED TO PEN-Y-PASS: 84 MILES
Holyhead Mountain (Anglesey): 220m

Prior to exercise, especially long-distance exercise, experts advise you to load up on carbohydrates in preparation for the calorie-consuming exertion ahead. It was a mantra I had taken to a new level. If I wasn't cycling, walking or sleeping, I was eating: my accelerated metabolism meant my belly was forever rumbling. Buffet breakfasts – the chance to shovel in as much food as physically possible, without the shame of ordering it (and paying for it) – held a particular attraction. It is therefore fortunate for the Swallow Falls Hotel, an impressive white-painted building a mile north of Betws-y-Coed, that not every guest consumes a full English breakfast, three bowls of cereal, six rounds of toast and jam, three mugs of tea and a pint of orange juice. That little lot would keep me going until elevenses.

My destination was Pen-y-pass, a short uphill hop of nine miles from Betws-y-Coed. However, should one wish to go via Holyhead, as I did, it is a journey almost 10 times that length. Anglesey's Holyhead Mountain is positioned awkwardly on the distant northwest tip of Holy Island. Just to complicate matters, Fi was meeting me at the famous Pen-y-pass youth hostel at five o'clock, giving me eight hours to complete my mission.

The first hour of the day was bliss: a benign ascent to Llyn Ogwen, a lake sandwiched by the jagged finger of Tryfan and the rounded hump of Carnedd Dafydd, before a swooping descent, where the road overlooked the flat-bottomed, glacial-gouged Nant Ffrancon. Soon after, under a cloudless sky in coastal Bangor, I pulled out my increasingly journey-beaten diary to record the early morning events. 'For the first time I stopped thinking about the time, where I was going, what I was doing, why I was doing it and where the next meal was coming from. I was lost in the pure exhilaration of the moment.' The tide had turned.

Thomas Telford's suspension bridge took bicycle and rider across the Menai Strait into Ynys Mon, the ancient Isle of Anglesey, where low flats replaced the stirring mountains of the mainland. For 18 uninteresting miles I focused on the tarmac of the A5, the old main road running almost parallel to the newer four-lane frenzy of the A55. Another Telford construction, the 1,300-yard long Stanley Embankment, saw me onto my third island of the day, Holy Island.

Holyhead Mountain is a mountain in name only. Generally, unless a hill exceeds 610 metres, it can't claim mountain status. Unfortunately for Holyhead Mountain, it falls 390 metres short. Rising 220 metres above sea level, the hill is easily the lowest Welsh county top and was the ninth shortest on my list of 92. Nevertheless, this pocket-sized peak doesn't suffer from small hill syndrome, because it oozes the qualities that define a mountain. Legendary Lakeland writer Alfred Wainwright would have agreed: 'The difference between a hill and a mountain depends on appearance, not on altitude and is thus arbitrary and a matter of personal opinion. Grass predominates on a hill, rock on a mountain. A hill is smooth, a mountain rough.' Wainwright was talking about Scafell Pike, England's highest mountain, yet his assertion is entirely appropriate for Holyhead Mountain. Anglesey's immense and shiny block of granite positively sneers, 'I may be small but I'm perfectly formed.'

Balanced on one of the UK's extremities, Holyhead Mountain has an end-of-the-world feel to it. The mountain's slopes end abruptly in cliffs and the sea laps on three sides. Holyhead lies far below, the harbour breakwater snaking out into the blue ocean. Much is packed on to this little mountain. Climbers come to tackle its challenging rock faces, bird watchers flock to point their binoculars at the wildlife around the South Stack lighthouse, and historians pore over the Roman, Neolithic and Bronze Age remains that litter the mountain's lower slopes.

No visit to Anglesey is complete without a trip to Llanfairpwllgwyngyll or, to give the town its full title, Llanfairpwllgwyngyllgogerychwyrndrobwllllantysiliogog ogoch – the longest place name in Britain. It is thanks to those 57 letters that the town has been invaded by tacky tourism, bringing an endless stream of coach tours to the doors of its railway station. Apart from the obligatory photograph with the station sign in the background, there seemed little else to do or see – except in the station foyer, where a multitude of signposts pointed to destinations around the world, giving the mileage to each one. I had just notched up 1,000 miles, and according to the sign that was the equivalent of riding from Anglesey to Iceland. If I'd chosen a different journey, I could now have been bathing in hot springs and perusing the sights of Reykjavik rather than battling with traffic on the Britannia Bridge.

Once in Llanberis, only the stone-wall-lined mountain road that climbs to the summit of Pen-y-pass remained. The last time I had endeavoured to bicycle as far in a single day – in excess of 80 miles – was the Home Counties horror between Saffron Walden and Jordans. That day, arriving ashen-faced and shaking with exhaustion, my body had capitulated and my thoughts had concentrated on giving up. Today, a different person sat in the saddle, someone brimming with assurance, whose spirits soared and pace quickened as if the slope didn't exist.

The road brushed the edge of lakes Padarn and Peris, nosed through Nant Peris and drifted by a glacial boulder crawling with climbers. Sheep-dotted scree slopes towered peerlessly above, Crib Goch to the west, Glyder Fawr to the east. Not a breath of wind. The sun in the heavens. Nature at her architectural peak. One man riding his bicycle. So joyous, so uplifting were these simple moments, that when I reached the short strip of level ground at Pen-y-pass, arrival was tinged with disappointment. I wanted to do it again. Such times of perfection, when body, mind and nature synchronise, come so rarely.

Fi was sitting on a bench outside the hostel, grinning in the sunshine. 'You took your time,' she said, pointing at her watch. It was one minute past five o'clock.

DAY 20 – PEN-Y-PASS TO BETWS-Y-COED: 9 MILES
Snowdon (Caenarfonshire): 1,085m

The Pen-y-pass youth hostel stands on the 359-metre lip of the road pass between Capel Curig and Llanberis.

Opposite the hostel buildings there is a modestly-sized car park, which, by 10 o'clock every morning – regardless of the weather – is teeming with cars and minibuses, out of which pour hundreds of walkers clad in boots and Goretex, ready to climb Mount Snowdon. Similar scenes are played out inside the hostel walls, with walkers consuming energy bars and bananas while scrutinising forecasts and studying maps.

Life at Pen-y-pass has been a walkers' and climbers' haunt for more than a century. Before serving its current function, the hostel buildings accommodated the Gorphwysfa Hotel. In the first half of the 20th century, the mountaineer and poet Geoffrey Winthrop Young organised Easter parties at the hotel for walkers, and in a declaration of love once described its position as 'lodged upon the rim of space... the highest roosting place on the island.'

The history of the building is celebrated on the hostel walls, from grainy black and white pictures to the poetry of Young. However, it is the visitors' book that is testament to Gorphwysfa's mark in mountaineering history. Over the decades, Aldous Huxley, the author of *Brave New World*, George Macaulay Trevelyan, the English historian, and Oscar Eckenstein, the English climber who pioneered modern crampons, all signed it. But one name stands out above all others, a man who died trying to go higher than all others: George Mallory. He and three companions, including his brother Robert, recorded their four-day stay at Gorphwysfa on April 14, 1913. The first to sign was Mallory, in joined-up but rather childish and looped handwriting. The page is on permanent display in the hostel lobby, preserved behind a pane of glass. Nearly 11 years and two months later, on 8 June 1924, Mallory, along with Sandy Irvine, died on the slopes of Everest as they attempted to be the first people to conquer the world's highest mountain.

Suitably inspired, Fi and I stepped into the early morning haze and joined the steady procession of Snowdon-bound walkers sauntering up the Pyg track. From the car park, it was a four-mile grind to the summit, but many of our fellow walkers seemed laden with enough gear for a 50-day trek to the North Pole. Their rucksacks were bulging with provisions and extra layers of clothing, while many clutched walking poles – the latest outdoor fad – in both hands. Within minutes they were dripping in sweat and realising that a woolly fleece and the latest hi-tech 'breathable' jacket might be cosy in the Arctic, but in the Mediterranean-like temperature of Snowdon they were redundant.

As we caught our first glimpse of the azure waters of Llyn Llydaw reservoir, we came to a junction. Ahead the Pyg track cut a route along the side of the mountain before zigzagging up to Snowdon's summit ridge. Meanwhile, a less worn path to the right led to the perilously steep cliffs of Crib Goch. A knife-edge arête with a vertical fall on one side and a very steep one on the other, the ridge became infamous in October 1999 when Jonathan Attwell, a 10-year-old Boy Scout, died after falling 150 metres. Crib Goch is no place for a little boy, and very often it is no place for a grown man. There is no margin for error. Even on a clear, windless day, an experienced and well-equipped walker could easily lose their footing on its jagged teeth.

HEIGHTS OF MADNESS

I'd climbed Crib Goch once before and wondered what all the fuss was about. But on that day, a blanket of heavy mist had been thrown across the ridge, hiding the precipitous drops. That day was particularly memorable because my dad – who had crossed it on several occasions before – did something he had rarely done, even when I was a child. He shouted at me. A few yards ahead of him and my brother, I was gambolling over slippery rocks, when he roared: 'For God's sake, be careful!' It was only then that I realised how treacherous Crib Goch could be.

After I'd told Fi the story of poor Jonathan, she made it clear that she wasn't going over Crib Goch. If I wanted to, I was welcome, and if I died, well, she'd told me so. In the end we stayed loyal to the safer, sun-drenched Pyg, following its doglegs as it reached up to the mountain's summit ridge. As soon as we arrived, the sun disappeared behind a wall of mist and we were buffeted by an ice-cold wind. Those people with woolly fleeces and windproof raincoats were now laughing at us, while their sticks were used to steady themselves against the swirling gusts.

Out of the mist appeared the tracks of the Snowdon Mountain Railway, which carries passengers from Llanberis to within 20 yards of the summit. For the walker who has spent the best part of two hours toiling up Snowdon's rocky slopes, it can make reaching the top of the UK's highest mountain outside Scotland an anticlimax. While Fi and I stood at the highest point, wind-blown and with teeth chattering, the couple next to us had just hopped off the train and sidled up a dozen manmade steps.

The concept of building a railway to the summit of one of the UK's most famous and revered mountains is lunacy. Suggest it now and you would be lynched by an angry mob who would rightly want to preserve the untarnished splendour of a mountain landscape. But because the four-mile rack and pinion railway has wound its way up Snowdon's slopes since the late 19th century, it is regarded as an institution rather than an insult. It was the monstrous building where the railway tracks ended that was the problem. When the railway began its life in 1896, the summit terminus was a hotel, before undergoing a conversion into Britain's highest restaurant in the 1930s. When Fi and I stepped through the door it was a falling-down café, worthy of Prince Charles' description as 'the highest slum in Wales'. We shared an pricey shortbread and a hot chocolate, before purchasing his and hers 'I climbed Snowdon the hard way' pin badges from the tourist shop.

It has all gone now. Four months after we stood at the top of Snowdon, the builders moved in and demolished the lot. In its place, a plush £8.3million centre, called Hafod Eryri, will welcome visitors to the UK's busiest mountain.

By two o'clock we were back in the Pen-y-pass car park. As I had now reached the summits of 25 county tops in 20 days, I decided to give myself the rest of the day off. Fi drove and I cycled the nine miles to Betws-y-Coed, where we booked ourselves into the scene of my breakfast-eating triumph, the Swallow Falls Hotel.

DAY 21 – BETWS-Y-COED TO BALA: 39 MILES
Moel Sych (Denbighshire & Montgomeryshire): 827m

We whiled away a lazy morning in Betws-y-Coed, a bustling village of tea rooms and outdoor shops in the shadow of Snowdonia's highest mountains. Hemmed in by the River Conwy, the Conwy Valley railway and a road carrying crawling Snowdon-bound traffic, the triangular village green was a splendid place to watch the world go by. Toddlers were taking their first tentative totter. Milk-white legs and torsos, which would be lobster red by the evening, were exposed for the first time that year. Meanwhile, a group of teenagers were having a competition to see who could gob a ball of spit the farthest.

Despite the commercialism of Snowdonia, this northwestern corner of Wales is very much the stronghold of the Welsh language. Locals gabbled in Cymraeg, making us imagine we were somewhere far more exotic than Betws-y-Coed. 'Dafyd!' a young mum hollered at her son, who a moment earlier had watched in horror as the ice cream he proudly clutched fell from cone to concrete. As a tantrum erupted, his mum launched into a tongue-twisting, throat-hacking rebuke.

Fi departed after lunch, leaving me alone again – for an hour or two at least. I was still standing in the car park outside the Swallow Falls Hotel, tinkering with gears and pumping up tyres, when my phone rang. It was Fi.

'Everything OK?' I asked cautiously. Of course it wasn't. A flurry of muffled tears was confirmation. 'What's happened? Have you had an accident?'

'The A5 is closed,' she complained. 'Between Pentre-wotsit and Shrewsbury.'

'Pentrefoelas?

'Yes, whatever the place is called. It's shut.'

At moments like these, it is sensible not to question the wisdom of a woman, even if, in all probability, she is utterly wrong. Just nod and agree, yes dear, black is white. I stated the obvious as gently as possible. 'Are you absolutely sure? That's a lot of road to close. It must be about 60 miles.'

'That's what the sign says.'

Convinced the main road between Wales and England must be closed, Fi announced she wasn't going home today and that she would meet me in Bala later that afternoon. Before I had time to make an excuse, she had rung off.

I took the country lanes to Bala. It was a Friday afternoon and I had visions of jams of agitated motorists sizzling in the sun on the UK's clogged motorways. As I cycled between Ryhd Iydan and Fran-goch, the only vehicle I met was a tractor.

Using Bala as a base, a trio of county tops were within striking distance, the summits of Denbighshire, Merionethshire and Montgomeryshire. At this juncture, I should come clean about an aspect of my journey I haven't yet mentioned. Although there are 92 counties, I didn't have to climb 92 peaks. Moel Sych, an 827-metre mountain in the Berwyn range, was the first such example I had come to. Straddling the border of Denbighshire and Montgomeryshire, it qualified as the highest point in both counties.

Reunited, Fi and I found a hostel where a matriarchal landlady marched us up two narrow flights of stairs to a room containing 11 single bed. Hostels tend to be relaxed, anything goes kind of places, with guests coming and going as they please. Not this one. We should have guessed from an ominous sign on the front door: 'Not tired? Climb a mountain.'

The room was split by a step into two halves, seven beds on one side, four on the other. Each bed had a little shelf with a Bible perched on top. The proprietor pulled across a curtain that partitioned the room. 'You can draw the curtain if you want some privacy. Don't pull the beds together though, because I'll hear. That'll be £11 each please.'

Our landlady was seemingly on a mission to educate the backpackers and travellers who chose to spend a night in Bala. On the reverse of the toilet door, a note pointed out: 'If you soil the toilet bowl, please scrub it after you to make it pleasant for the next person.' Fair enough perhaps, but then she went one step further, adding, 'Please do not put anything down the toilet you have not already eaten first, except toilet tissue and tampons.' And the final piece de resistance, 'Now wash your hands please.'

We moved on to the kitchen. 'No frying more than half a teaspoon of oil. No longer than 30 minutes gas per day. No cooking after 10 o'clock.'

'Is there anything we can do?' Fi whispered in my ear.

In the corridor, another sign implored: 'Be careful and considerate to others at all times.' Below the advice was an English translation of the Welsh National Anthem, the third one we had come across. As we were about to leave, the proprietor emerged from a kitchen.

'Make sure you're back before midnight because the lights will be off.'

'If we're late,' I replied, 'I'll make sure they are turned off again.'

'No,' she said with a smirk. 'You won't be able to. The lights are programmed not to come on after midnight. The power is switched off. Same thing in the bathrooms. No lights after midnight. OK?'

Still, despite all of its idiosyncrasies, it served us well and was a great place to stay.

Moel Sych lies at the lonesome heart of the Berwyns, Snowdonia's ugly sisters. The hills lack the jagged awe of Snowdonia and as a result, escape the heaving crowds of the National Park. The road clung to the eastern edge of Llyn Tegid, Wales' largest natural lake, passed the Bala Lake Railway and took off over the high pass to Llangynog. A steep hairpin road through woods catapulted me onto the moor, with the Berwyns – where a UFO is alleged to have crash-landed on a winter's night in 1974 – rising gently to the east. It was an euphoric 45 minutes of cycling, a gentle wind at my back and scarcely a car on the road.

There was one car that I was expecting, but never came – Fi's. Dismounting at the 486-metre crest of the pass, where the road dropped into Powys, the northern third of what used to be Montgomeryshire, I waited. Maybe my instructions had been too vague? 'Keep driving until the road stops climbing,' I'd said. At last, a silver shape emerged over the brow of the hill, and Fi, red-cheeked, confessed to taking a wrong turn, inadvertently driving the 12 miles around Llyn Tegid before joining the right road. She was having a bad day.

Moel Sych means 'dry hill' in Welsh, so why was it a sodden sponge where gurgling peat hags lay waiting to swallow us whole? Even the name failed to inspire: two blunt one-syllable words. Wooden boardwalks crossed the early bogs and prickly heather, but as the path rose to a cairn, the boardwalk ended. Ahead lay a mile-long sea of thick gorse and wet peat, with no discernible path. We slogged through the sticky bog without speaking and twice I had to rescue Fi's shoes from the sludge. This was no way to show a girl a good time.

A lifetime seemed to melt away before we arrived at the summit of this miserable mountain, crossed a sheep fence and found an untidy cairn atop a flat plateau. Not far to the northwest, the bare rocks of Cader Berwyn, every inch a mountain compared to Moel Sych, shimmered in the late evening light. Nevertheless, with Denbighshire falling away to the north and Montgomeryshire dropping to the south, our endeavour had earned us two county tops for the price of one.

On Ordnance Survey maps, Cader Berwyn and Moel Sych share the identical, but rounded-off height of 827 metres above sea level. Taking the level of these mountains to finite measurements reveals that Moel Sych rises a whole 30 centimetres higher than its neighbour, so regardless of Cader Berwyn boasting the aesthetic hallmarks of the worthy boss of the Berwyn range, it is Moel Sych that claims the honour.

A year and half after Fi and I had reached Moel Sych's summit, Cader Berwyn was vindicated. A fresh survey revealed a south summit on Cader Berwyn topped out at 830 metres, making it three metres higher than Moel Sych. Because the highest points of both peaks sit squarely on the dividing line between Denbighshire and Montgomeryshire, it would appear Cader Berwyn therefore overtakes Moel Sych as the loftiest ground in these two counties. It is a claim, however, that demands closer scrutiny. Again, according to Ordnance Survey, Cader Berwyn's south summit does not occupy the county boundary. Instead it stands around 100 yards from the line on the Montgomeryshire side.

All this means the following. Yes, Cader Berwyn is the highest mountain in Montgomeryshire. Yes, Cader Berwyn is the highest point of the Berwyn range. But – for what it is worth – Moel Sych remains the summit of Denbighshire, whether the people of that county want it or not.

It was nine o'clock when I began the descent to Bala, the retreating sun casting a tall shadow of my bicycle across the moor, as if it were a penny-farthing. The sun had dipped below the mountains as I glided into the town, where clouds of midges had formed a welcoming party on the shore of Llyn Tegid.

We traipsed along one side of the main street and back the other way without finding anywhere suitable to eat. I had just dragged my girlfriend across a thousand bogs on a never-ending mountainside. The least I could do was buy her dinner and – in some small way – make up for it. Yet pub menus were either too grand or only stretched as far as a chip butty. With great relief to our parched mouths and rumbling stomachs, we spotted the neon light of a pizzeria, still serving food at ten o'clock.

DAY 22 – BALA TO ABERDYFI: 43 MILES
Aran Fawddwy (Merionethshire): 905m

'*Bore da,*' smiled an old woman as I pedalled into Llanuwchllyn. I'd only cycled five miles along the southern bank of Llyn Tegid before the path to my next mountain appeared. I was back in the Snowdonia National Park to climb the little-known Aran Fawddwy, Merionethshire's county top. When walkers come to Snowdonia's southern reaches they tend to ignore Aran Fawddwy in favour of its celebrated neighbours, Arenig Fawr and Cadair Idris.

It was Fi's last day with me – unless the traffic fairy waved her roadworks wand – and we strolled up the sheep-dotted slopes hand in hand. It was the fifth consecutive day of unbroken sunshine and the tantrums of the Home Counties seemed a lifetime ago. However, the romantic mood soured somewhat as I broke the news that I had chosen the longest route up Aran Fawddwy, a ten-mile round trip. Soon we were trudging up steep inclines, Fi plodding a few yards behind, head down, silently swearing. 'Are you sure you're OK?' I asked for the tenth time that hour.

'Yes,' she snarled. 'If you ask me again...'

We walked on in silence.

'I reckon once we get to the top of this slope we'll be on the summit,' I declared confidently.

As I reached what I hoped would be the top, I looked up in anticipation. It wasn't the summit. 'Look, I'm sorry,' I said to the arriving Fi. 'Slight miscalculation. False summit. We've got to walk over there.' I pointed a mile away to the west and bit my lip. Her momentary glance of pure hatred was enough.

By the time we reached the summit of Aran Fawddwy – the highest point of a ridge stretching from Llyn Tegid east to the Dovey Valley – we had made up. Wonderfully alone on this sun-blasted plinth, we sat eating lunch and marvelling at the views across what seemed like all of Wales.

In search of shade and sustenance after a long descent, Fi drove us to Bala, where we retreated to a grassy spot next to Llyn Tegid. Although it was a peaceful scene with swimmers gliding across the millpond waters and children dashing in and out of the shallows, there was an unspoken tension between Fi and I. Nothing could paper over a very large crack. Our three days of adventure were over and she was returning home that night. I felt an awful pang of guilt. My 92-county quest was so self-centred. It was all about me – my escape, my dream, my journey. Where did she fit in? In truth, she didn't. There was no way she could, or would, cycle with me across the UK. We both knew that.

Fi drove me back to Llanuwchllyn and tossed my belongings into the dust. She was upset because her selfish boyfriend – someone who was meant to care about her – was going to abandon her again. I didn't say much. There was a brief embrace and I waved forlornly as her car disappeared down the road.

There was nothing to be gained from pondering. I shook the dust from my clothes, rammed them into my bag and pedalled towards Dolgellau. As I edged nearer to the Welsh coast, the dull ache of sadness was replaced by the exhilaration of solo travel again. Once I escaped Dolgellau, a sandy estuary leading to Barmouth Bay opened up before me. The road stuck to the coast and swept through Llwyngwril, Llangelynin, Rhoselefain and Bryncrug, before taking a sharp left to Aberdyfi.

Tonight I was staying in a house in this seaside town, and my host Mike Bendall hobbled down to the end of his driveway to meet me. He pointed his stick to a leg in plaster and smiled, 'It's on the mend. Great to meet you, Jonathan' – he called me by my proper name – 'I've heard all about your travels.'

Mike and Jill were friends of my parents; they had met while on holiday in Scotland three years earlier. Jill showed me to a bedroom, pointed out a shower and insisted she wash all my clothes. They were an ideal support team. Mike dug out his collection of maps and planned my route to Machynlleth and all the way to Pembrokeshire, while Jill provided the sustenance – double helpings of Moroccan shepherd's pie followed by apple pie and cream.

DAY 23 – ABERDYFI TO TREGARON: 64 MILES
Plynlimon Fawr (Cardiganshire): 752m

Nant-y-Moch. It was a name etched on my memory. I had spent a day standing in the River Rheidol, the watercourse that flows from the Nant-y-Moch Reservoir, during an A-level geography field trip. I could still recall the depth and velocity of the Rheidol and draw a neat cross-section of the riverbed, and I certainly hadn't forgotten how cold the water had been as it lapped over my wellies. Following the creation of two dams to generate hydroelectric power in 1964, water was allowed to flood the Cardiganshire valley, swallowing the hamlet of Nant-y-Moch, although a graveyard's contents and Iron Age cairns were relocated. Today the waters of Nant-y-Moch Reservoir lap the lower reaches of Plynlimon Fawr – a peak dubbed bland and boring by a section of the walking fraternity. At least I had company: my parents had driven west to tackle the mountain with me.

Dad unfolded the map across the car bonnet. 'If we head this way,' he said, running a finger along the blue line of the River Hengwm, 'I'm sure we'll find a path to the summit.' He flashed a reassuring smile at Mum: 'Just a short walk.' How many times had we heard that before? Unsurprisingly, an hour later we were sloshing through pools of water and tripping over grass tussocks, hopelessly lost. Dad scrutinised the map again.

'We've gone the wrong way, haven't we?' I suggested.

'No,' he replied stiffly. 'Just a different way.'

The different way escaped the tiresome tussocks before following a 4x4 track to the edge of Llyn Llygad Rheidol, a lake immediately to the east of Plynlimon Fawr. The path to the summit disappeared up a steep grassy slope high above our heads.

'No way,' Mum said, shaking her head. 'I'm not going up there.'

For 20 minutes, faced with false summit after false summit, we coaxed and cajoled her upwards. As the land became almost horizontal again, before rearing up to the true summit, Mum went on strike. 'Not another step further.'

Dad and I left her sitting on a smooth boulder, guarding the picnic basket and clambered to the stony top of Plynlimon Fawr. Bland? If rounded hills and shimmering lakes are bland, then yes, it's bland. Thrilling? Not particularly. Unlike neighbours in the north and south, Snowdonia and the Brecon Beacons, the central Cambrians lack an awe factor. They roll in serene green bumps, filling an onlooker with respect rather than wonder.

Dad breathed deeply, as if he was mentally preparing to break devastating news or utter some profound words. Instead he observed, 'I guess most of the county tops are pretty uneventful, much of a muchness.'

Uneventful? Although I remained silent, I took the word as a stinging slight on my journey. If you want eventful, I decided, I'll give you eventful.

We left the summit by an alternative route, walking towards a series of small cliffs above Llyn Llygad Rheidol. Navigating a way across fields of boulders, we soon came to the start of the line of cliffs, no more than a few metres high. The first precipice had a convenient ledge we were able shuffle along, one at a time. The second cliff was a different proposition. Its surface was cloaked in slippery wet moss and halfway across it demanded a leap of faith between a pair of outcrops. I scampered over untroubled, but it was a fearful prospect for someone twice my age, nearly twice my weight and unused to the terrain of a mountainside.

Dad reached the edge and paused. The outcrops were only a large step apart, but the stakes were high. Miss the ledge and there's a good chance a tumble will end with a 'plop' into Llyn Llygad Rheidol far below. Dad hesitated.

'Just jump,' I mocked. 'Come on.'

He leaped, right foot landing on firm ground, left foot flailing in clean air. It wasn't a pretty sight. Dad flung out both arms, clinging to the rock as his flapping leg madly sought a platform. After a second of panic, he wriggled unceremoniously onto safe ground. As blood poured from gashes on a knee and shin, I tried not to laugh. 'Uneventful, eh?'

After my parents had left, I drifted south but as dusk fell, I grew increasingly anxious. I had found nowhere to spend the night. Between Devil's Bridge and Pontrhydfendigaid, there were only a handful of tiny villages. Now I was in Tregaron, the biggest place for miles around, but as I cycled a lap of the town I could see no accommodation. All evening I had been attempting to make contact with a remote hostel in the Arfon Groes Valley, three miles northwest of Tregaron, but each time the phone rang out. I knew this particular hostel had been earmarked for closure and assumed the axe had already fallen. Nevertheless, it was my only hope – although a slender one – and making my way through high-hedged lanes, I knew that if this failed I was on the streets.

The gates were padlocked. The lights were off. The place seemed deserted. After scaling the metal gates, I peered through the glass. Inside, the walls were lined with bunk beds, each with a neatly folded blanket and pillow on top. It was still a hostel after all. A hostel I couldn't get into. Standing on the front porch, I twisted the doorknob – in desperation, rather than expectation – and to my surprise the door swung upon.

'Hello,' I called out. 'Anyone there?' No one answered. Tiptoeing across the threshold, I pushed open the kitchen door, murmuring 'Hello?' again. Feeling like an intruder, I toured the bedrooms and the bathrooms. Not a soul. The hostel was like an abandoned ship. The silence unnerved me. Surely there was an axe murderer lurking behind a door waiting to pounce, or a bloodied corpse festering in a shower cubicle?

Then it became clear. Blaencaron, as it was known, was one of the UK's last remaining unmanned hostels, where guests were trusted to pay for their night's stay. Not for much longer, however – posters indicated that the Youth Hostel Association planned to close it, along with nearby hostels at Ty'n Cornel and Dolgoch. In response, a campaign had swung into action to maintain the buildings as hostels.

The valley was now plunged in darkness, but I was safe, ensconced in a hostel where I was the only guest. Curling up on a sofa, my stomach full of rice and tea, I began to revel in my quiet surroundings. Rarely had I experienced such tranquillity, such freedom of thought. The silence made a tremendous knock on the outside door, a noise that echoed around the empty building, all the more startling. Rooted to the spot, I watched the door swing open. It was 11 o'clock. The hostel was in the middle of nowhere. Who could this be? The axe murderer? I gripped a saucepan and waited.

An old man with a flat cap and orange braces ambled through the doorway. I loosened my grip on the saucepan. 'Evening,' he roared, taking a seat at one of the kitchen tables. 'I saw the light and just thought I'd check that everything is as it should be.' The man spoke in a Welsh accent so thick I could barely comprehend his words, but he was no axe murderer, so I took a chair opposite, smiling and nodding politely as he spoke. He looked around the room, his gaze stopping on one of the campaign posters calling for the hostel to remain open. 'Have you seen what they want to do with this place? Close it down. Bloody fools they are, the lot of them. What would people like you do without this place?' Not be scared senseless by some local is what I could have said, but I resisted the urge.

Ten minutes later, still muttering about the 'bloody fools', he shuffled out of the door, leaving me alone again. This time I bolted the front door behind him, just in case the next visitor was the axe murderer.

FIVE

THE SUNDAY NIGHT BLUES – THE BRECON BEACONS –
WALES' BEST-KEPT SECRET – BONKING IN BRECON – A
WELSH HEATWAVE – THERE'S ONLY ONE ROI DE LA
ROUTE IN MERTHYR TYDFIL – PEN-Y-FAN – 'WE DON'T
GET MANY ARGENTINEANS IN ABERGAVENNY' – A
BRIEF ENGLISH INTERLUDE

DAY 24 – TREGARON TO NEWPORT: 64 MILES
Foel Cwmcerwyn (Pembrokeshire): 536m

It was Sir Bob Geldof who asked: 'Tell me why? I don't like
Mondays.' I can tell you why I don't like Mondays. For me,
Monday isn't a 24-hour block between two midnights.
Monday starts at around six o'clock on Sunday evening.
Just as you are tucking into beans on toast in front of
Songs of Praise, a wave of gloom slips unseen into the
room. The Sunday night blues. The unconfined joy of
finishing work on Friday evening seems only seconds ago.
Time has melted away. The weekend has vanished and
another five days of drudgery beckon.

It is Monday morning and an alarm clock is screaming
in your ear, the most wretched sound in creation. You've
just had two days off – pottering around the house,
reading the paper, catching up on the gardening – but, for
some unfathomable reason you feel exhausted, as if
you've run a marathon in your sleep. The cure? Press the

snooze button. Another 10 minutes won't hurt. Only it does. Again that dreadful din cuts through silent slumber, forcing you out of bed. Now you're rushing. You've missed your slot in the bathroom. There is no time for breakfast and the house keys are hiding down the back of the sofa. You arrive at work late and everyone is already at their desks, tapping keyboards and looking busy. They glance up and grunt.

My working Mondays tended to run a similar course. First, check the newsroom diary, where on a typical morning I would spy my initials next to a funeral at noon and a council planning meeting at three o'clock. Overwhelmed with the good news, I would traipse back to my desk, keeping my eyes fixed on the floor to avoid the glare of my editor. At precisely 20 minutes past eight, the ill-tempered reporter sitting opposite would be overcome by caffeine deficiency and suggest I make her a coffee. I oblige. 'Anyone else want one?' The grunters perk up and nod. I might as well be running a café. Tea with milk and sugar, herbal tea, hot water for Annabel who is 'on a diet', black coffee, decaffeinated coffee, coffee with whipped cream and a cherry on top, whiskey on the rocks, sex on the beach. There are, of course, no clean mugs, meaning a treasure hunt neatly fills the gap until 10 o'clock.

But Monday was never as bad as I imagined it would be. By lunchtime it was no different to a Tuesday or a Wednesday. Obviously not like a Friday though. The funeral is a happy send-off and I'm in and out of the council meeting within an hour. Soon it is six o'clock and I'm walking home. Monday is over for another week and the Sunday night blues are a distant memory.

Waking up in Blaencaron, it was the fourth Monday morning of my journey. I didn't need an alarm clock to rouse me. The sun beaming through the window was like a kiss on the cheek. Unemployment had a peculiar affect on me. At first, far from feeling footloose and free of responsibility, I was racked with guilt. While everyone else was doing an honest day's work, I was gallivanting across England and Wales, or as my ex-editor put it, 'away with the fairies'. Today, that guilt had evaporated and roaring along the sun-drenched lanes of central Wales, I didn't have a care in the world. After detesting it for two years, Monday was my new favourite day of the week, for no other could stir such powerful feelings of freedom.

I steered a course to the southwest, coasting through Llanddewi Brefi, home of Little Britain's 'the only gay in the village', before reaching Lampeter. From the little university town, the straightforward approach to Pembrokeshire's Foel Cwmcerwyn was to venture along the Cardigan to Haverfordwest road, which climbs over the spine of the Preseli Hills. At its highest point the route touches 404 metres, representing a serious test of my cycling legs. Even in Lampeter, some 30 miles shy of the Preseli Hills, the high pass consumed my thoughts. To some cyclists, bicycle riding is defined as pedalling uphill. This hardy breed of half-human, half-goat has no time for pottering about on flat terrain. Their bread and butter is grinding up an incline, the steeper the better, and getting a strange thrill out of the suffering it brings. It was a category I thought – or I'd like to think – I fell into.

The climb began in Brynberian, where the flat road charged upwards in cruel, thigh-burning fashion. I stayed in the saddle, churning the pedals, fighting the incline. Rumbling across the metal bars of a cattle grid, the road emerged onto scorched open moorland. A warm morning had turned into a sweltering afternoon. While the sun had been life-affirming in Dartmoor, now its dry rays were sucking that life from my limbs. Beads of salty sweat stung my eyes and my nose felt as if it could combust spontaneously. My engine was overheating, causing me to suffer badly, but there was still a mile to go. I lifted my backside from the saddle to ease the tension in my legs and dared look up to the pass. The road curled hideously, hiding the final torture. After ten minutes of wobbling progress, 'why am I doing this?' histrionics, ice cream hallucinations and indiscriminate cursing at passing cars, Wales became horizontal again. I threw down my bicycle and rolled onto a grass verge, shaking with dehydration and exhaustion.

With no prospect of finding water or food here, I wasted no time in setting off to discover the summit of Foel Cwmcerwyn. Desperate to escape the searing sun, I dived under the cover of the Pantmaenog Forest. There was no path, so I headed the logical way of an adventurer looking for the highest point – up. Nearing a clearing, I ducked under a tree branch, but another unseen stick jabbed me in the shoulder. I was already weakened by dehydration and the pain was intense, as if I had been stabbed with a knife. Holding back a trickle of blood, I concentrated on putting one foot in front of the other until I reached the hilltop.

Although Foel Cwmcerwyn is six miles inland, the hill is included within the boundary of the Pembrokeshire

Coast National Park. From the summit, I followed the jagged progress of the coast from St David's Head to Strumble Head. Not that I cared a jot – all I could think about was water, and gallons of it.

The road was almost exclusively downhill to the coast, but even the slightest rise made my legs feel as if they would crumble into a pile of dust. I made for Newport Sands, where I envisaged a cooling late-afternoon swim, followed by a leisurely and large dinner. 'Newport Sands: golden sandy beaches and a refreshment kiosk,' a tourist leaflet had boasted in Lampeter. Perhaps I should have checked the small print, for when I arrived, the beach was a miserable grey strip of sand doubling as a car park, while the kiosk displayed an unhelpful 'closed' sign in the window.

After retracing my route to neighbouring Newport, I hid under the covers of a bed in the town's youth hostel. My face was the colour of beetroot and my eyes were bloodshot and puffy. Far from resembling a well-honed athlete, I looked as if I was on the verge of collapse. I had ridden 64 miles – a modest but certainly not massive distance – yet the blistering heat and 1,600 yards of uphill cycling had reduced me to a pitiable state. Typical, I thought, as I gazed at the ceiling. It's Monday, isn't it?

DAY 25 – NEWPORT TO BRECON: 87 MILES
Fan Foel (Carmarthenshire): 781m

To the west lay the 520-square-mile slab of the Brecon Beacons National Park, extending from Llandeilo to Hay-on-Wye. From west to east, the National Park encompasses Black Mountain, Fforest Fawr, the Brecon Beacons and, rather confusingly, the Black Mountains, where Wales meets England. Four county tops lie within the National Park and a fifth just outside its boundary in north Glamorgan. Fan Foel straddles the Carmarthenshire and Brecknockshire border near Llandeusant. The great wedge-shaped Pen y Fan, the highest mountain in South Wales, casts an unmistakable presence over the old county town of Brecon. Chwarel y Fan, in Monmouthshire, and Black Mountain, in Herefordshire, stare at each other across the national divide. The fifth top, Glamorgan's Craig-y-Llyn, rises west of the twisting A4061 between Hirwaun and Treherbert.

The previous day's capitulation had made me fear the worst. Had I cracked? I cycled nervously away from Newport, agonising over every ache and niggle. But out of my tentative state grew confidence, a feeling that by noon had spawned a 50-mile dash to Llandeilo. Not long after, I was immersed in Black Mountain territory, a quiet place where rocky escarpments escape suddenly from smooth grassy humps.

Alone among the hills, I followed a path of grass and mud as it wound its way around a mineral-water-clear lake to the 749-metre Bannau Sir Gaer, where a walker exuding a man-of-the-mountains air stood admiring the view from the top.

'It's beautiful, isn't it?' said Dave, after introducing himself and telling me he lived close by in Gwynthe. 'I brought an Everest climber up here once and he reckoned this view was Wales' best kept secret. Its beauty is in its loneliness. I've been out here for five hours today and you're only the second person I've seen. The only paths are sheep tracks and there are no worn-out trails like you'll find around Pen y Fan.'

Dave's eyes lit up as I told him my story.

'You'll want to know all about the history of these hills then,' he said, and stepped towards the precipitous edge high above the lake. He pointed down towards the water I had skirted minutes earlier. 'That's Llyn y Fan Fach, a place where fairies are said to live.' As Dave spoke, he lowered his voice to a hushed whisper, as if fluttering fairies could eavesdrop on our conversation and cast a wicked spell. 'A local farmer saw a fairy woman rise from the lake while he was tending his cattle. For three successive days, the farmer returned, offering the woman three different types of bread.'

Dave had the story down to a tee, a clear sign he had told it too many times before.

'She refused the first two types of bread, but on the third day he presented her with lightly baked bread and she agreed to marry him. The woman disappeared into the lake, resurfacing again with her father and identical sister. The father said the farmer could marry his daughter providing he could choose between her and her sister... it's never simple with women, is it? Now where was I? Ah, yes. The farmer chose right and they married. But he was warned that should he strike his wife three times, the fairy woman would disappear into the lake forever. Sure enough, the farmer did, and years later after he struck that third blow, she came back up the valley and vanished into the lake.'

As we gazed down at the depths of Llyn y Fan Fach, Dave broke the silence. 'Good story, isn't it? Sad, though. Some say the farmer made it up because he wanted to marry a woman from a rival area.'

Pacing up the slope to Fan Foel, there was renewed vigour in every step. These weren't lifeless mountains and lakes. They were living and breathing, haunted by fairies and echoing in history. Soon I was standing on the summit of Fan Foel, my right leg in Brecknockshire and my left leg in Carmarthenshire. I shared the moment with a couple from Hertford who had their binoculars focused on a dot in the sky.

'It's a red kite,' the man said excitedly. 'Third one today.'

In 2002, Llandeilo-based Cambria Archaeology set about protecting a burial cairn on the summit of Fan Foel that walkers were treating as any old stone cairn. Intrigued, archaeologists excavated the site and made a stunning discovery. They unearthed a rectangular stone tomb and inside they found the cremated bones of a 12-year-old girl, along with the remains of two pigs and what might have been a dog. Experts at the University of Groningen dated the remains to 2000BC, while surrounding soil samples showed up microscopic pollen grains, indicating that the girl was buried with a floral tribute of meadowsweet.

As one of the local summits, Fan Foel would have been visible to the many farming communities that existed around Llandeusant 4,000 years earlier. The girl, possibly the daughter of a local chieftain, would have been a sacrifice, with locals hoping her virginity would make the surrounding land fertile. It was remarkable to think that over the 40 intervening centuries, thousands of people had tossed a stone on top of her unknown grave.

A glucose tablet pushed into my palm by Dave was all I had eaten since Llandeilo, five hours earlier. While runners hit 'the wall', us cyclists are a romantic lot. We 'bonk'. Bonking is avoidable and therefore a self-inflicted torture: a mix of exhaustion, dehydration and stomach-wrenching hunger, which leads to overwhelming lethargy. I have done some serious bonking in my time and today I was bonking like never before. It started on the descent from Fan Foel and manifested itself on the cross-country road to Trecastle. Between Sennybridge and Brecon, it became a dream-like state where my concept of danger disappeared. As cars whizzed past, I found it hard to steer a straight course. Rather like being hideously drunk, it was an hour of my life I couldn't account for. My mind was blank and all my body knew was to just keep on pedalling.

At the first shop in Brecon I grabbed a packet of chocolate biscuits from a shelf and ate every last one. The calorie-laden biscuits didn't even scratch the surface of my hunger, and it took two cans of fizzy drink, a litre of water, a banana and fish and chips to bring me back to life.

A short way out of the town centre, I came to a line of pubs and chose the one that offered the cheapest bed and breakfast, a £25 room in a wooden chalet behind the Gremlin. I opened the door, drew the curtains, tore off my clothes and flung myself onto the bed.

DAY 26 – BRECON TO TALYBONT-ON-USK: 54 MILES
Craig y Llyn (Glamorgan): 600m
Pen y Fan (Brecknockshire): 886m

No bonking today, I ordered myself, as I wheeled my bicycle to the front of the Gremlin. So an hour later, when I glimpsed an ice cream van at the crest of the mountain road between Brecon and Merthyr Tydfil, I didn't hesitate to pull over and treat myself. I joined the back of a long queue of Army recruits who were cooling off after a hot climb to the top of Fan Fawr.

The Brecon Beacons are synonymous with the Army. Opposite the ice cream van was the Storey Arms Centre, the starting point for the so-called Fan Dance, a 15-mile SAS selection exercise, intended to break the mental and physical will of recruits. With a two-stone Bergen pack on their backs, troops climb Pen y Fan and Cribyn, follow a Roman road to Torpantau, before retracing their route to the Storey Arms – all in under four hours. For those who haven't fallen by the wayside, this is only the beginning. The Long Drag is held on the last day of the three weeks of selection. Recruits' rucksacks now weigh four stone and have to be lugged across 40 miles of Brecon Beacons in 20 hours.

Avoiding the kamikaze sheep that lay spread-eagled across the tarmac, I raced to Hirwaun, from where the zigzagging road towards Treherbert deposited me at Craig y Llyn picnic site. I was in Glamorgan, a county bounded by the Brecon Beacons and the Bristol Channel. Here in Wales' densely populated industrial heartland I would find deep, narrow valleys scarred by the collapse of the coal mining industry. But in this corner of north Glamorgan, mining still lived on – for now. Nestling in the Hirwaun valley below Craig y Llyn was Tower Colliery, Wales' last deep mine. After beginning life in 1864, it was closed in 1994 by the National Coal Board, which insisted it was uneconomic. Unwilling to accept it was the end, 239 determined miners, led by Tyrone O'Sullivan, used their £8,000 redundancy payments to buy out the pit and it re-opened a year later. With the coal seams exhausted, the colliery closed again on 25 January 2008 – this time for good.

Glamorgan's county top was not as inspiring. A rubbish-strewn Forestry Commission track passed a burned out car, an abandoned chest of drawers and a lone red stiletto before emerging into a clearing in the woods, where the summit lay next to a rusty radio transmitter.

'Revolution!' screamed the front-page splash on *The Independent*. 'Britain is in the grip of a cycling revolution as clogged roads, concern at global warming caused by air pollution and the quest for improved fitness persuade millions to opt for pedal power.' I read on. Bicycle journeys in London are up, users of the National Cycle Network are up and overall journeys made by bicycle are up.

I wasn't about to crack open the champagne. Motorists and cyclists have an uneasy relationship. Cycling, we are told, is good for our health and the pollution-free cure for our traffic-clogged roads. But be honest. Cyclists can be frustrating and unpredictable, rarely signal their intent or move painfully slowly. Many motorists would love to swat the environmentally conscious smugness off the faces of Lycra lunatics like an annoying insect. I know. I've been there. I despised them when I was learning to drive. What do you do? Overtake or hang back? Or lose patience and drive over them, hoping your instructor didn't notice? The night before my test, I prayed a wobbling cyclist wouldn't lurch out from some invisible crevice, dashing my chances of passing. In the end it wasn't a cyclist that made me fail. It was my bad driving.

Enter the actor Nigel Havers, stage right. 'I absolutely hate cyclists,' he told *The Independent*. 'If they use the roads for free and they don't have to pay any tax, they must obey the rules. The rules are that you stop at a red traffic light. I'm at one now and four cyclists just went through. They go up a one-way street the wrong way. One just smacked the side of my car with his hand. It's unbelievable behaviour.'

Obey the rules of the road? Like car drivers do? Where do I start? Drink-driving. Speeding. Jumping red lights. Reading a map while driving. Using mobile phones. Fiddling with the stereo. Eating. Not bothering with a seatbelt. Discarding litter. Tossing cigarette butts. Not to mention picking at a snotty nose, while their vehicle spews a cocktail of planet-annihilating chemicals into the atmosphere.

Quite simply, the UK lacks a cycling culture. Sustrans could add another 10,000 miles to its National Cycle Network and Lance Armstrong could be elected as the next Prime Minister. It wouldn't make a blind bit of difference. Take the French. They have a 100-year love affair with the bicycle, thanks largely to the Tour de France. It's a culture that can't be replicated overnight.

It's a bit like continental style drinking. 'Let's open pubs longer,' we said in 2005, 'and the British will drink more sensibly.' Of course we won't. We're British. We'll still get legless. We're just not like the French.

Across La Manche even the amateur is king of the road, or *roi de la route*, as they say. I was once cycling through the Romanche Valley to Bourg d'Oisans when a battered Fiat paused behind me. When there was no traffic coming the other way the car drew level. Were I in the UK, I'd have braced myself for some smart comment, a shower of spit or a string of obscenities. Instead a gnarled hand gently touched me on the back and the passenger, an old lady, murmured, '*Courage*'.

Cyclists flout the rules of the road. Everybody knows that. And when we do, don't uptight motorists take it so seriously, as if we've mugged their grandmother? What do they expect? Isn't an essential part of cycling that opportunity to show a streak of anarchism? As for me, I'm as guilty as the rest, having lost count of the number of times I have breezed through a red light. Car drivers won't believe me, but sometimes it is safer to get away from traffic lights, to keep up the momentum of motion. What motorists must remember is that a cyclist gambles with his or her life every time they set rubber onto UK roads. Crossing a red light is only another throw of the dice. And in the wider scheme of road safety, aren't there hundreds of potential flash points far more serious than a cyclist running a red light? I was getting quite het up about cyclists' rights until a juggernaut trundled past my right ear bringing me to my senses. There was only one *roi de la route* in Merthyr Tydfil.

Retreating to the narrow lanes of the National Park, I had hoped for some respite. I was busy penning a letter in my mind to *The Independent* when I passed a sign for Pontsticill, prior to rounding a bend. As I turned the corner, a jeep was approaching in the opposite direction. Our paths would cross in a matter of moments. Nothing unusual in that. But then suddenly a car lurched from behind the jeep, veered into my lane and accelerated. The driver of the jeep slammed on his brakes. It was no use. The three of us were on a collision course.

As the grim reaper, in the guise of a black Saab, neared, I could see the faces inside. The passengers in the rear seats were leaning forward, their arms wrapped around the headrests, cheering the driver on. The driver cut a different figure. His arms were locked on the steering wheel, a stunned expression on his face. His bit of fun was never meant to end like this: the death of a cyclist. The Saab was almost on top of me now. As I felt a warm draught of air, I accepted that this was the end. I had reached 31 county tops, more than a third of the way. It had been a brave effort. I shut my eyes and waited. The wing mirror brushed the top of my thigh. I gasped and wobbled, but stayed on two wheels. I was alive. Adrenaline pounded through my veins. I'd never felt more alive. 'I'm invincible!' I roared.

The trio of wedges, Corn Du, Cribyn and Pen y Fan, are a sight to behold. From the south, glaciated sandstone slopes rise serenely, ending at a flat summit plateau. The land then takes a vertical plunge down sheer grassy cliffs, giving the appearance of a vast tidal wave poised to break over Brecon. The highest of the three, Pen y Fan, has been called the most dangerous mountain in Wales because the climate can change so rapidly, though whether the mountain is more dangerous than the perilous ridges of Snowdonia is doubtful.

The most popular starting point for walkers tackling Pen y Fan is the Storey Arms Centre on the A470, where the Army recruits and I had enjoyed an ice cream six hours earlier. Fewer choose to start their climb from the Neuadd Reservoir to the southwest of the mountain, and that is where I left my bicycle, under a corrugated iron shelter below the top dam. The path followed the margins of the reservoir, but the water level was so low that the orange rescue buoys were marooned 100 yards from the lake's edge. Sheep tracks led me to the pass between Cribyn and Fan y Big, Brown Willy's fiercest competitor in the naughtiest mountain name stakes, and not long afterwards I was standing on top of Pen y Fan, alone in the soft evening haze.

With night falling, I cycled into a wall of flies alongside the Talybont Reservoir. If I kept my head up they would zoom into my eyes, blinding me for a moment. If I lowered my head, the insects would ricochet off my helmet with a thud. Once I reached Talybont-on-Usk, my left eye was so sore I could hardly open it, and I raced into the gents in the Star Inn. No wonder I was in pain. I recovered the bodies of five of the little black critters, who were drowning in my left eyeball, while another two had taken up residence in my right eye. With my sight returned, I ordered a pint in the Star Inn, where the chattering hue and smoky air was reassuring after a lonely day in the hills. I wolfed down chicken balti, chips, rice and naan bread, before inching my way through the darkness to a hostel below the Talybont dam.

A man strolled out of the building to meet me. 'Mr Muir? We've been expecting you.' It was an ominous welcome, even more so when we got into the light and my companion was revealed to be a 6ft 6in giant, with a gelled Mohican on the top of his head.

'This is the youth hostel, isn't it?' I asked, fearing I might have unwittingly got caught up with the Talybont Mafia.

DAY 27 – TALYBONT-ON-USK TO CAPEL-Y-FFIN: 34 MILES
Chwarel y Fan (Monmouthshire): 679m
Black Mountain (Herefordshire): 700m

'How do you think you'll do in the World Cup?'

'Excuse me?' I said, looking up from *The Worst Journey in the World* as a lean Welshman limbered up in front of me. He was jogging on the spot, panting. 'Semi-finals? England-Argentina final maybe? Can you imagine?'

The World Cup was starting tomorrow and football fever was sweeping the UK, even though England was the only home nation that had made it to Germany.

'Ah, you mean...'

I wore my Argentina cycling jersey every day. Apart from a couple of comments in Devon and Somerset, it had been ignored up until now. Perhaps I was beginning to look like I could be from Argentina? My pale white skin of a month ago was tanned and my beard was coming on nicely, even if it lacked the thickness of a Reinhold Messner. All that let me down was my hair, which was steadily being bleached blond in the sun. 'Sorry, mate,' I said. 'I'm not actually from Argentina. I'm English. I just like this shirt.'

'Oh,' he said, his voice tinged with disappointment. 'We don't get many Argentineans in Abergavenny. Plenty of English, though.'

I had set off early that day because the mercury was forecasted to tip 30C. Even by 11 o'clock, when I'd started along the road that snakes its way through the Vale of Ewyas en route to Gospel Pass, I was melting. The sultry heat was beginning to get to me. Sun was better than rain, but while rain drained my spirits, the sun sapped my strength. The heat had already got the better of me twice in the past three days, leaving me nauseated in Newport and bonked in Brecon. With that in mind, I retreated to the shade of the 12th-century Llanthony Priory to contemplate the trudge to Chwarel y Fan.

I was impatient to get the walk over and done with, and because of Chwarel y Fan's modest height, I didn't bother looking for a path. Heading straight up, I followed a narrow sheep track through high ferns, which brought me to an ocean of calf-deep gorse. I'd have found more shade in the Sahara. As the sun frazzled my thoughts and unsteadied my step, I might as well have had a radiator strapped to my face. Swearing really loudly in the direction of the sun helped, but it didn't prevent me becoming delusional. After seeing a snake earlier in the day, I was convinced I would disturb another one. It would bite me and unable to suck out the poison, I would die a lonely death on this godforsaken hillside.

After an interminable slog, I escaped the gorse and clambered on to Chwarel y Fan's summit ridge. The ridge sloped gently to the highest point, marked by a pile of stones standing sentinel over two valleys, my starting point in the Vale of Ewyas and Grwyne Fawr to the west. Following a wide path downhill, I reached the valley floor in a quarter of the time it had taken to get up.

The road had followed the course of the Afon Honddu since leaving Llanvihangel, but as I neared Gospel Pass, the winding strip of tarmac reached up to a gap in the hills between the tastefully-named Lord Hereford's Knob and Hay Bluff. As I arrived at the top of the last incline, I was greeted with a view across the Wye Valley and the hills of Radnorshire that was resplendent enough to warm the heart of any Welshman or woman.

As attractive as Lord Hereford's Knob sounded, I set off east towards the great hulk of Black Mountain. The afternoon heat had subsided and on reaching Hay Bluff I swung south to join Offa's Dyke, a track that follows the boundary line of Wales and England. One might expect a summit of a mountain to be obvious, a towering peak dominating its surroundings. Not the flat plateau of Black Mountain. I stopped at a point where Offa's Dyke seemed to go no higher, though with the eye alone it was hard to tell. I could have been standing on the summit or as much as 100 yards away. But being Herefordshire's county top I had to be in England, so I stood to the east of Offa's Dyke and turned my back on Wales.

DAY 28 – CAPEL-Y-FFIN TO HEREFORD: 56 MILES
Great Rhos (Radnorshire): 660m

Rising three miles to the northwest of the tenth-century village of New Radnor is Great Rhos, the green dome summit of Radnorshire. A multitude of signs warn the walker about a great swathe of land on the mountain's southern slopes, which is used as an ammunition testing area. Walkers must not stray onto the land when red flags are hoisted, the signs instruct. Today, the red flags were flying, but presumably the hundreds of sheep grazing in the 'danger area' were not at risk of being struck by a flying bullet. Still, I wasn't going to take the chance and followed a grassy track that led around the perimeter of the firing zone.

On the Black Mountain look-a-like summit, I came across a middle-aged man in a flat cap and raincoat, who was in the process of lowering an aerial and packing up radio equipment. Each item was carefully ordered into individual Tupperware containers before he put them all into one large Tupperware box. Then he pulled out yet another item of Tupperware containing what resembled a beetroot sandwich. As he didn't look like he was going to tell me what he was up to, I asked.

'I thought you'd want to know,' Tupperware man laughed smugly. 'People always do.'

I instantly wished I had not let curiosity get the better of me.

'I use the radio to talk to people on other mountains. It's called Summits on the Air,' he explained. 'You must have heard of it?'

'Um... no.'

Summits on the Air sounds like it could be the next extreme-sport craze. In reality, it involves a group of walkers who communicate with one another from specific high points across the globe. 'It combines my two interests,' he said, 'walking and radios.'

Each qualifying mountain is designated a score. Ben Nevis, for instance, earns ten because of its height, while the lower Aran Fawddwy gets eight and Great Rhos just four. However, the scoring system appears somewhat biased in the favour of British hills and mountains. While a walker can earn ten points for climbing Scafell Pike or Ben Nevis, ten points in Switzerland is harder to come by. You have to climb the 3,970-metre Eiger to earn that. Why does this matter you ask? Well, there are prestigious prizes on offer. Top mountain chasers are presented with the Mountain Goat award and the losers get the Shack Sloth plaque.

Tupperware man said he'd been on the summit for 90 minutes and in that time had spoken to Ben Nevis. 'I mean someone on Ben Nevis,' he quickly corrected himself.

I wondered what they could possibly talk about.

'Hello, Great Rhos here, anybody there?'

'This is Ben Nevis. What's the view like?'

'Wonderful. Yours?'

'Great.'

'What's the weather like?'

'Windy.'

'Windy here too.'

'Better go – I've got the Matterhorn on the other line.'

'I'm doing the county tops,' I said.

'Oh right,' Tupperware man acknowledged without a shred of excitement.

'On my own, continuous journey, just cycling and walking – in 92 days.'

'I think I'll head over to Gwaunceste Hill. Only three points though.'

Having failed to impress Tupperware man, I left him alone on the summit to drool over his next hill and descended to New Radnor.

My prize for completing the 13 Welsh county tops was three glorious days off. Cycling to Hereford, I realised I needed them badly. Pain in my right knee was beginning to trouble me and another day of light-headedness was more than I could take. As I rode into Hereford railway station, the 3.39 train to Bromsgrove was waiting at the platform. As it rolled out of town, I raised a bottle to my lips, draining the last warm water in a little toast to Wales.

DAY 29 TO 31 – BROMSGROVE

I must have been in an idealistic mood. I was sitting at home reading the back of a cereal packet when I was overcome with an urge to buy a tent. Before I knew it, I was in an army surplus store in Kidderminster, handing over £25 for a one-man contraption.

Camping would solve all my problems. Fed up with being a slave to bed and breakfast, hotel and hostel, I could do away with the last boundary to my freedom with a tent. My little green shelter would make me the footloose traveller I longed to be. If I saw a favourable place to park myself, maybe on a beach, next to a lake or halfway up a mountain, I would pitch my tent. No hassle.

There was one major drawback. To carry the extra equipment I needed to fit panniers to my bicycle. Formerly a lightweight travelling machine, it was now a mobile suitcase, in need of a sign warning 'wide load'. Antoine de Saint-Exupéry would be spinning in his grave.

SIX

THE WILDS OF WARWICKSHIRE – GABBY LOGAN AND GABBY YORATH ARE THE SAME PERSON – THE VILLAGE IDIOT – LEICESTERSHIRE'S ANSWER TO THE BERMUDA TRIANGLE – CAMPING ON THE BOUNDARY – HILLS OF GOLD – ENGLAND'S LOWEST COUNTY – BORING FIELD – THE WISE WORDS OF H.G WELLS

DAY 32 – HEREFORD TO WELLESBOURNE: 75 MILES
Ebrington Hill (Warwickshire): 261m

Camping. What springs to mind at the prospect of spending a night under canvas? Toasting marshmallows on a crackling fire, while gazing up at twinkling stars? Curling up in a warm sleeping bag and waking to the sound of twittering birds? Get real. The drip-drip-drip of washed-out Cub camps, raw dawns in the Alps and the wretched darkness of solo camping – those were the images that sprung to my mind. Too late I had remembered – I hate camping.

With a day of meandering across Herefordshire, Gloucestershire and Warwickshire behind me, I was determined to spend my first night in the great outdoors. There were still four hours till dusk, ample time to find a place to pitch my tent. How difficult could it be? Even though my map failed to show such useful titbits of information as camping sites, I cycled towards

Stratford-upon-Avon confident that finding one would be a simple task.

Sure enough it was. In Tiddington, touring caravans were sprawled across the south bank of the River Avon, but a notice on a metal gate stated simply: 'No tents'. Why were tents so unpopular? I imagined a gang of vigilante campers roaming the Warwickshire countryside setting fire to caravans, sabotaging waste-water pipes and holding middle-aged couples and their golden Labradors hostage.

My next hope was a hostel in Alveston; a refurbished Georgian mansion set in three acres of grounds.

'We don't allow camping,' the warden said firmly.

'But, you've got three acres of land,' I moaned. 'Why can't I pitch a tent on one little bit of it?'

'Sorry, we're not allowed,' she said. 'But we do have beds free if you want to stay tonight.'

I hesitated, hovering on one foot, my mind thrown into limbo. Just stay here, my brain urged. Don't make things more complicated than they need to be.

'Thanks, but I want to camp,' I replied.

After 15 minutes of feeling sorry for myself, I came to a caravan park, where white boxes were arranged in neat rows on numbered pitches and there was even a separate grassy area for tents. Running my eyes down the price list, I gawked at the fee – £10 per night per tent. 'Daylight bloody robbery,' I muttered aloud. The hostel in Alveston only charged a couple of pounds more, and for that I didn't have to sleep in a field.

Deciding it was too expensive, I set off to explore the outskirts of Wellesbourne, looking for somewhere wild to camp. Wild camping is illegal in England, but with a little native intelligence I reckoned I could find a secluded pitch for the night. As I scouted the edge of a playing field, the corner of a farmer's crop and even one of Wellesbourne's large roundabouts, a wave of daunting reality washed over me. I'd never done this before. The thought of being found while I lay sleeping, semi-clothed and defenceless in my tiny tent filled me with dread. I followed my instincts, which shouted at me not to wild camp tonight. Instead I propped my cycle outside the Stag's Head and took a nosy stroll around the pub to see if there was a beer garden I could pitch my tent in. I found a prime square of soft grass between two tables. All I needed now was to persuade the landlord to let me stay.

A man and a woman were serving behind the bar, and deciding my charms might be more disarming on the woman, I waited until the former had sloped off to collect empty glasses.

'I'm trying to find somewhere to camp tonight. You don't know of anywhere, do you?' I decided not to ask directly. Hopefully, she would suggest the pub garden and I'd say: 'Ooh, I couldn't possibly. Really? Are you sure? Oh, OK, I'd be delighted. Bacon and eggs for breakfast? If you insist.'

'I'd say you could camp in the garden behind the pub,' she said.

She had fallen for it. 'Are you sure?' I replied, trying to muffle my excitement.

She backtracked. 'Actually, it's full of stuff for a wedding that we're holding on Saturday. There will be no room.'

In my head, I bellowed at her. There's room. There's definitely room. But only a meek begging voice came out: 'It's a very small tent. You won't know I'm there.'

She wasn't budging. 'No, I really don't think there's space. I'm sorry, I don't know what else to suggest.'

Defeated, I ordered sausage and chips and sulked at a table next to a double act of pot-bellied boozers. One was completely bald, his head as smooth and polished as a snooker ball. The other had a few remaining Bobby Charlton-style wisps of hair, enough to comb over his scalp. The World Cup was now in full swing and on a TV in the bar, Brazil were playing Croatia. As the cameraman – it must have been a man – swept across the crowd, he focussed on Brazil's glamorous female following, many of them clad only skimpy yellow and green bikinis.

'Ooh yeah, I'd give her one,' Snooker Ball chortled.

'She's a bit skinny for my liking. I like a bit of meat to hang on to,' Comb-over argued.

Snooker Ball was staring open-mouthed at the screen. 'Just look at the tits on that,' he gasped. 'Ooh yeah, I'd give her one as well. Bang her senseless, I would.'

I smiled at him, resisting the urge to ask whether he thought she would mind being 'banged senseless' by a bald, tubby Warwickshire fiftysomething.

Comb-over was clearly a football connoisseur, a student of the beautiful game. 'Ronaldo, you fat bastard,' he barked at the TV. 'My old man's 82 and he's faster than you.'

As the barmaid scurried past collecting glasses and emptying ashtrays, I eyed her with an 'I'll be sleeping on the streets tonight and it is all your fault' glare.

Another profound colloquy was underway at the bar. Again women and football were the night's specialist subjects. This time ITV's football presenter Gabby Logan was the topic of conversation.

'So Gabby Logan and Gabby Yorath are the same person? Well, I never knew that. Why did she change her name?'

'She got married to that Scottish rugby player, didn't she, stupid.'

'You know I always thought they looked similar. I used to say it to the wife. Wait till I tell her that they're the same woman.'

It had been a day of transition. The thrilling ups and downs of Wales had given way to the horizontal terrain and prosaic roads of Herefordshire and Gloucestershire. Under forbidding skies I had ducked below the M50 and dived over the M5. Rain clouds had chased me all morning, finally catching up with me in Tewkesbury where I'd sheltered under the forecourt of a petrol station. Spray from the wet road had flicked across my back as I sped past Snowshill's scented lavender fields and through Chipping Campden's Cotswold splendour, en route to the Warwickshire border. Ebrington Hill hunkers on the outlying fringe of Shakespeare's county and a road signposted to Ilmington had led me across the boundary. To my right, Warwickshire's county top lay in an unremarkable field of dripping grass, while to my left, two large satellite dishes and a pylon reared their ugly heads.

It was full time. I skulked out of the Stag's Head, giving the barmaid a final 'I hope I don't freeze to death' look. My tail between my legs, I cycled back to the caravan park, wondering how four hours of my life had become absorbed by procrastination.

DAY 33 – WELLESBOURNE TO MARKET BOSWORTH: 73 MILES
Arbury Hill (Northamptonshire): 225m

I unzipped the flysheet and watched the light of dawn creep across the sky. I was bitterly cold. My sleeping bag was designed for temperatures down to zero, adequate I had assumed for the wilds of Warwickshire. Overnight, the mercury had plummeted until my teeth chattered and my feet felt like blocks of ice. I tried to lull myself back to sleep, but the ground was as hard as rock and knotted clumps of grass protruded into my back and shoulders. An hour later, I gave up, unzipping the flysheet again. Now the sky was grey and forlorn. The birds weren't singing. Pulling cobwebs off my face, I trudged barefoot along a track to a portable building, a glorified wash room, where I splashed my face with water piped straight from the Arctic. I packed up, paid up and cycled away. I had confirmed that I hate camping.

Soaked by a claustrophobic mizzle, I edged through Leamington Spa's rush-hour traffic before crossing the Northamptonshire border between Napton-on-the-Hill and Staverton. Arbury Hill stands on the county's eastern reaches and from its slopes the River Nene begins a 91-mile journey through Northamptonshire, Cambridgeshire and Lincolnshire to The Wash. There was no right of way so I made haste across muddy fields until I emerged onto a flat summit, dotted with clumps of stinging nettles and a flock of sheep. With steep earthworks on four sides and with a top so flat the sheep and I could have played cricket, it was clear that Arbury Hill had not been sculpted by nature alone. Like many UK summits, it had been irrevocably altered by the presence of an Iron Age fort, which had once stood astride Northamptonshire's highest point.

As I searched for a café in Daventry, an elderly man with grey hair in a ponytail stopped me and muttered something unintelligible about my bicycle. Assuming my propensity to attract the village idiot had returned, I was thinking up an excuse to move on when his ramblings struck a chord.

'I used to live on a narrow boat and I'd spend the whole day on my bicycle, just exploring,' he said. 'I'd start at six o'clock and cycle until it was dark – 70, 80 or 90 miles.'

I could see my elderly friend was going a little misty-eyed. To him, I was a reincarnation of what he used to be.

'I'd visit cathedrals, monuments, all the things that have shaped our local history. You can't do that in a car. You miss so much. It was a wonderful life.' He tilted his head near mine to proffer some final advice. 'Always make time for the lovely ladies.'

My Northamptonshire sojourn lasted less than three hours. Warwickshire lured me back across the border and I cycled north to Rugby, where I darted into the plush new visitor centre to shelter from the rain. I really wished I hadn't. For when I told the female versions of The Two Ronnies – one short and round, the other tall with glasses

– that I was searching for a campsite, they threw themselves into action. Problems arose because of a misunderstanding: I obviously hadn't made it clear that I had to cycle to my destination. After each phone call, they would return to the counter and ask, 'Is Birmingham too far?' or 'Will you be able to get to Chesterfield tonight?' or 'I can find you a bed and breakfast in Moscow.' Almost all the campsites were full, didn't answer or wouldn't accommodate tents. Finally, a site in Market Bosworth, some 25 miles north, would welcome me, provided I arrived before six o'clock.

Zooming north, I was set to meet my deadline with time to spare. However – and let this be a warning to all – I hadn't accounted for Leicestershire's version of the Bermuda Triangle: the wedge of land imprisoned by the M1, M6 and M69. As soon as I crossed the M6 I could sense the presence of higher forces afflicting my mind, with strange air currents – not the inability to read a map – sending me spinning in circles. Claybrooke Magna was pleasant the first time around and tolerable on the second lap. On our third meeting, I wanted to torch the damn place.

It was after six o'clock when I reached Market Bosworth and found the site reception closed. The decision was made for me. Tonight I had to camp wild. After a dinner at the Red Lion, I laid my tent out on the springy grass of the town's cricket pitch. Unless Market Bosworth played night cricket there was no chance I'd be disturbed. It was on that cricket boundary in a rainy corner of southwest Leicestershire that I'm proud to say I lost my wild camping virginity.

DAY 34 – MARKET BOSWORTH TO UPPINGHAM: 53 MILES
Bardon Hill (Leicestershire): 278m
Cold Overton Park (Rutland): 197m

There be gold in them there hills... well, a tiny bit at least. The precious metals locked away in Leicestershire's low-lying bumps may not have attracted the euphoria that surrounded the 19th-century gold rushes in Australia or South Africa, but hey, even if there's only enough gold to make a ring, who cares? Gold is gold.

There are few places in the UK where urban and rural collide so dramatically as at Bardon Hill, for Leicestershire's highest low-lying bump is also a Site of Special Scientific Interest. Following the Ivanhoe Way, I strolled through lush woods, where rare migrants such as ring ouzels, woodlark and buzzards have been known to visit. Stepping up to the summit I saw that Bardon Hill is also an island in a sea of concrete and industry. To one side, the sun reflected off the flat white roofs of a sprawling industrial estate and a plume of smoke curled from the lips of a towering chimney. Below, a vast bowl-shaped quarry had been gouged out, with diggers scurrying across the mine like ants building a nest. The rock, a mix of vivid red and grey, has been mined for nearly 400 years. The grey rocks were formed first, the deposits of volcanic eruptions when Leicestershire lay at the bottom of a tropical ocean. Some 200 million years later, when the county was a dry desert, wind-blown dust and sand coated the volcanic rock. Today the red rock is removed so the durable volcanic rock beneath can be quarried and used in the construction of roads.

The county of Rutland disappeared in 1974, when it was divided up between Leicestershire and Northamptonshire, only to return in 1999 and reclaim its crown as England's smallest county. It measures just 17 miles across and is home to only two towns, Oakham and Uppingham, so Rutland's county top was not going to be a towering peak to set pulses racing. I inched my way east through a maze of villages – Copt Oak, Swithland, Queniborough, Barsby, Twyford, Somerby and Cold Overton – before I located the roof of Rutland, a grassy knoll only a handful of steps across the Leicestershire border. Under the watchful eye of a British Telecom mast, I waded through a field of long grass until I found the flat summit, marked by a triangulation pillar hiding behind a hedge.

What I'd missed most on my journey were those simple pleasures we all take for granted, like putting the kettle on, raiding the fridge or soaking in a bath. Apart from an icy cold splash of the face in Wellesbourne, I hadn't washed since leaving Hereford two and a half days earlier – two and a half days of sweat, mud, toil and more sweat. I was beginning to stink. Even the sheep on the summit of Arbury Hill had eyed me with disdain. Fortunately, the prospect of a shower was on hand, as I had arranged to stay with two journalist friends in Uppingham. Jenny was the chief political correspondent for the *Leicester Mercury*, while Matt manned the news desk at the *Evening Telegraph* in Peterborough.

Jenny hugged me, sniffed the air and quickly let go,

probably wishing she hadn't gone in for the embrace. Keeping arms pinned to my sides to prevent the escape of noxious gases, I politely asked if I might use their shower. Handing me a towel and a bottle of bleach, Jenny left me to it.

DAY 35 – UPPINGHAM TO CAMBRIDGE: 65 MILES
Boring Field (Huntingdonshire): 80m

Unlike Rutland, Huntingdonshire is no longer a county in its own right, having been demoted to a district council sub-section of Cambridgeshire. Huntingdonshire does, however, hold two of the UK's geographic distinctions. At Holme Fen, six miles south of Peterborough, the land dips to 2.7 metres below sea level, the lowest point in the UK. Meanwhile, Huntingdonshire's highest point rises only to 80 metres, making the county's summit the lowest of the highs. Boring Field, as it tends to be aptly called, sits on the present-day Cambridgeshire border with Bedfordshire, between the villages Covington and Hargrave, not far from England's largest natural lake, Grafham Water.

I parked my bicycle under a concrete water tower next to Three Shires House, where for centuries the boundaries of Bedfordshire, Cambridgeshire and Huntingdonshire had converged. The drive of the house resembled Steptoe's scrapyard. A coach was propped up on jacks, battered old cars were crammed into every free crevice, while doors, bonnets, tyres, wheels and exhausts sat in rusting heaps. A sign warned: 'Loose dogs, stay in your car.' A sorry-looking mongrel hobbled towards me and let out a hoarse woof. It looked like its years of mauling trespassers were long gone. Alerted by the bark, a man leaned out of an upstairs window and introduced himself as Sam.

'OK to walk through your yard?' I asked.

'Fine,' he replied. 'Help yourself.'

Negotiating a haphazard way through decades of accumulated junk, I reached a path blocked by a high wall of stinging nettles. Hacking through the jungle, I felt like an explorer on the verge of discovering a lost land. Instead I found the rusting hulk of a Sunbeam Rapier before emerging on to the edge of a field of barley. I could see why this place was called Boring Field. The contours rose so gradually you could be forgiven for thinking the land was flat. It was not really fitting to call Boring Field a highest point; that would bring shame on the exclusive club of county summits. A hedgerow between two decidedly boring fields marked the top and upon arriving there, in my mind I re-christened this lowly spot Steptoe's Rise.

It was mid-Friday afternoon when I reached Cambridge, a 65-mile jaunt from Uppingham. Deciding to knock off early, I joined the hordes of sunbathers on Parker's Piece. As I lay on the grass, the city reminded me of the words of HG Wells: 'When I see an adult on a bicycle, I do not despair for the future of the human race.' Cambridge is a city of cyclists and the presence of so many bicycles filled my heart with a warm glow. An hour earlier, on the road between St Neots and Cambridge, I'd been a stranger in a world of petrolheads. Now I was among friends, a place where cyclists really were the *rois de la route*. I watched as every variety of bicycle drifted past, from slick road racers to chunky-tyre mountain bikes and 'sit up and beg' Dutch machines loaded down with bells, wicker baskets and panniers. There is nowhere else in the UK, except perhaps Oxford, which demonstrates the classless appeal of pedal power. There were carefree schoolchildren, posh students in boaters, pretty waitresses on their way to work, wise old professors and smartly dressed business folk.

Wrenching myself away from Parker's Piece, I followed in the slipstream of one particularly pert-bottomed female cyclist who was heading towards the railway station. It was a lovely sight, one of those things they fail to mention in the *Lonely Planet* entry for Cambridge. As the city's hostel loomed to my left, I pulled up, watching the pert bottom disappear around a corner.

Above: The first of many… on the summit of Brown Willy.

Below: Day 15 and Worcestershire Beacon in the Malvern Hills, 'the most beautiful silhouette in the world'.

Above: Holyhead Mountain in Anglesey, officially it is 390 meters too short to be classed as a mountain. Who cares? It *looks* like a mountain.

Below: The Snowdon Mountain Railway, which has been running since the late 19th century. On foot it takes the best part of two hours to reach the summit… but at least you can look the cashier in the eye when you buy your 'I climbed Snowdon the hard way' badge at the souvenir shop.

Above left: Fi on Moel Sych, which means 'dry hill' in Welsh. It was, of course, soaking wet and I had to rescue her shoes from the sodden peat bog twice.

Above right: Day 22: The wonderfully dry Aran Fawddwy.

Below: Great Rhos, not the best place to wander off and explore.

Above: Day 48 found me visiting the Old Man of Coniston in the Lake District. Tremendous name. Tremendous mountain.

Below: The following day it was the turn of Scafell Pike. Never had I encountered so many false summits…

Striding Edge. I felt privileged
just to see it.

Above left: 'You let a red flag and a story about unexploded shells put you off? Soft, are you?' The troublesome Mickle Fell. Eventually, I decided to risk it…

Above right: By day 54, I'd made it to Scotland.

Below: Feeling reflective in Broad Law… having been mauled by thousands of midges.

Above: The view from the summit of Ben Lawers, the seventh highest mountain in Scotland. Over the years the sheer number of visitors have caused terrible erosion to the footpaths.

Below: Mixed messages near Glas Maol.

Above: The welcome sanctuary of the Corrour bothy in the Cairngorms.
Below: The last day, the last summit: on Ben Nevis with Roger, my dad.

SEVEN

**A PROUD DAY TO BE ARGENTINEAN – A 100-MILE RIDE
– 'NEVER RIDE JUST TO PROVE YOURSELF'– A
PTERODACTYL, A CUP FINAL AND A FUNERAL –
MECHANICAL MELTDOWN – PLAYING SCRABBLE IN
KING'S LYNN – 'STAFFORDSHIRE, BLOODY
STAFFORDSHIRE' – DYKES, FIELDS AND HEDGES –
LINCOLNSHIRE'S HIGHEST CABBAGE PATCH**

DAY 36 – CAMBRIDGE TO SHERINGHAM: 100 MILES
Great Wood (Suffolk): 128m

I rode along Suffolk's poppy-lined roads bristling with
pride. It was a great day to be Argentinean. The football
team – my boys – had thumped Serbia and Montenegro 6-
0 in a World Cup group game last night. The second goal,
scored by the midfielder Esteban Cambiasso, climaxed a
sensational 24-pass move. 'Is this the greatest World Cup
goal of all time?' asked the *Daily Mail*.

Sitting on a bench overlooking Bury St Edmunds
Abbey, I opened *The Worst Journey in the World*. I had
reached page 12. I was averaging around two paragraphs
a day, so I wasn't making terribly good progress. Captain
Scott's expedition had not even reached Antarctica, but
the crew were busy exploring the uninhabited Atlantic
island of South Trinidad. I managed to read another
paragraph before I was disturbed.

'Great game.'

Standing in front of me was a middle-aged man sucking on a lollipop smothered in hundreds and thousands.

'The Ar-gen-tina foot-ball game,' he mouthed slowly, assuming I was foreign or a little slow. 'That second goal – have you ever seen anything like it? I was jumping around my living room like a nutter.' He took a thoughtful suck of his lolly. 'We don't get many Argentineans in Bury St Edmunds.'

I breathed deeply. 'Look, I'm English, alright? I just happened to go to Argentina on a holiday and I bought back this shirt.'

My little outburst made me feel better, but I resolved that the next time someone assumed I was Argentinean, I would fulfil their fantasies. I put down the book to concoct a story that would explain my South American heritage.

By this time, I'd already wandered 30 miles from Cambridge and ticked off Suffolk's 128-metre county top, which was the third lowest on my list (after Huntingdonshire and Norfolk). A swathe of land encompassing the villages of Chedburgh, Depden and Rede rises above the 100-metre mark and this plateau reaches its zenith just north of Chedburgh. After bumping down a narrow lane, I was opposite a towering Arqiva communications mast and standing on the edge of a field of sweet peas – Suffolk's highest point.

Perhaps it was the manner of the Argentina victory, but the previous night I'd been struck by illusions of grandeur and seriously contemplated the prospect of a 100-mile ride. East Anglia was the one area of England I had little enthusiasm for. In fact, I hated it. Flat, maybe.

Dull, definitely. The solution was to get it over and done with in a day. From Cambridge, a 100-mile journey would see me to the north Norfolk coast and within touching distance of Beacon Hill, a lowly tump rising between Cromer and Sheringham. As I cycled between Thetford and Watton, I decided to go for broke. The roads were pancake-flat and although the air was muggy, there wasn't a breath of wind to bother me. If I was going to notch a 100-mile day on this trip, today would be the day.

Nevertheless, it is not a challenge to be taken lightly. Riding 100 miles in a single day is a cyclist's magical barrier, rather like the 26.2 miles of a marathon is to a runner. To go that far not only requires determination, but also an ability to keep motivated in the face of utter boredom. Driving 100 miles is a fair way, let alone attempting the distance on two wheels powered by two tired legs. Bonking was on my mind and avoiding it the priority. So, ice cream in one hand, bottle of water in the other, I draped myself across bags of coal outside a petrol station in Dereham.

'You remind me of an old cartoon,' a motorist observed as he filled up with unleaded. 'It was of an exhausted cyclist sitting outside a petrol station. He had a water bottle in one hand and the air pump in the other. You look a bit like that,' he chuckled.

There is an old saying by Paul de Vivie, the late-19th-century founder of French bicycle touring:

> Eat before you are hungry.
> Drink before you are thirsty.
> Rest before you are tired.

Cover up before you are cold.
Peel off before you are hot.
Don't drink or smoke on tour.
Never ride just to prove yourself.

Apart from drinking or smoking, I had broken every one of his seven golden rules. No amount of ice cream or water was going to rescue me now. The bonk whacked me like a sledgehammer. With a dry mouth and hollow stomach, I reached Holt, still eight miles from destination Sheringham. My eyes may have been open but my brain was asleep, conjuring up a succession of bizarre hallucinations.

A pterodactyl flew overhead. Swooping down, the creature's giant talons grasped my jersey, lifting me off the saddle. 'You're a dinosaur, aren't you?' I pointed out, as we flew upwards. 'I didn't think you existed any more?' The pterodactyl didn't answer. Dinosaurs don't talk, even in dreams. With the winged beast's grip slowly loosening, it let go, sending me tumbling to earth. I landed in soft snow on the side of the road. The creature swooped down again and stood next to me for a second, before lunging at my ear, ripping it clean off. Blood gushed from the wound, turning the snow red.

I was no longer in Norfolk. I was at Wembley Stadium. It was the FA Cup final and Aston Villa were drawing with Birmingham City, extra time looming. 'The referee's looked at his watch again,' I commentated in my head. 'There's only seconds to go. This is Villa's last chance to win it. McCann in the centre circle... to Angel... passes to Barry... back to Angel. Muir's free in the centre if Angel can find him... that's a wonderful ball from the Colombian. Muir... it's there! He's done it –an unstoppable strike! And that's it... the final whistle. The Birmingham players slump to their knees. Villa have won the Cup. Muir is the hero.'

Before I could get my hands on the trophy, there was a whistle of air and a thud, followed by a muffled but ghastly scream. A juggernaut had clipped my bicycle, catapulting me off my mount. My body disappeared under its churning wheels, the hot rubber ripping through my fragile skin, tearing limbs and shattering bones. An ambulance came but there was nothing the paramedics could do. My injuries were too severe. I was pronounced dead at the scene. The mangled wreckage of my bicycle lay on the verge, as police officers pored over the blood-spattered scene.

A week later, I was standing behind the vicar at my funeral. There were rows of mourners, family of course, some school and university friends and a handful of former colleagues. It's a good turn out, I thought. 'He died what he loved doing most,' Dad said tearfully in the eulogy. 'I'm going to continue his journey. I don't think I'll manage it in 92 days, but it's what he would have wanted...'

As the cry of seagulls filled the air and the smell of fish and chips wafted up my nostrils, I knew I was in Sheringham. I glanced down at the mileometer as it flashed up the supposedly golden figure of 100 miles. Prising my bent-double frame from the bicycle, I glared at it with disgust. I snarled at the hostel warden, throwing my money across the counter. I couldn't open the dormitory door, then I couldn't open the packet of soap. Finally, I lost my temper when the shower water wasn't warm. More than anything, I hated myself for forcing my body to ride 100 crazy miles.

DAY 37 – SHERINGHAM TO KING'S LYNN: 56 MILES
Roman Camp (Norfolk): 103m

Whenever I spoke to people about my journey, they would joke about joining me for the Norfolk leg. 'Because it's the flat bit,' they would say. They never did join me, of course, but they were right – Norfolk is flat. In fact, the county is so flat that only a single patch of land punctures the air above 100 metres. This precious spot is known as Roman Camp, a clearing on the summit of the otherwise tree-smothered Beacon Hill. A National Trust pamphlet helpfully set the scene: 'Roman Camp is the highest point in Norfolk and on clear days gives a lovely view over the North Sea. There is nothing between you and the North Pole here.' Except, that is, for hundreds of miles of sea, the Arctic ice caps, some polar bears, a bearded explorer and the odd oil rig.

'The name Roman Camp was coined in the late 19th century,' the pamphlet continued, 'but there is no evidence that the Romans had a camp here.' It was an easy mistake to make. Suspicious-looking earthworks on the summit of a hill? Must be those pesky Romans. They get everywhere. Should we excavate the earthworks just to check? No, don't bother – just in case we're wrong. Anyway, it's bound to be the Romans, so let's call it Roman Camp. The tourists will love it.

HEIGHTS OF MADNESS

The earthworks actually mark the site of a long-gone look-out station. From the 14th century, Beacon Hill was used as a vantage point for pirate watch. When danger emerged on the horizon, the beacon would have been lit, and during 1588, when the Spanish Armada threatened English shores, it would have burned at its brightest. Today, any would-be invaders would be caught on the CCTV camera that keeps a beady eye on walkers using the Norfolk Coast Path, passing only a few paces to the west of Roman Camp.

My greatest fear on this odyssey wasn't physical exhaustion. Nor was it loneliness. And it certainly wasn't the rain forecast to sweep across Norfolk that afternoon. What made me push the panic button was something far worse, something I couldn't control or do anything about. Mechanical failure. Cycling was my passion and my escape, but did I understand the inner workings of my machine? Did I heck. My technical knowledge stretched as far as gluing a patch over a puncture. At anything else – the gears, brakes, wheels, chain – I was clueless. It once took me three days and endless rattling to realise a spoke had snapped on my front wheel. To someone who doesn't know a triple drivetrain from a rear derailleur, or a crankset from a groupset, the mechanics of a bicycle were a confusion of unfathomable jargon.

The inevitable happened in Castle Rising, six miles shy of King's Lynn. There I was, pedalling happily along, when my rear wheel decided to stop turning. In the blink of an eye my cycle slowed from 15mph to zero. Expletives rushed through my mind and a roadside hedge welcomed me with outstretched, sharpened arms. Cars rushed past.

No one stopped. I clutched a pedal and tried to spin the wheel. It wouldn't budge. I tried it again, a little harder, but still no movement. What was wrong with it? Perhaps there was a problem with the sprocket set? Or maybe the dual pivot brakes? Pulling back my foot like David Beckham about to whip in a free kick, I booted the pedal as hard as I could. There was an awful crunching of metal on metal, but the wheel spun freely again. Job done. Who says I'm not mechanically minded?

For the third night in a row, I shirked camping and booked into a hostel, in a wing of King's Lynn's 500-year-old Chantry College building. There were three other guests: a slow on the uptake South African, a brash Irishman from Cork and a Portsmouth woman, unemployed after being made redundant the previous week. Where else would you go after losing a job?

Cork pulled a Scrabble box from a shelf. 'Let's play.'

'I don't know the rules,' said Portsmouth.

'What's Scrabble?' asked South Africa.

'Everyone pick out seven letters,' I ordered, taking charge. 'I'll explain as we go along.'

Portsmouth started. 'Giveth. Two, three, seven, eight, nine, 13. Double word score, 26,' she announced proudly.

'Giveth? Not exactly a common word nowadays, is it?' I suggested.

'It's in the Bible, isn't it?'

Next up was South Africa, who started with Portsmouth's 'g' and laid another six tiles on the board to spell out g-n-i-d-e-e-f. He looked up and smiled. I looked at Portsmouth. Portsmouth looked at me. We both looked at South Africa.

'What's that meant to be?' I asked.

'Feeding,' he said triumphantly.

'Ah, feeding. I thought…' My words trailed off as South Africa beamed, revelling in an incredible start to his Scrabble career. I hadn't the heart to tell him he couldn't spell words backwards.

Cork grabbed the board and spun it round to face him. 'Right, my go. I've got a cracker for you, w-h-o-r-e, whore. How about that then?'

Portsmouth and I giggled like schoolchildren. South Africa looked puzzled.

'It's spelt with a w,' Cork boomed. 'I know that for a fact. If anyone does, I do.'

'Enough,' I said. 'You can have it then, I suppose.'

'Of course I can. Whore. It's a good word is whore.'

It soon came round to Cork's turn again. This time he wasn't so quick off the mark, staring at the board and back to his letters with all the adroit preparation of a Scrabble grand master. 'Wog,' he revealed at last, flashing a grin at the three of us.

'Um… you can't have that. To be honest, it's not politically correct and I doubt it's in the dictionary.' I had suddenly turned into Mr Sensible.

Cork wasn't giving up on his word. 'How about if I add an "s" at the end? Wogs.'

'No, that's worse.'

'Call yourself a journalist? Who says the words have to be in the dictionary? I bet it's in the Irish dictionary. Your English dictionary is wrong.'

As we waited for Portsmouth to play her next turn, South Africa broke into spontaneous laughter.

'What's so funny?' demanded Cork.

'I just realised what a whore is,' South Africa choked. 'Rude.'

'Jesus, man, that was ten minutes ago,' Cork blasted. 'What is wrong with you?'

On Cork's third go he came up with the word 'ebe'.

'What's an ebe then?' queried Portsmouth.

'Ebe? You've never heard of an ebe? What are you like? It's a small animal. It's furry. Like a hamster. A bit smaller though. Shy little buggers they are, only coming out at night. You'll only find them in Northern Ireland. That's why you haven't heard of them.'

South Africa took an eternity to play each turn, his confused face contorted in mental agony. After a promising start he was now struggling to come up with an offering longer than two letters. Stubbornly refusing help, he laid down his customary two tiles for the fourth successive turn.

'Zo?' I questioned. 'What's that then?'

'No silly, oz. As in Australia. One and ten is eleven. Triple word score makes it 33.'

'We know,' said Portsmouth, 'but it's slang.'

'You can't use slang?' South Africa said turning towards me. 'What's slang?'

And so South Africa was awarded the highest score of the game. Judging by the simple expression of glee that lifted his features, it was a story he will be telling his grandchildren in 40 years time.

When Portsmouth placed the letters o-r-e-d after the word honk, I began to see why she had been fired. 'Honkored,' she declared aloud. A warning to all compilers of dictionaries: do not give this woman a job.

It was midnight when we realised we had been playing with two sets of letters that had been mixed into one bag. I had won, announced scorekeeper Portsmouth. Despite his 33, South Africa was rock bottom, and had Norris McWhirter been present, he might now have been in the Guinness Book of Records for the lowest ever score in a Scrabble game. Runner-up Cork was still muttering as we packed the game away. 'No wonder he won, bloody cheat. He made the rules up.'

DAY 38 – KING'S LYNN TO MARKET RASEN: 82 MILES
Wolds Top (Lincolnshire): 168m

Crouched on hands and knees, the mechanic scrutinised my sick rear wheel. 'Where are you trying to get to?'

'Lincolnshire.'

'No chance.'

'What?'

'No chance. You need a new wheel.'

'Have you got a new wheel?

'No.'

My eyes glazed over as the man launched into an explanation involving barrels, bearings and cones, and how my barrels, bearings and cones were worn out. Basically, the wheel was buggered. Or very nearly buggered. There was a solution. Two days from now, my older brother James was due to join up with me in Staffordshire, meaning he would be able to bring a replacement wheel from Bromsgrove. A hurried phone call later and it was agreed.

'Right,' I said to the mechanic. 'I need to get to Staffordshire now. Via Derbyshire.'

'Staffordshire? Bloody Staffordshire is miles away! You're off your head.' He was a positive fellow. 'You'll be lucky to get out of King's Lynn,' he predicted, as I wheeled the cycle out of the shop. 'Good luck. You'll need it.'

In the 1948 book, *The English Counties Illustrated*, J. Wentworth Day gave his verdict on my next county.

> Lincolnshire, that broad, bright land, which lies 75 miles long by 45 miles wide, between the Humber and The Wash, its face to the bitter North Sea, its back to the mosses of Yorkshire and the wide fields of Nottinghamshire, Leicester and Rutland, is no place for weaklings in stature or bad farmers. It has something of the bleak independence of Norfolk but more of the harsher, more northerly, characteristics of Yorkshire. It is halfway house between East Anglia and the north. And it stands as a buffer between the North Sea, whence came the Vikings and the Danish raiders, and the warmer wetter Midlands.

Today, Lincolnshire is a confused county. On the one hand, it is a natural paradise, where wolds roll under wide skies. On the other, it is a place where man has meddled with nature by creating dead-straight ditches and planting copious amounts of yellow oilseed rape. At Walpole Cross Keys, midway between the River Great

Ouse and the River Nene, I reached Lincolnshire's eastern fringe. Here the grim side of the county was plain to see. It was a truly dreadful place. The A16 was hell on earth for a cyclist, an appallingly lorry-clogged road. As for the Fens? Field, dyke, field, dyke, hedge, field, dyke, field, dyke… you get the picture. Don't imagine it for too long or you'll want to drown yourself in a dyke. And across those mind-numbingly monotonous fens swept ceaseless southwesterlies that delayed my desperate efforts to escape this flat desert. Wentworth Day was right. Lincolnshire was no place for weaklings.

Heroically, my battered bicycle battled on for 80 miles to Market Rasen, where I arrived at the edge of the Lincolnshire Wolds, a line of low-lying hills that run from Spilsby to the Humber. The highest point in the Wolds and the summit of Lincolnshire is the imaginatively named Wolds Top. The map indicated I would find a triangulation pillar close to a radar station near Normanby le Wold. Sure enough, a high mast – topped with what looked like an enormous golf ball – guided me to the area. Finding the summit was trickier. Impatiently, I waded into a one-metre high field of sweet peas. A dozen steps later, one metre turned to two, and stalks were towering above my head, dwarfing me like a character in *Honey, I Shrunk the Kids*. Taking a different approach, I followed a track around the perimeter of the field.

When in doubt, I pulled out my trusty GPS, which had stored on it the grid reference of every county top. As I paced along the track, I watched as the GPS indicated I was gaining on the summit… 200 yards… 100 yards… 80 yards… 50 yards… until I knew the top must be just around the corner, in a field adjacent to the sweet pea jungle. The anticipation was overwhelming. What secrets might the summit of Lincolnshire hold? Thirty yards... 20 yards... I turned the corner. Ahead was a cabbage patch. There must be some mistake. I checked the GPS. This was definitely it. Standing alone in Lincolnshire's highest cabbage patch, I pondered the question I had asked myself 38 days ago in Okehampton. Why?

EIGHT

COLLIDING WITH METAL BARS – WHAT COMES
AROUND GOES AROUND – THE CENTRE OF ENGLAND
– A FRUSTRATED GIRLFRIEND – LACKING MOTIVATION
– A 60-SECOND VISIT TO STAFFORDSHIRE –
EMERGENCY REPAIRS – KINDER SCOUT – WILD
WEATHER – DAYS OFF

DAY 39 – MARKET RASEN TO DARLEY DALE: 73 MILES
Newtonwood Lane (Nottinghamshire): 204m

One stretch of Lincolnshire's western boundary with
Nottinghamshire follows the meandering River Trent, and
one particular toll bridge, between Dunham and Newton
on Trent, welcomes travellers to the land of Robin Hood. A
queue of cars paused before a lowered barrier, waiting to
pay a man in a little kiosk. In turn, each driver would hand
over a fistful of change, the metal barrier would spring up
and off they would go into Nottinghamshire. As cyclists
were allowed to cross this bridge without charge, there
was no need for me to stop at the kiosk. So when there was
only one car in front, I decided I would slip under the
barrier the next time it was raised.

Up it went. The car swept underneath, cyclist in its
slipstream. Unfortunately, my acceleration was not as
swift as a BMW's, meaning the barrier was suddenly

147

falling back down with me still on the Lincolnshire side of it. My brain – already at fault for this miscalculation – told me I wouldn't make it, only my body didn't react.

I was lucky in Hungerford, fortunate in Castle Rising. Now surely my nine lives were up? Broken arm? Broken collarbone? Either way the journey was surely over. The barrier was horizontal when we met. There was an almighty thud as I waited to be catapulted off my mount, but to my surprise I remained upright. I stopped, turned around and watched the barrier trundling across the floor towards the next car in the queue. Never mind the barrier doing me damage – I had ripped the thing clean out of its socket. Embarrassed? I was proud. The attendant rushed out of his kiosk to rescue the rolling rod, shouting: 'You've ripped me barrier off!'

'Yeah, it seems that way. I'm really sorry. It was an accident though,' I mumbled, while clutching my right arm and making appropriate pained expressions.

'Are you OK?'

'It's pretty sore,' I winced. 'I can't move it. I think it could be broken.'

'Do you want me to call an ambulance?'

'You know, it's feeling a lot better. Look, I can move it a bit.'

'Right, stay here. You'll have to pay for this,' the attendant said, as he scurried to the nearby Tollbridge House to talk to his boss.

Seconds later, out came the man in charge, shaking his head. 'Flamin' cyclists. We let you cross for free and this is what happens. It's gonna cost you a tenner that. We'll have to get the bleedin' thing welded back on.'

I pretended I didn't have £10, and only by promising to put the cash in an envelope later that day was I permitted passage into Nottinghamshire.

Five miles up the road, I realised there was such a thing as karma. My sickly rear wheel had developed an ominous rattle, and changing gears was accompanied by a meaty clunk. Nevertheless, each one of my bicycle's 24 gears continued to function with relative mechanical precision. That was until karma struck on the A57 between Tuxford and Ollerton. The gear cable – which runs from handlebar to rear wheel – had snapped, so in a heartbeat my bicycle had lost 21 gears, leaving only three.

Of course there was no bicycle shop in Ollerton. Karma, you see? The nearest one was nine miles away in Mansfield. Or – where a wrong turn led me – Sutton in Ashfield, some 12 miles distant.

Nottinghamshire's county top is found in the corner of a muddy field off Newtonwood Lane, a rural road rising a mile west of the M1's Tibshelf services. For purists, Newtonwood Lane will always remain the true summit of Nottinghamshire, because it is the county's highest natural point. However, the emergence of a rival means it has lost its crown as the county's highest point. Rising to 205 metres – a single metre taller – are the landscaped spoil tips of the former Silverhill Colliery, on the northwestern outskirts of Sutton in Ashfield. So take your pick: natural or unnatural. Nottinghamshire County Council has and they say the highest point is Silverhill Colliery. Personally, I don't think it really matters.

The lowly, unspectacular summit of Newtonwood Lane, which straddles the boundary of Derbyshire and

Nottinghamshire, symbolically marked the end of my eight-day flat interlude. Beyond the M1 rose the brooding mass of the Peak District: I was back among the hills. After passing through Morton – the 'centre of England' – the rollercoaster road between Clay Cross and Matlock reminded me of what I had been missing, with a series of strength-sapping climbs blasting away the cobwebs.

In a race against rain, I threw up my tent in a field opposite a pub in Darley Dale, while four teenagers laughed at my efforts. With the tent up, I ran across to the Square and Compass, stopping outside the lads' tents. They were clearly bored and tent-bound because of the rain. The lads' holiday had not turned out as they had hoped.

'I'm going to the pub. Do you want me to bring you out some beers?' I asked.

'Yeah mate, cheers,' they echoed in unison, delving into their pockets in search of change.

'Well, tough shit. You shouldn't have laughed.'

I watched England draw 2-2 with Sweden, an outcome that meant England would play Ecuador in the second round of the World Cup, before calling Fi. Earlier that day she would have found out the result of her degree (a 2:1). As soon as she answered I sensed the voice of an inebriated woman. 'Well done,' I said. 'I knew you'd do it.' I was unprepared for the verbal onslaught that was to follow.

'What do you care? You're not here to celebrate with me, are you? You're off gallivanting around the country on a bloody bicycle.'

I didn't have an answer. Not that she gave me time to

babble one, because the phone had already been slammed down. What could I do? Call off the journey? Run into her arms? That wouldn't satisfy either of us. For the moment, I did what all men excel at – doing nothing.

DAY 40 – DARLEY DALE TO EDALE: 36 MILES
Cheeks Hill (Staffordshire): 520m
Kinder Scout (Derbyshire): 636m

I departed from my campground by the River Derwent at nine o'clock, giving me one hour to cover the 15 miles to Axe Edge Moor, where James would be waiting for me with a shiny new wheel. As it transpired, the journey became three hours of purgatory, the most frustrating of 40 days in the saddle. There were a number of reasons.

First, I wasn't in the mood. It's just one of those things, isn't it? Sometimes you wake up raring to go, while at other times you just... well... can't be bothered. Life is too much effort. Packing away the tent was exhausting, loading up panniers laborious and even the thought of brushing my teeth was too much like hard work. There were thirty-plus miles of Peak District cycling to pedal, and the summits of Staffordshire and Derbyshire to conquer. Tantalising in theory, but in wind and rain, on top of consecutive days of eyeballs-out effort? I'll leave it thanks. It was moments like these when I knew I had to find some motivation, a chink of hope to drag me onto the bicycle, whether it was the promise of a day off in a week's time or a Mars Bar at the next village store. Anything to keep the mind sane and the legs moving.

Second, the terrain. Come back the Fens, all is forgiven. The ride started with a hideous climb through Darley Bridge. For cold, stiff and unresponsive legs to be forced into such strenuous activity so early in the day was a mistake. They trembled like jelly, as if cycling was an alien concept. Taking pity on them, I stopped in Winster, craving energy and enthusiasm. That promised Mars Bar helped. After the initial long uphill drag, I was taken along a series of never-ending ups and downs as the road wandered through Youlgreave and Middleton. Just after Arbor Low stone circle, country lanes finally emerged onto the main A515 to Buxton, which brings me neatly to my next excuse.

Third, the wind – enemy-in-chief to cyclists. At least the tree-lined country lanes had been sheltered. Pedalling north on the A515, a cruel wind peppered me with blows like a boxer, not one of them big enough for a knock out, but each one draining me of what little strength remained.

Fourth, mechanical capitulation. My bicycle had been brave. Since Castle Rising, I had nursed it through three days and 180 miles, but now the end was near. The bearings were now so badly worn that one in every three pedal strokes failed to drive the rear wheel. Gradually, it became two out of three, and then, with Axe Edge Moor on the horizon but still three miles distant, life was extinguished. It was painless, just a final defiant clunk and the bearings gave up. The pedals still spun frantically, but they were no longer turning the wheel. Faced with no other alternative, I dismounted and pushed the last three miles.

It was midday when I hauled myself on to the A54, the main route between Leek and Buxton, which at its highest point rubs shoulders with Axe Edge Moor. Leaving my woes behind for half an hour, James and I made our way across the moor to the top of Staffordshire. It was the county where I would spend the least amount of time – roughly 60 seconds. Arriving at a stone wall on Cheeks Hill, we had reached the place where Staffordshire meets Derbyshire, and where the former can go no higher.

It was time for emergency surgery. Off came both front and rear wheels, exchanged for fresh ones, and the job was rounded off with a brand new chain. My bicycle had been resuscitated and boarding what felt like a new machine, I swept down the hill to Buxton, with James' Mini Cooper giving chase.

We met again in Edale, the starting point of the Pennine Way, a 268-mile trail along the spine of England, taking in the Peak District, Yorkshire Dales and the Cheviots, before reaching its climax in the Scottish borders.

Kinder Scout – bleak, boggy and exposed, a place where the weather can change in the blink of the eye – is the summit of both Derbyshire and the Peak District. However, Kinder Scout is more than a mountain. It is a national treasure and one of the UK's renowned high places, largely thanks to the Mass Trespass of 1932 – the turning point for a series of events that saw England's once restricted countryside opened up to the public. Six years after the Second World War had ended, the Peak District became Britain's first National Park and a vast swathe of moorland to the north of Edale was classified as open country. At last, in 2003, 'right to roam' legislation opened up land previously forbidden to the rambler.

Here is how the *Guardian* marked the momentous day of 24 April 1932.

> Four or five hundred ramblers, mostly from Manchester, trespassed in mass on Kinder Scout today. They fought a brief but vigorous hand-to-hand struggle with a number of keepers specially enrolled for the occasion. This they won with ease, and then marched to Ashop Head, where they held a meeting before returning in triumph to Hayfield. Their triumph was short-lived, for there the police met them, halted them, combed their ranks for suspects, and detained five men. Another man had been detained earlier in the day.

In 1932, less than a one per cent of the Peak District was designated open land, at a time when economic depression meant the cheapest pastime for folk in Leeds, Manchester and Sheffield was to ramble across the moors. Yet places such as Kinder Scout were strictly off-limits and gamekeepers patrolled the grouse moors for the sake of the privileged few. On that famous day, the trespassers massed in Hayfield and set off for the mountain, where they were met by gamekeepers armed with sticks. The rabble fought the wardens with the belts from their trousers and their bare hands, before marching triumphantly towards to the summit of Kinder Scout.

Today's rabble-rousers are the numerous children that

scamper over the mountain, for Kinder Scout is a favourite of school, Scouting and Duke of Edinburgh excursions. James and I followed a pack of map-clutching youngsters, their bags loaded up with chocolate bars, fizzy pop and waterproofs, along what our map described as the 'alternative' Pennine Way. Overtaking the youngsters one-by-one we arrived at a cluster of buildings in Upper Booth and here the path turned north towards the steep zigzags of Jacob's Ladder.

As we approached Kinder Low, a mere three metres shorter than Kinder Scout, a lashing wind flung sand into our faces. We were on top of a mountain, but by the looks of Kinder Low we could have been at the beach. The ground was sandy, the peat hag resembled seaweed and Kinder Low's triangulation pillar was the guiding lighthouse. We waded into the rolling waves of peat in search of Kinder Scout's top. Three times we thought we had made it and each time doubted ourselves. The roof of the Peak District is so flat that we could have walked for a quarter of a mile in each direction from where we stood and still been on an almost identical level. Even the GPS was uncertain. Eventually, we settled on a pile of stones with a pair of wooden sticks poking out.

DAY 41 – EDALE TO HUDDERSFIELD: 45 MILES
Black Hill (Cheshire): 582m

Shivering and chilled to the bone, I woke long before the dawn chorus. There were no more garments to pull on, for any item of clothing I wasn't wearing was stretched out between bag and tent to form a makeshift mattress. The layers offered precious little respite from cold ground. Adding to my discomfort was a steady six-week weight loss, meaning bones jutted out from where there was once a barrier of fat. Feeling thin and weak, all I could do was curl my legs to my chest and listen to the wind roaring through the trees.

In the perishing first light of day, I sprinted a couple of laps around the campsite to bring life back to fingers and toes, then paid 60p for the pleasure of six minutes of hot shower water. James had driven home after a night at Edale's Old Nag's Head, leaving me with a veritable feast for breakfast: apples, cherries and oranges. Instead I opted for a packet of smoky bacon crisps and a mint chocolate-chip bar. Calories were what I needed, not fruit, for between Edale and Black Hill stood two fearsome mountain roads, Snake Pass and Holme Moss, both of which would be buffeted by wild winds and cloaked in mist.

There was something of the masochist in me today, a realisation that I was about to be stretched to my physical and mental limits. The ascent of Snake Pass was close to a cycling impossibility, with tremendous walls of wind a notch away from halting my progress altogether. Holme Moss was dreadful, a test of attrition and bloody-mindedness bordering on stupidity. Keep pedalling and it will end. This can't go on forever, I told myself. At the 524-metre zenith of Holme Moss it did end. Black Hill was now just a mile away across an invisible stretch of moorland to the west. An eerie blanket of grey mist had been thrown across this high ground, reducing visibility to no more than 15 yards. Out of the darkness fell icy slants of rain, drilling against my forehead. A map would be near useless in such a flat and featureless landscape, even before it was enveloped in mist. Not that I had a map.

At this point, you might be feeling sorry for me. I'm dripping wet, teeth are chattering and just for good measure I'm on the verge of getting lost. A galloping mountain hare was my sole companion. Don't feel sorry for me. This was my office, a place where I was in my element. The exhilaration was overwhelming: the wind roaring in my ears, the pang of uncertainty, the gasping cold, the utter loneliness.

Had I tackled Cheshire's top by following the route of the Pennine Way from Crowden, a convenient path of stone slabs would have led me to the summit of Black Hill. As it was, my way involved a trudge over waves of inky black peat. My destination, the Ordnance Survey triangulation pillar heralding the highest point, rested on the shoulders of a plinth of concrete. Presumably the pillar occupies this elevated position to prevent it from being sucked beneath. When the Royal Engineers first laid a pillar in the 19th century, the soldiers had to slog through deep sludgy peat to reach this point, earning the summit its nickname, the Soldier's Lump.

Undoubtedly, I would never have found Black Hill without the GPS. But that was the easy bit: it was getting back that posed the problem. My saviour turned out to be the towering 228-metre radio transmitter perched atop Holme Moss, standing close to the road. I knew that making for the mast would guide me to safety. Occasionally the gloom lightened enough for me to glimpse the aerial and the five sets of stay levels keeping it upright.

Before long, I was back on the bicycle, charging down the hairpins of Holme Moss to Holmfirth. Even with fingers numbed by cold and the dark clouds above looking as if they might rain forever, I wore a demented grin of satisfaction. It was days like these – the filthy weather and slogs across barren moor days – that shaped my journey, and what I knew I'd recall when I was old and grey.

Inevitably, as I sought refuge in a Holmfirth café, the adrenaline ebbed away, my wet clothes clinging to my skin like limpets on a seashore rock. It was my last cycling for a week, for I had promised to take Fi to Edinburgh, and I was due to travel to her family home in Lytham St Annes tonight. That morning, Burnley or even Preston had been my ambitious target destinations, from where I would catch a train to the Fylde coast. Consulting my road map, Burnley looked an age away, while reaching Preston in ever worsening weather was unthinkable. Instead I took the easy option, cycling eight miles north to Huddersfield where I gleefully jumped on a westbound train.

DAY 42 TO 47 – LYTHAM ST ANNES & EDINBURGH

Days off. When I couldn't have one, I craved one. When I got one, I was like a bear with a sore head, unable to keep still or relax. And what happened when I had six days off in a row? Every darn one was sunny and warm: perfect cycling and walking conditions. I had the itchiest feet in Scotland.

Fi and I trawled Princes Street, visited the castle, ate at her favourite vegetarian restaurant and debated the architectural merits of the Scottish Parliament building. But the moment that would stick in my mind was the view from the top of Arthur's Seat. From this 251-metre perch above the Firth of Forth, I could see hills and mountains I longed to be on, among them West Lomond, the top of Fife, and Clackmannanshire's Ben Cleuch, the highest of the Ochil Hills. Knowing I'd be there soon enough, I kept my thoughts to myself. To utter them would have deflated the moment.

NINE

**HALIFAX – SHARING MY BED WITH A RAT – IN THE BOOT
MARKS OF ALFRED WAINWRIGHT – THE OLD MAN OF
CONISTON – UNCLE DIEGO – MY ORREST HEAD
MOMENT – SCAFELL PIKE – THE EXHILARATION OF
STRIDING EDGE – CROSSING A MILITARY FIRING ZONE**

DAY 48 – HUDDERSFIELD TO INGLETON: 57 MILES

No place is quite so symbolic of the north as the West
Yorkshire town of Halifax. Growing up in the Midlands,
even in the 1980s, the north seemed a far-flung location,
where people spoke in a peculiar accent, wore flat caps
and called you by the name of a bird. Halifax first came
into my consciousness when the town's football team
visited my local club Bromsgrove Rovers in the mid-
1990s. Throughout the game, Rovers fans hummed the
theme tune to the classic Hovis bread advert, a tune
punctuated only by the occasional taunt of, 'Oi, keeper,
show us your whippet.' That reassuring Hovis tune: that
was the north – freshly baked bread and boys on old
bicycles pedalling up cobbled streets steeper than an Alp.

The A629 isn't built of cobs, but it led me to a place
where my Halifax fantasies were more suited, Haworth.
The former manufacturing village, four miles south of
Keighley, is famous the world over for its association with

the Bronte sisters, Anne, Charlotte and Emily. The family's former Georgian residence is now the Bronte Parsonage Museum, where Emily's *Wuthering Heights*, Anne's *The Tenant of Wildfell Hall* and Charlotte's *Jane Eyre* were all penned. Eating a pasty, I sat patiently outside the museum, waiting for a photographer. Why a photographer? Well, while I was 'resting' in Edinburgh, a freelance journalist had contacted me to say she had been commissioned to write a feature on my journey for the *Sunday Herald*, hence the need for an accompanying photograph. Eventually, the photographer turned up – half an hour late – and we made our way to nearby Penistone Hill, where the backdrop was a little more countrified than Haworth's tourist shops.

I had never been professionally photographed before – sorry, as a former colleague Mike doesn't count – and I can tell you, it was a painful experience. In search of the perfect shot, the photographer made me contort my body in ways I didn't think possible. An arm or leg was never quite in the right place.

'Bring your arm forward a little,' he would coax. 'No, your right arm. Tilt your head slightly. Move your knee out. A bit more? And smile.'

Smile? Another inch and the bones in my arm will snap. I don't know how Kate Moss puts up with it.

My next assignment, Lancashire's Old Man of Coniston, was still 50 miles away, so today was a chance to get re-acquainted with my cycle after six days out of the saddle. From Haworth, I roared down dale to Keighley, flying past the Keighley and Worth Valley Railway, the backdrop of *The Railway Children*. After Skipton, cycling on the A65 became a tedious grind along the southern edge of the Yorkshire Dales. The road brought me to Ingleton, the 'home of caves and waterfalls', according to a road sign, where I camped in the first site I saw, a field under the imposing gaze of Yorkshire's giant hill, Ingleborough.

DAY 49 – INGLETON TO SKELWITH BRIDGE: 53 MILES
The Old Man of Coniston (Lancashire): 803m

Another early morning wake-up call, but this time it wasn't the cold. There was a mouse – or maybe a rat, definitely a rat, a big fat black one – not only inside my tent, but perched clumsily on my toes. Can you imagine the sheer horror? Waking in the middle of the night to find a dirty great rodent running amok in your bedroom? I screamed – loud enough to alert the entire campsite – and launched emergency evacuation procedures, baling out in record time. As my vision grew accustomed to the darkness, I could see part of my tent had collapsed. Of the two poles to hold the structure up – a long hoop over my head and a short one over my feet – the smaller one was in bits.

'You all right out there?' came a concerned voice from a neighbouring tent.

'Fine. It's all fine,' I reported, feeling a little embarrassed. Ratty was nothing more sinister than a tent pole where it should not have been.

Obeying the list of historic county tops was a blessing, permitting me to tackle three classic Lakeland fells, the Old Man of Coniston, Scafell Pike and

Helvellyn. Cumbria now encompasses the entire Lake District, but rewind three decades and the land was split between Cumberland, Westmorland and the Furness tranche of Lancashire. Westmorland may be long gone but the county name lives on in numerous guises: the town of Appleby-in-Westmorland, the newspaper the *Westmorland Gazette*, the Westmorland Geological Survey and the annual Westmorland County Agricultural Show.

The traditional boundary of Westmorland and Lancashire ran through Kirkby Lonsdale, where I paused to admire Ruskin's View across the River Lune, the Howgills, Calf Top, Brownthwaite Pike, Gragareth and Ingleborough. In 1875, the poet described this outlook 'as one of the loveliest in England, therefore the world'. Beside the sign celebrating Ruskin's words was a metal plaque, almost hidden by the undergrowth. Placed by the Parish Council of Kirkby Lonsdale, it commemorated the merging of Westmorland into the new county of Cumbria on 1 April 1974.

Travelling west on the A590 towards Barrow-in-Furness, I had officially reached the Lake District. But pedalling along this winding mini-motorway of thundering traffic, I wondered how such a ribbon of concrete could fall within the boundaries of England's most beautiful and biggest National Park. Released from purgatory in Newby Bridge, within seconds I was rubbing shoulders with the western shore of Lake Windermere, approaching a slice of Lakeland sprinkled with literary stardust.

In Near Sawrey a procession of tourists had come to

see the 17th-century cottage called Hill Top Farm, once owned by Beatrix Potter and now managed by the National Trust. After spending summer holidays at Hill Top, the young Beatrix would return to her London home clutching a suitcase of nicknamed pets. For this lonely youngster, these creatures became her friends and inspiration. The JK Rowling of her era, Potter's genius was not recognised until her mid-thirties, by which time she had received seven knock-backs from publishers. Potter published her first book, *The Tale of Peter Rabbit*, herself in 1901, before being signed up the following year. In 1905, she purchased Hill Top, and although she never lived there permanently, two literary heroes did, Tom Kitten and Samuel Whiskers. Over the course of the following years she filled the cottage with mementos from her life, turning the property into what it is today – a shrine to the author.

Potter could have been the legendary Lakeland writer. Unfortunately for her, a man named William Wordsworth – he of 'I wandered lonely as a cloud' fame – came before her. On the narrow road between Near Sawrey and Hawkshead, I was trapped between two coaches, the first crammed with children pulling faces at me from the back seat, and the second filled with white-haired senior citizens. They had all come in search of Wordsworth. Hawkshead is one of a number of Lake District locations boasting of their association with the poet. On the same list is Cockermouth, where he was born; Grasmere and Rydal, where he lived; and Grasmere again, where he died. Hawkshead adds another piece to the Wordsworth jigsaw because the village gave him an education.

Testament to the fact is Wordsworth's wooden desk inside what was once Hawkshead Grammar School on which he carved his name.

But I was here to climb mountains, not discuss Lakeland writers, so I made off in the direction of Hawkshead Hill. As I rolled over the low pass, the Old Man of Coniston stared down at me. Tremendous name. Tremendous mountain. The great joy of my journey was the element of surprise. Apart from its height and county, I knew nothing of the Old Man. Even the eccentricity of the five-word name excited me. There is, however, a simple explanation. 'Man' is a commonly used term for summit, while 'old' originates from the Norse word *alt*, meaning high.

Sauntering along a path above the churning Church Beck, I emerged into Coppermines Valley, where I discovered a steep mountainside littered with the rusted remains of age-old slate mines. It led Hunter Davies, in his 1979 book *A Walk Around the Lakes*, to describe the Old Man as 'an old cheese, full of holes and mounds where man has been hacking it about over the centuries'. My guide was a £1 pamphlet produced by a local industrial history group calling itself the Cumbria Amenity Trust. The leaflet was as thorough and detailed as even a quarry enthusiast could have demanded. Simple as I am, the introduction sufficed.

> Coniston has had a very prosperous past. Extensive deposits of copper ore have been worked in the mountains above the village from the late 1590s until the Coniston Mine closed in

1895. But copper wasn't the only valuable deposit in the hills.

Originally slate was worked to provide material to roof the houses of the expanding communities of northern England during the Industrial Revolution. More recently, the beautiful 'greenslate', for which Coniston has become internationally known, is being extracted to clad and decorate some of the most prestigious buildings on all continents of the world.

The workings of slate from the Old Man's silver-grey vein is known to have taken place for at least 500 years and there is some evidence that it may have started much earlier, shortly after the Norman Conquest. During the ascent of the mountain today, you are passing remains of man's activities covering nearly 1,000 years.

I make no apology for turning to the words, drawings and opining of Alfred Wainwright over subsequent pages. To write about Lakeland mountains and not consult Wainwright is akin to analysing the Second World War with no reference to Winston Churchill. Born in Blackburn in 1907, Wainwright made his first visit to the Lakes in 1930 and climbed the 239-metre Orrest Head, near Windermere. In his own words, Wainwright was at once 'enslaved' by the beauty of Lakeland. In 1952 – and now living closer to the Lakes in Kendal – Wainwright dedicated his life's purpose to the outdoors. The result was seven hand-written and hand-drawn books, encapsulating 214 Lakeland hills and mountains, collectively known today as *Wainwright's*.

Never mind waterproofs, walking boots or a compass – the essential accessory on any Lakeland adventure is one of Wainwright's labours of love. For my purposes, I was drawn to a Wainwright-sketched cartoon depicting summiteers on the Old Man. In a stereotypical slur or 'typical summit scene' as Wainwright called it, he drew a flock of tourists who point excitedly towards Blackpool Tower and Morecambe Bay to the south. Meanwhile, a band of Boy Scouts stand to attention next to the summit cairn. On the far right sits a lone adventurer, a 'solitary fellwalker, bless him, looking north to the hills'.

Standing on the roof of historic Lancashire, I wasn't alone, although Blackpool failed to distract our small number. Nervously, all eyes were focussed on black storm clouds whipping their way towards the Old Man. We had just enough time to make out the shape of the Barrow peninsula, admire the cliffs of Dow Crag and glimpse the towers of Sellafield power station before each in turn was obscured by a sea of damp mist. To the north, England's highest land and my next challenge, Scafell Pike, was already immersed in the storm. Sure that the Old Man was next in line, I turned on my heels and descended to Coniston.

As I propped my bicycle against a pub wall, a roar came from within the building. Roberto Ayala, the central defender, had nodded Argentina into a 1-0 lead against the World Cup hosts Germany. I strutted in, trying to look broody and macho – an image not advanced by sporting Spandex. 'I'm related to Maradona,' I explained to the man sitting next to me.

With a pint glass poised at his lips, he eyed me suspiciously. 'You don't look very Argentinean... or sound it. 'Ere, Mick,' he said, nudging his neighbour. 'This bloke says he's from Argentina and knows Maradona. Say something in Spanish or Argentinean or whatever you lot speak.'

'*Lo hace siempre llueve este tanto en julio?*'

The pair looked at me blankly, their furrowed brows taking a few seconds to soften. 'We don't get many Argentineans in Coniston.'

'I lived there till I was 10. My mother is Argentinean but met my English father when he was on business in Buenos Aires.

'And Maradona?'

'You mean Uncle Diego.'

I watched as the cogs of their alcohol-affected brains processed this information.

'OK, I've got it... So your mum is his...'

'Sister.'

'Jesus. What's he like?'

'Top bloke. And you know what? Remember the Hand of God goal in 1986? You know the one against England? It's a myth. He used his head.'

'No way...'

Last night I was sharing my bed with a rat – or at least I thought I was. Tonight I was staying in the height of luxury, as a guest of family friends who ran a bed and breakfast in Skelwith Bridge. My host, Cornelia, showed me to Little Loughrigg, otherwise known as my room, where I found little packets of soap, fluffy towels, a choice of beds and a Sky TV remote control. All for free. Imagine my excitement after days of roughing it in muddy fields and being the millionth person to attempt sleep in the same squeaky hostel bed? Then there was the view from the window: down to Elterwater – the smallest of Lakeland's 18 lakes (the rest are tarns) – and the mountains of Great and Little Langdale, their slopes turned orange by the setting sun.

'Jonny,' Cornelia's husband Roger called up the stairs, 'fish and chips are here.'

God bless Elterwater Park Country Guest House.

DAY 50: SKELWITH BRIDGE TO SKELWITH BRIDGE VIA BOOT: 23 MILES
Scafell Pike (Cumberland): 978m

A soft mattress and thick duvet should have been the ideal ingredients for a sound night's sleep. But something was missing. Perhaps it was the absence of the early morning nip in the air, or the now familiar sensation of hard, unfriendly ground? I lay awake, obsessing about Scafell Pike, as if this mountain were an absent lover.

I was no stranger to England's highest peak. Three years earlier, I had been among a gang of students who ventured north to the Lake District when we should have been taking notes in a media law lecture. Without a map and with limited experience, we left a car at Wasdale Head and step-stoned across Lingmell Beck, before beginning an absurd hike up Lingmell, the acutely steep-sided mountain to the north west of Scafell Pike. Being of varying fitness, the five of us were soon straggled across the mountainside, while light was fast fading on this October afternoon. Bringing up the rear was a ginger-haired chap called Julian, who clutched a plastic bag containing a Wisden cricket annual and a wad of scribbles on contempt and libel. Need I elaborate further on our lack of preparation?

I was first to behold the vista from Lingmell's summit, before a companion some way behind phoned to say he and the others were turning back. As it would soon be dark, I was advised to do likewise. Laughing down the phone, I continued onwards to Scafell Pike. Exhilaration, respect, trepidation. They were just a snapshot of the feelings pulsing through me as I stood alone on England's summit. A jet pierced the silence with a thunderous roar as it arced through Wasdale Head below, seemingly close enough to touch. In a black flash, it was gone, leaving the air still again. I was spellbound, mesmerised by mountains. My Orrest Head moment had arrived.

Two years later, again in late October, I returned, tackling the mountain from Dungeon Ghyll in Great Langdale. As I crested Bow Fell, a thick mist descended, but unconcerned I pressed on to a col named Esk Hause, where the path reared up to Scafell Pike. The track – two yards wide moments earlier – seemed to vanish in a puff of mist and clambering over identical boulders, I wandered hopelessly in circles, totally lost. Wearing shorts, carrying only a bottle of water and a banana for sustenance, along with a map that was sodden and torn, I was unprepared for the dangers posed by Lakeland mountains.

Then the battery on my mobile phone died. Trying to control panic, I skirted a featureless plateau, searching for a way down. Any way. North, south, east or west – just a way down. There didn't seem to be one, with every potential route leading to a gully with an invisible drop. The wall of mist made me claustrophobic; lakes and mountains had disappeared and the ghostly whiteness was now closing in on its latest victim.

After what felt like an eternity, I spied a cairn, then another and another, and I knew this was a path to safety. Thank heavens for these piles of stones laid out by generations of walkers who had trod this way before. Now sure of the route, I didn't open the map again. Reaching the road, the feel of a flat surface under my feet was bliss. I heaved a sigh of relief. It had been a close one, but I had made it. Then an awful realisation swept over me. Where was Dungeon Ghyll? Where was my car? I don't remember this bridge being here before. Hang on, I don't even recognise this road. Reluctant to bow to the grim reality of my hideous mistake, I flagged down a car and asked where on earth I was.

'This is Seathwaite, of course,' came the reply.

Foul language is not big and is not clever, but in this instance it was entirely appropriate. Shit, shit and shit again.

I had descended into the wrong valley. Instead of heading west to Great Langdale, I had drifted north to Borrowdale. The light of day was already fading when I knocked on the door of the mountain rescue and begged – for what I don't know. What was the man meant to do? Charter a helicopter and fly me back to Dungeon Ghyll?

'It's at least six miles away over the mountains. You can't possibly attempt it now,' he told me. 'It will be dark soon and too dangerous to go back up there.'

Unable to drive me to Dungeon Ghyll – he had a night class in Penrith to get to – he loaned me £10 and a fleece two sizes too big. I hitchhiked, for the first and only time in my life, to Keswick, where I caught a bus to Ambleside, and sought refuge in the hostel, with all my belongings still six miles up the road in Dungeon Ghyll.

So you see, walking on Scafell Pike had a habit of being eventful.

The two passes between Little Langdale and Boot, Wrynose and Hardknott, were the hardest road cycling I had ever come across in England, if not the United Kingdom. And – I'm sticking my neck out here – I would wager there is nothing tougher in Europe. Longer, yes – by miles. But nothing as viciously steep – up to 33 per cent, and for long stretches a punishing 25 per cent. The pain inflicted upon cyclists climbing these ski slopes is inhuman. Minute after minute of gritted teeth, screwed-up faces, burning thighs, throbbing knees, lactic acid overdose and unrelenting suffering. Wrynose – long and steep – was horrifying. Hardknott – shorter but sheerer – was even worse. But if you can conquer the gruesome twosome, you can conquer anything.

A conqueror myself, I arrived in Boot only to be told I was in the wrong place to begin an ascent of Scafell Pike.

'You should have stopped three miles up the road,' an assistant in the Post Office informed me. 'You're way out.'

My error had been a simple one. Some months earlier, I had noted that in *Book Four* of Wainwright's *Pictorial*

Guides to the Lakeland Fells, the author had described the six-mile route between Boot and Sca Fell as 'delightful'. Sca Fell and Scafell Pike are part of the same massif, but they are two different mountains, separated by a mile of challenging terrain and the formidable cliffs of Broad Stand. I wasn't so much in the 'wrong' place to climb Scafell Pike, more an unusual place. Unwilling to swallow my pride and cycle back to the foot of Hardknott and the 'right' place, I set forth from Boot. Sca Fell and Scafell Pike? I'll climb them both.

What followed was an interminably long and lonely walk. Without *Book Four*, I could not have known that the 'delightful' walk Wainwright spoke about was along a so-called Terrace Route, which included an ascent of Slight Side and a ridge walk to the summit of Sca Fell. I was some distance to the west, tramping across a maze of tussocks to Burnmoor Tarn. Following the channel of Hardrigg Gill, I began to ascend Sca Fell's immense western face, a steep-sloping wall of rough grass and boulders that gave the appearance of reaching up to the heavens. Never had I encountered so many false summits, until at last I came to the true stony summit. Beyond, still some way to the west, lay England's (and naturally Cumberland's) highest ground.

I struck up conversation with a walker sporting impressive sweat patches around his armpits and chest. When I told him about my quest, he took a step back and grinned. 'You bugger,' he chuckled, in a Liverpool twang. 'You've nicked my idea. Where did you think of that then? Young lad like you. I was going to do it myself, just for fun like.'

Reaching Scafell Pike required a further arduous down and up effort. After descending Sca Fell by the Foxes Tarn path, which is effectively a ravine that follows the course of a stream, the route swung north under Broad Stand. From Mickledore, an obvious track then led across wobbly boulders to Scafell Pike.

There were 25 satisfied-looking faces on the summit, at least half of them children. Hill snobs have been known to look down their noses at Scafell Pike, casting it as an overcrowded mountain of day-trippers and picnickers. So what? Whether the mountain is climbed from Borrowdale, Eskdale, Langdale or Wasdale, what an achievement. Each one us had reached the summit of England. No higher can we go. And on Monday morning, when the children who had scaled Scafell Pike returned to their schools, they will have proudly told their pals: 'I climbed England's highest mountain.' They will, hopefully, be inspired, and such an adventure should surely be a rite of passage to adulthood for every youngster growing up in England.

Although the first recorded ascent of Scafell Pike was by Samuel Taylor Coleridge in 1802, it is at this juncture – and the scene of my 49th county summit – that I again turn to the words of Wainwright.

> This is it: the Mecca of all weary pilgrims in Lakeland; the place of many ceremonies and celebrations; of bonfires and birthday parties; the ultimate; the supreme; the one objective above all others; the highest ground in England; the top of Scafell Pike.

As I walked into the Boot Inn, a referee was waving a red card in the face of Wayne Rooney. A Cristiano Ronaldo wink and three missed penalties later, England had crashed out of the World Cup. At least I had the return grind over Hardknott and Wrynose to look forward to.

DAY 51 – SKELWITH BRIDGE TO POOLEY BRIDGE: 23 MILES
Helvellyn (Westmorland): 950m

Today was destined to be my triumphant 15 minutes of fame; the day my exploits would be splashed across the *Sunday Herald*, a national newspaper, albeit a Scottish one. I said goodbye to Cornelia and zoomed to Ambleside at breakneck speed, desperate to get my hands on a copy. The first newsagent had sold out; the second didn't stock it; the third had one copy left and I handed over £1.20.

I leafed through the sport section. There was the Rooney dismissal and a post-mortem of English defeat. Andy Murray had reached the second week of Wimbledon after beating the tournament's number three seed, Andy Roddick. Norwegian Thor Hushovd had been victorious in the prologue of the Tour de France, after two of the pre-race favourites were forced to withdraw. Meanwhile, Cameron McNeish, the doyen of Scottish hillwalking, took readers on a circular stroll through the Angus glens. I checked the main body of the newspaper, the magazine and in desperation the business section. A tale of 92 counties in 92 days was nowhere to be seen.

Shrugging off the disappointment, I made for The

Struggle, a devil of a three-mile grind from the shores of Lake Windermere to Kirkstone Pass. After 20 tortuous minutes, the end appeared in the shape of the Kirkstone Pass Inn, but The Struggle had a sting in its tail – a 20 per cent toil up its final slope.

Pain and pleasure. That is my simple definition of cycling. Take The Struggle or Hardknott Pass, for instance. What starts as mild inconvenience turns to discomfort, increasing to pain and excruciating agony. Then there is the pleasure. The Struggle met the top of Kirkstone Pass and nose-dived to Ullswater, a joyous 10 minutes of freewheeling frenzy, cruising at 35mph, the pain utterly forgotten. Until the next time, that is.

As I laboured up the flank of Birkhouse Moor, the east shoulder of Helvellyn, I wondered what all the fuss was about. After all, Helvellyn is the most climbed mountain in the Lake District, even more popular than Wainwright's 'one objective above all others', Scafell Pike. But there seemed nothing to distinguish Helvellyn from any of its high Lakeland neighbours.

Reaching the beginning of Striding Edge, boredom dissipated in a glance. Had I ever experienced such mouth-watering anticipation on a mountain? Ahead was a breathtakingly narrow arête – around 300 yards long and at times just a single yard wide – rising and falling in a series of whalebacks, before climaxing in a tremendously steep pull to the summit plateau. 'Striding Edge is the finest ridge there is in Lakeland,' said Wainwright, giving this place his seal of approval. Such fearful beauty, lovingly carved by nature – I could only feel privileged to gaze upon it.

With the right mindset and friendly weather, Striding Edge is as safe as houses – providing a walker does not take a tumble. I trod swiftly but carefully, elated, on top of the world. Just a short time earlier, I had been climbing a run-of-the-mill mountain – if such a thing exists in the Lake District. Now, sitting on top of England's third highest peak, eating a lunch of bread and biscuits, I had conquered one of the greatest.

There are three Helvellyn monuments worthy of mention. Typically, two of them are in memory of men who have lost their lives. A stone memorial close to the summit of Helvellyn pays tribute to Charles Gough of Winchester, who fell to his death in 1805. Would-be rescuers discovered Gough's body after being alerted by the whining of the poet's faithful terrier, which had stayed at his master's side for three months. On Striding Edge, an octagonal metal plaque recalls another Helvellyn victim: 'In memory of Robert Dixon, Rookings, Patterdale, who was killed on this place on the 27th day of Nov 1856, when following the Patterdale fox hounds.' On a lighter note, a third monument celebrates a momentous day in December 1926, when John Leeming and Bert Hinkler became the first people to land an aeroplane, an Avro 585 Gosport, 'on a mountain in Great Britain'.

As I descended Swirral Edge, cool air was replaced by a sweltering humidity. Shortly after the confluence of Glenridding and Redtarn becks, a natural bath of clear mountain water, around two yards wide and a yard deep, beckoned me to bathe. In a rare moment of spontaneity in this conditioned world, I stripped off my T-shirt and shorts before lowering myself into the beck. Bobbing up and down in the water, I would disappear under the surface momentarily, emerging with a gasp. It was a moment of perfection to rival the Pass of Llanberis.

I went no further than Pooley Bridge that night, craving another night in the midst of Lakeland peaks. The east bank of Ullswater was covered in sprawling campsites, a jumble of multi-coloured canvases, caravans, cars and squawking children. In the end, I found Cross Dormant campsite, where I was the only guest. As thunder crashed overhead, I lay in my sleeping bag reliving a breathless day: The Struggle, Kirkstone Pass, Striding Edge, Helvellyn, Glenridding Beck and Ullswater. At last, I had answered my editor's question. Today was why.

DAY 52 – POOLEY BRIDGE TO ALSTON: 69 MILES
Burnhope Seat (Durham): 746m

The UK can provide challenging environments, but extreme? I'm afraid not. There is no desert, jungle or ice to negotiate. Earthquakes are small and uncommon, and there is not much chance of Edinburgh Castle being blasted into the air from its extinct volcano-top perch. Our spiders and snakes are a bunch of softies, and the locals are friendly enough, generally frowning upon cannibalism or kidnap. The list of potential hazards while cycling through England is not an extensive one: punctures (highly likely), sunburn (unlikely) and getting rained on (certain). Strangely, having my feet blown off by explosive ammunition, evading Army tanks or dodging bullets did not enter my thoughts.

179

So who would have thought that an obscure corner of Yorkshire could throw up such dangers? The 788-metre Mickle Fell lies deep, very deep, inside the Warcop Range, a MoD firing zone. The ominous words 'danger area' – sometimes in capitals just to ram home the point – are sprinkled across a map of this area like confetti. It means Mickle Fell, standing four miles north of the Brough to Middleton-in-Teesdale road, and across rarely walked moorland terrain, is an extremely tricky customer.

This is the problem. There is MoD land. Then there is MoD land with a red warning flag flying. And then there is MoD land with the red warning flag flying and which also happens to be privately owned grouse moor. On a patch of grass close to where Durham meets Yorkshire there were two signs. On the first, the landowner, Strathmore Estates, indicated that I would need written permission from the head gamekeeper before setting foot on the moor. On the second, the MoD instructed that when a red flag was hoisted, on no condition could I set foot on the moor. In short, two excellent reasons not to set foot on the moor.

So, what to do? I had no qualms about trespassing. If I were caught I would play the ignorant card. Sign? What sign? I didn't see a sign. Besides, according to new right to roam laws, wasn't I entitled to walk across private land? As I weighed up the options a man in a jeep pulled up, got out and attached a lamp to the flagpole.

'How do?' he muttered in my direction.

'I want to walk up to Mickle Fell. Should I risk it?' I asked, nodding my head towards the pair of signs.

He looked surprised. 'There's a shooting range, but

it's on the other side of the valley to this one. The chance of you being hit is small. The problem is that this area was used as a tank practice ground in the Second World War and there's still unexploded material lying across the moor.'

The deafening ring of alarm bells sounded in my brain, awakening a memory in a crevice of my mind. Months earlier, I had typed Mickle Fell into Google and come across a gruesome story of a walker whose leg had been blown off by an unexploded shell. Maybe it was made up? Maybe it was true? Either way it troubled me greatly.

'So you think it would be stupid to risk it?'

Against the might of the MoD and Strathmore Estates, I had no desire to climb Mickle Fell, but I was in a quandary. As the highest point in the historic county of Yorkshire, Mickle Fell was on the list. It was one of the 92. I had to climb it. I knew that when the doubts ebbed away – which they inevitably would – I would think how cowardly I must have been for not taking the risk.

'You see that?' he said, pointing to the red flag. 'You're not going anywhere.'

'Are they firing tomorrow?'

'All week.'

'All *week*?'

'You really want to climb this mountain, don't you?'

Mickle Fell was out of bounds for a week. I ran that realisation around my head. What was I going to do? If the red flag was down tomorrow I could easily come back, but all week? I reckoned I'd be near Edinburgh in seven days. A detour back to Yorkshire was out of the question, but I couldn't stand on the summit of Ben

Nevis knowing that one county top had eluded me. That would be failure.

Back on my bicycle, I descended for two miles to Grains o'th Beck Bridge and spotted a 'public footpath' sign pointing on to the moor. Sick with fear, I climbed for 20 paranoid minutes, convinced my next step would be on a 60-year-old shell. Who was I kidding? I was never going to reach Mickle Fell from here. It was still six miles away, a 12-mile round trip. I turned back and ran, desperate to escape the moor's clutches. As I approached the road, a 4x4 vehicle with tinted windows was parked in a lay-by next to my bicycle. I stopped and shuddered. A gamekeeper or someone from the military? Drawing level with the car I felt like I was watching myself on a cinema screen. The window would wind down an inch, a barrel of a gun would appear and bang – my brains are splattered across Mickle Fell.

As I retrieved my cycle, the window lowered with a whirr. Staring out was a grey-haired old man and a fresh-faced grandson, dead ringers for the characters in the Werther's Original TV advert.

'Lovely day for it,' the grandad said cheerfully.

I reached Middleton-in-Teesdale and pedalled north to Alston, all the while trying to clear my mind of Mickle Fell. It had become the axis of my universe. Global warming? Poverty? Aids? No, Mickle Fell – two words that two hours earlier had simply been a scribble on a piece of paper – had now become the most important thing on the planet.

The B6277 climbed through Forest-in-Teesdale and Langdon Beck, before eventually rising to 598 metres.

Burnhope Seat, the highest point in County Durham, lay two miles to the west of the road's peak, on top of slopes littered with ski tows. The walk was a depressing, tiring slog through ankle-deep gorse; the summit a flat plateau surrounded by peat hags. Frankly, Burnhope Seat was a disappointing place, a poor advert for the splendid county it tops.

DAY 53 – ALSTON TO WALL: 50 MILES
Mickle Fell (Yorkshire): 788m

I spotted him at breakfast. Peeling nose, tan lines, smug expression – it must be a Pennine Way walker. He scoffed at my cowardice. 'You let a red flag and a story about unexploded shells put you off? Soft, are you? Must be, you're from the south.'

Bob was a local man and the surrounding hills and fells were his back garden. In a reassuring northern tone, he said that the red flag almost always flew on Mickle Fell, but it did not deter walking groups from reaching the summit. However, in a note of caution, he added, 'At the end of the day, it's up to you. There could be someone from the military there, but more likely a gamekeeper looking after his birds. But what's the worst that can happen?'

'I get shot?'

'That's a possibility.'

I wobbled up Alston's cobbles and retraced yesterday's tyre marks, past Burnhope Seat, over the 598-metre pass and down to Langdon Beck. En route, I devised a new plan of attack. I would not return to the ill fated

Middleton-in-Teesdale to Brough road. Instead, when I reached Langdon Beck, I followed a lane towards the Cow Green Reservoir. A third of the way to the man-made lake, I picked up a track that led me on foot through a field of Galloway cows to Widdybank Farm, where I would be able to join the Pennine Way. Under the cliffs of Falcon Clints, the path clung to the banks of the River Tees and I caught up with another Pennine Way walker, who had stopped to consult his guidebook.

Mike, an Essex man, told me he had left his job at Ford six months earlier and having walked part of the Pennine Way route many moons ago, he wanted to do the lot in one go. As we walked, he waxed lyrical about the wildlife, the inspiration of the hills and freedom of the path. I did not want to challenge his new-found freedom, but the greatest danger of designated long-distance footpaths is that walkers develop a head-down attitude, ignoring the treasures waiting just a few steps off route. Before I'd met Mike, I had stopped four separate walkers coming towards me and asked them what they knew of Mickle Fell. The stock responses were 'What's Mickle Fell'? and 'Is it on the Pennine Way'?

I asked the same question of my companion. Mike flicked through his Pennine Way guidebook, one that describes every bend, every step, every inch of the 268-mile route, destroying the mystery of exploring and finding your own way. No stone is left unturned.

'Cross a stile and after ten yards you'll pass a large pile of dog excrement. This fascinating lump of fossilised turd is believed to date back to the early 20th century and may have been deposited by a Labrador cross called Spike, though some experts argue it could have been the work of a German Shepherd known as Fido.

'Continue southeast where you'll pass the remains of a mouldy cheese and pickle sandwich left by Janice Cleggingbottom, from Llandudno. She only made it as far as Horton-in-Ribblesdale after twisting her knee on Pen-y-Ghent.'

Something like that, anyway.

'It's not in the guidebook,' Mick announced.

At Cauldron Snout – a creamy waterfall bubbling beneath the Cow Green Reservoir – Mike continued north, leaving me to search for the best place to cross the chocolate-coloured waters of the Tees. Mickle Fell was close now. I could see its green dome, perhaps two or three miles away. I just needed to hold my nerve.

My first mistake was taking off my footwear. The second was flinging them to the opposite bank. The riverbed was made up of smooth tennis ball sized rocks, slippery as fish, while the water was flowing faster than I had anticipated. Trainers would have given me some grip, while bare feet gave me none. A third of the way across, I stood rooted to the spot for some 20 seconds, fearful that a step, forward or back, would see me swimming down the Tees towards Middlesbrough. Gingerly, I lowered my hands into the murk and clutched the boulders on the river bottom. Water pounded my chest, but squatting on all fours, my centre of gravity lowered, I managed to move across in clumsy crab movements until I reached the safety of the other bank.

The land climbed steeply away from the river to the start of the 'danger zone', marked by warning signs at 100-

yard intervals stretching into the distance. The MoD really did not want me here. The slopes were breathless and silent, the quiet punctuated only by jack-in-the-box grouse springing from invisible nests in the gorse and making hideous 'go-bak, go-bak' calls. When disturbed, an adult was usually followed by several chicks squawking at high decibels, the suddenness of their flight sending my pulse soaring. My ears were pricked like a nervous rabbit, fearing every sound – the rustle of the wind or a chirruping bird – would lead to my imminent death. Convinced I would be rumbled, I played out paranoid scenarios in my head. A tank would trundle over the hills and I would be surrounded by gun-toting soldiers.

No one came. No military personnel. No gamekeepers. I stood on no landmines. My pace quickened as gorse gave way to short grass and I followed faint 4x4 tracks to a large stone cairn – the summit of Mickle Fell. I punched the air as adrenaline, endorphins and manic elation created an intoxicating mix in my brain. This was sex, drugs and alcohol rolled into one heady concoction. Cauldron Snout was now just a frothy dot. Cow Green Reservoir glinted in the sunshine. Teesdale sparkled. The tragedy is that more people are not able to gaze upon this view.

TEN

CARTER BAR – SERENADING SHEEP – IN THE DARKEST MOMENTS, THINK OF CAPTAIN SCOTT – A HILL NAMED CAIRNPAPPLE – 'LET'S HOPE HE HASN'T UNDERESTIMATED THE MAGNITUDE OF SCOTLAND'S HILLS AND MOUNTAINS' – 'RATHER YOU THAN ME, LADDIE' – GOING THE WRONG WAY – THE STORM – QUEUING FOR BREAKFAST – BIRTHDAY CELEBRATIONS ON MERRICK

DAY 54 – WALL TO KIRK YETHOLM: 58 MILES
Hangingstone Hill (Roxburghshire): 743m
The Cheviot (Northumberland): 815m

There is only way to arrive in Scotland. The Dumfriesshire town of Gretna Green may boast romantic connotations, but there is nothing romantic about the A76, the dual carriageway that propels motorists from England to Scotland. No, there is only way to enter Scotland: Carter Bar. By 2018, this 417-metre pass in the Cheviot Hills will have marked the boundary of England and Scotland for a millennium. Looking out from this lofty, windswept perch, across rolling green countryside and knobbly hills, provides a stupendous first glimpse of Scotland.

Made up of laybys on either side of the A68, there is little glamour about Carter Bar. A food van was doing a steady trade in bacon sandwiches, while a bagpiper struck up every time the occasional coach of tourists unloaded. Meanwhile, day-trippers posed for photographs in front of two large boulders, one on either side of the A68, bearing the word Scotland and England on opposite faces.

The border was laid down in 1018, when King Malcolm II defeated the Anglo-Saxons at Carham on Tweed. When Alexander III died in 1286, two and a half centuries of calm were followed by three centuries of conflict that saw a Scottish army march over Carter Bar to the Battle of Otterburn in 1388. Then came the era of the Border Reivers, a period of regular skirmishes on both sides of the border, until the last battle, the Redswire Fray in 1585. In 1701, peace was (more or less) established with the signing of the Treaty of Union to create the UK.

My first taste of Scottish soil came on the A68's wide hairpins, which spill down towards Jedburgh. Although I was now in Scotland, I still had unfinished business in England. The Cheviot, Northumberland's highest point – my final and 40th English summit – is best tackled from Kirk Yetholm, a Scottish village. Coincidentally, after spending a night in Edale at southern end of the Pennine Way, Kirk Yetholm – the Border Hotel to be precise – stands at the northern end.

Whenever I'm hungry, I think of the Cheviot. And whenever I think of the Cheviot, I recall awful gut-wrenching hunger. Grossly underestimating the distance from Kirk Yetholm to the Cheviot, via Roxburghshire's Hangingstone Hill, I was ready for a walk of six miles, perhaps seven at a push. I couldn't have been more wrong. The walk turned into a 12-mile march of attrition.

Carrying only a packet of pub-bought cheese and onion crisps, a chocolate bar and bottle of water, I cycled a mile out of Kirk Yetholm, as far as the road would allow, before the Pennine Way turned into grass. A zigzagging path climbed across a mountainside dotted with cows and up to a hilltop called The Schil. I ate the crisps, licking every crumb from the packet, a square of chocolate and swigged at the water. Fatigue had already zapped me, with hunger slowing my pace and thoughts.

In a dip before Auchope Cairn, I stumbled into a mountain refuge hut. What a relief this would be to a weary walker in winter or bad conditions. Maybe there was some food here? I scouted around the musty interior, finding only an empty baked beans can. What I would do for beans on toast. I peered into a bag of rubbish hanging from a hook on the wall, shocked that I would even contemplate taking something that had been thrown away.

I eyed up a tube of half-full toothpaste, a mind-racing discovery, taking me back to a story from my youth when my family spent holidays on a caravan site close to the north Cornish coast. The story – without doubt heavily embellished, because I've never been able to properly verify it – was about a man who purchased a tube of toothpaste in St Agnes, before falling down an old tin-mine shaft on his way home. Nine days later he was rescued, surviving his ordeal – with minty fresh breath – thanks to eating the toothpaste. I picked up the tube. Colgate. I preferred Macleans. I put it back. I wasn't that desperate. Not yet.

Struggling up a relentless slope to the summit of

Auchope Cairn, I set my sights on a pair of walkers and their Dalmatian, who were making even slower progress than I was. Catching them, I announced where I was going and moaned, 'But I'm so hungry.' They either had no food or failed to take the hint. A dog biscuit would have sufficed. A wooden boardwalk surrounded by bog brought me to the non-descript Hangingstone Hill, with the Cheviot still three-quarters of a mile away. At last, I crested the whaleback roof of the Cheviots and arrived at the range's summit, a place so flat it obscured any sort of view.

The next two hours were a blur. Somehow I escaped the Cheviot, stumbling back to my bicycle. On the descent, I did a good deal of talking out loud to grazing animals. I also developed a worrying knowledge of the lyrics of every Elton John song he had ever written. I performed, to a herd of cows, a hysterical rendition of 'Rocket Man' and later serenaded a pair of bemused sheep with a wholly original version of 'The Bitch is Back'.

The relief to get down was almost unbearable. Emotions flooded out in a torrent of eye-stinging salty tears. As I rode slowly to Kirk Yetholm, twilight set the scene for a moment of sheer bliss, a magical culmination to a day of endurance. Two badgers snuffled in the grass at the roadside, just a few yards ahead, gloriously ignorant of my approach. I'd only ever seen these wild animals dead, their stinking bloodstained carcasses rotting in the road. Alive, their white and black fur had all the brilliance and vitality of a hair model. I watched them for a few seconds, until one sniffed the air and two heads looked my way, beady eyes entranced by this unexpected visitor. An instant later, they were running past me, one to my left, one to my right, their claws scratching along the road.

DAY 55 – KIRK YETHOLM TO NORTH BERWICK: 57 MILES
Meikle Says Law (East Lothian): 525m
Meikle Says Law (Berwickshire): 522m

Meikle Says Law – a moorland plateau amid the Lammermuir Hills – is home to two county summits, although not in identical places. The top of East Lothian was marked by a standard triangulation pillar on the hill's highest point, while Berwickshire's marginally inferior summit lay a minute's walk to the southwest.

The rolling Lammermuirs have the veneer of a wild, untamed land, where there are few settlements, roads and paths. Don't be fooled. These hills are irrevocably tainted by man. The open, bare landscape points to deforestation, while crackling electricity pylons bulldoze their way across the countryside. To the east was the most recent blot, a windfarm, where turbine blades turned lazily in the breeze. Wind power opponents had made their feelings abundantly clear. 'No more wind turbines in the Lammermuir Hills,' a roadside banner demanded. I was inclined to agree. If wind power really is the solution to the UK's energy needs, then surely turbines could be erected somewhere less damaging than the Lammermuirs? Where is the sense in spoiling the environment to save the environment?

Several hours later, I was holed up in my little shelter on a North Berwick camping ground. Pitched next door was a Millennium Dome-sized tent, filled with games and giggles. A family's simple pleasures were in sharp contrast to my miserable mood, as I plunged depths of despair not experienced since Okehampton. Hurriedly scrawling down my thoughts before shadows prevented me from seeing the words, my journal entry gave away my feelings.

> Sometimes, like today, things just aren't great. I feel low, lonely and lacking in motivation. After 55 days, my body is beginning to suffer, to fall apart. Now when I hit a climb, my bicycle seems to park, rather than hurry up. My average daily distances are going down. At times, the boredom of sitting on the bicycle is overwhelming. Walking is tedious, always a slog. My legs aren't recovering. I doubt they'll ever get over that day on the Cheviot.
>
> I knew it was going to be a bad one from the off. I was up at six o'clock – kept awake by two snorers in the top bunks. The chap opposite had the nerve to poke me in the ribs when it wasn't me snoring. I was lying awake suppressing the urge to smother them both with a pillow. I mustn't resort to murder. I'm too tired to even shed a tear about how I feel right now. Such self-pity. I'm a wimp. I bet Captain Scott didn't get upset when the chips were down. Stiff upper lip. Mind you, at least he had

companions. The loneliness is the worst thing, the fact I'm lying here in this small, dark, hard pit, with not a soul to talk to.

I was guilty of underestimating the scale of my journey, which I was beginning to realise would surpass 5,000 miles. That is Cape Town to Marrakech, or London to Kathmandu. Was 92 days really enough time to cover 5,000 miles? Psychologically, completing the 53 English and Welsh county tops had seemed like the end. Indeed, the highs of Scafell Pike and Helvellyn, along with the triumph of Mickle Fell, would have been a fitting finale. In the exhilaration of those glorious moments, I had almost forgotten that there were another 40 days – if I were to end the journey on the 92nd day – to the finish line on Ben Nevis.

There were still 2,500 miles to go. Ahead I had to fight my way across Scotland's central belt, conquer the Southern Uplands, complete a lap of Northern Ireland, visit the Isle of Arran, clamber up eight Munros, venture into the Cairngorms, cycle as far north as Shetland, before pedalling 250 punishing miles into the teeth of prevailing southwesterlies to Fort William. There were 36 hills and mountains left, half of them higher than 700 metres. And if they were not many miles from the nearest road or civilisation, they were pitched out on a limb, propelling me to the corners of Scotland and Northern Ireland.

A 92-day journey? It seemed an impossible task.

DAY 56 – NORTH BERWICK TO EDINBURGH: 26 MILES

Cycling does not get much better than the marathon distance between North Berwick and Edinburgh. After manicured golf fairways, there were sandy beaches, where white horses lashed the Firth of Forth coast. As heavy clouds rested above the land, a clear blue sky opened over the water, with shafts of sunlight reflecting off the frothy surface. Soon I was bearing down on Cockenzie's imposing power station, a vision of functionality in comparison to the natural splendour of Arthur's Seat rising behind it.

It was 7 July, the first anniversary of the London bus and underground bombings. At 11 o'clock, it was anticipated that the country would fall silent to pay tribute to the 52 victims. At 11 o'clock in Edinburgh's main thoroughfare, Princes Street, there wasn't an obvious flicker of emotion. Tourists kept touring. Pipers kept piping. Buses kept bussing. Shoppers kept shopping. Perhaps that was the way it should have been, carrying on regardless.

DAY 57 – EDINBURGH TO AIRDRIE: 48 MILES
Cairnpapple Hill (West Lothian): 312m

With expectations of a low, unremarkable summit amid the Bathgate Hills, I pedalled eastwards in search of Cairnpapple. With a name more suited to a Pacific island or a tropical fruit than a West Lothian tump, Cairnpapple had the ring of an intriguing place. That meant it was bound to be dreadful. So I was surprised – no, stunned – to find Scotland's lowest county summit was a 5,500-year-old prehistoric site. Having already encountered county tops doubling as back gardens, MoD land and cabbage patches, I was cock-a-hoop to add my first museum to the list.

Despite its ancient history, Cairnpapple was only excavated in the late 1940s. It seems someone glanced up one day, perhaps from nearby Bathgate or Torphichen, and thought, There's a strange looking hill – let's dig it up. So they did. As excavation leader Professor Stuart Piggott and his team of archaeologists patiently chipped away at the ground, they made a series of astonishing discoveries that exposed centuries of hidden history. Cairnpapple Hill had been a monument, a beacon and a place of worship long before the area was became known as West Lothian. In 1992, Rodney Castleden would declare in *Neolithic Britain*, 'Cairnpapple stands virtually alone in British archaeology in offering evidence of such long-sustained religious observance at a particular spot; it thus has a virtually unique claim to being a holy place.'

According to my £1.95 Historic Scotland souvenir guide, life on Cairnpapple began 5,500 years ago, when early Neolithic man started fires here and left behind pottery and axes. Some 500 years later, a 24-stick ceremonial henge was erected around the top of the hill. Bronze Age man turned Cairnpapple into a cemetery, when 'burials were placed under cairns, in stone-lined boxes called cists, in shallow graves and in unlined pits. Some were cremations, others were interments of unburned graves. A few were buried with belongings, mostly pottery vessels, but also including items of wood and animal bone.'

Apart from an ugly concrete bunker built to preserve ancient burials at the centre of the monument, Cairnpapple Hill is an open-air museum. But was it the summit of West Lothian? Looking to the south, the land dipped before climbing again to two hills of similar height. I visited them both to be sure I had stood on the roof of West Lothian. The first was called The Knook, where a summit toposcope pointed towards ten hills or mountains that I had climbed or was due to scale. Ben Lomond was 43 miles away and Ben Lawers just 49 miles – but it would be another fortnight before I would touch their slopes. The third point was the most non-descript of the three but it was marked by a triangulation pillar; I made for it in the knowledge that one of these three must count as West Lothian's summit.

I was going to Airdrie. Not the most uplifting sentence in the English language I appreciate, but for me the Lanarkshire town represented respite and companionship, for I was staying with Laura, an ex-housemate from Cheltenham. Firm friends on one hand, we also shared a love-hate relationship. In 18 months, her ability as a natural alarm clock – a siren that would sound at one or two o'clock in the morning – drove me to distraction. Her favourite alcohol-induced trick, ably assisted by her accomplice Jenny, was to charge into my ground-floor room in the early hours of the morning, before throwing herself on top of my sleeping body. Not in a sexual way, you understand. In a sweating neat vodka kind of way.

'Jonny, you look so skinny,' Laura screeched on her

first glance at me. Her mother Theresa looked me up and down, from drawn face to protruding collar bones, narrowing waist and two chicken legs. My weight had dipped below ten stone for the first time in a decade.

'You do look thin,' Theresa agreed, with a little more tact than her daughter, and darted into the kitchen to rectify the situation. Before the perspiration had dried on my forehead, she had plonked a vat of melon, blueberries and strawberries on my lap. As I swallowed the last mouthful, she swapped the empty bowl for a full plate of sausage, fried egg and black pudding barms, with tea and chocolate biscuits for dessert. Moments after the feast had been devoured she emerged from the kitchen. 'What do you want for your dinner?'

I was granted a rest between meals, giving Laura and I time to drive across town to visit her 82-year-old Granda, who lay in bed drinking sherry and eating crisps. To his ears, my English lilt clearly sounded like Punjabi, while Laura's Glaswegian burr made perfect sense. Every time I uttered a few words, he would turn to Laura with the cheeky smile of a schoolboy and bellow, 'Translate!'

DAY 58 – AIRDRIE

Sometimes it takes someone who flits into your consciousness for only a few moments to put your life into perspective. For the first time, Fiona Russell's article in the *Sunday Herald,* made me look at the enormity of my journey.

Jonny Muir cycled across the Scottish border on Wednesday. Nothing remarkable in that you might think, except that by the time the 24-year-old reached Carter Bar he had been cycling for almost seven weeks, taking in the highest points in more than 50 counties in England and Wales – and will be set to tackle the highest hills and mountains in all 33 Scottish counties.

Muir has spent 42 days in the saddle, cycling to and between 52 historic county tops in England and Wales. So far he has covered almost 2,500 bike miles, averaging 60 miles a day. His lowest summit of 80m was in Huntingdonshire, while the highest, Snowdon, in Caernarfonshire, was 1,085m.

In one day, he cycled more than 100 miles. In one six-day period, he cycled 350 miles to tick off seven county peaks. On three occasions, he reached three summits in one day. He has climbed an average of 1.3 hills or mountains per day. And this doesn't include the miles walked when mountaintops have been unreachable by bike. So far, he's worn out three wheels, two sets of brake pads, a chain, three tyres, snapped one gear cable and had five punctures.

Was this really about me, some daft adventurer who tens of thousands of people would be reading about over their cornflakes? I needed to scamper up a mountain before breakfast or swim across the Clyde to prove my madness.

Instead, I got out of bed, wandered down the stairs, sat on the sofa and turned on the TV, moving only to answer a call of nature. In fact, I didn't even step outside. And still the tea and biscuits came. This was better than any five-star hotel. I did nothing, finding it astonishing how fast time drifts when one does nothing. In a day of sport, Roger Federer beat Rafael Nadal in the Wimbledon final and Zinedine Zidane butted Marco Materazzi in the chest before Italy beat France on penalties in the World Cup final. Before I knew it, darkness had fallen and it was time for bed.

DAY 59 – AIRDRIE TO INNERLEITHEN: 60 MILES
Culter Fell (Lanarkshire): 748m

'Rather you than me, laddie.' It was an oft-repeated phrase thrown at me most mornings, but on this occasion I couldn't disagree with the Airdrie granny. It was an insipid morning. I was bloated and a little hung over. The sky was grey and my route – a leapfrog across the M8 followed by brief tours of Wishaw, Carluke and Lanark – was predominantly urban. After reaching the most northerly extent of my journey so far in Edinburgh, I had been forced to turn south. The county summits of six shires, Ayr, Dumfries, Kirkcudbright, Lanark, Peebles and Wigtown, along with Midlothian, were scattered haphazardly across the map of southern Scotland, proving particularly unhelpful to those wanting to climb them.

Lanarkshire's Culter Fell came first, a 748-metre

peak in the Southern Uplands, rising six miles south of Biggar. A single-track road ran alongside Coulter Reservoir, where I entrusted my bicycle to a trio of inquisitive sheep. A steep climb brought me to the summit of Knock Hill, before a gentler slope led to Culter Fell's upper limits. A swaying metal fence a few inches to the west of a triangulation pillar indicated the border between Lanarkshire and Peeblesshire. On rare occasions such as these, I liked to stand straddling the boundary, amused by the concept that my right leg was in one county and my left leg in another. Other than that, I didn't linger long on this windswept and lonely summit.

DAY 60 – INNERLEITHEN TO LOCH OF THE LOWES: 46 MILES

Blackhope Scar (Midlothian): 651m
Broad Law (Selkirkshire & Peeblesshire): 840m

These were harsh days in the Borders: life was a struggle against incessant winds and the desire to fall asleep in the saddle. For 60 days I had been forcing my body through the same ritual with my mind dominated by identical thoughts and fears. Waking from a coma-like sleep on an Innerleithen campsite, I knew it would be tough again. You know how yesterday was a hard, long slog? my brain teased my aching limbs. Well, today's going to be harder and longer.

If I compiled a black list of hills and mountains, Blackhope Scar, some six miles northeast of Peebles, would be on it, right at the top with Burnhope Seat. Awful places. From the off, I was irritated, for Blackhope Scar's location in the Moorfoot Hills meant I had to cycle north – the opposite direction I ultimately needed to go. Starting along a muddy track, something was amiss. My legs were stiff and resented going uphill. That was normal. An owl swooping overhead, again and again, while making a repetitive cry was not. I felt uneasy. Maybe the bird was trying to tell me something? An hour later I realised it was: 'You're going the wrong way you blithering idiot.'

I should have cycled a further two miles north and climbed Blackhope Scar from what would have been a far more advantageous position. It was too late to turn back. Head down, I resumed a long march across trenches of filthy moor and twice had to haul a shoe free from pools of reeking slime. Getting to the summit made it all worthwhile. Actually, it didn't. The top was reminiscent of Black Hill and Burnhope Seat. Soaring peak? I'd be lucky. There was a metal fence stretching into the distance, a lonely pillar and an ocean of mud.

At Clappercleuch, I took the mountain road to the west alongside the long and narrow Megget Reservoir, one of Edinburgh's supplementary water suppliers. Before I reached a second reservoir called Talla, I came to the Megget stone – a slab of greywacke that once marked the county line of Peeblesshire and Selkirkshire. Today it was a useful prop for my bicycle. From the stone, it was a straightforward two-mile hike to Broad Law's green dome, where my final few strides to the shared summit of Peeblesshire and Selkirkshire were accompanied by a constant whirring sound from the spacecraft-like transmitter on top.

Exhausted and midge-bitten, I pitched my tent close to the edge of Loch of the Lowes and shuffled to the Tibbie Shiels Inn in search of food. The pub was named after its 19th-century landlady Isabella Shiels and is a stopping point on the 212-mile Southern Upland Way. Too late for a meal, I had to make do with a less-than-nourishing main course of salt and vinegar crisps, followed by a bar of chocolate. As I ate, a woman behind the bar said I wasn't the first unusual traveller to darken her door.

'Last week a man came in with a Scrabble board,' she said. 'He asked if I could find him an opponent. It was a strange request, but I managed to find someone. He said he was travelling across Scotland with his board and every night he'd find a new opponent to play a game against.'

Lost in thought, she chuckled to herself before pointing to a round certificate shaped like a beer mat and pinned to the wall. 'You see that? A group of men said they were visiting every pub in Britain. They must have been to a few. We're number ten thousand and something,' she said, squinting as she tried to make out the number on the certificate.

While 21st-century visitors to the Tibbie Shiels Inn are self-confessed oddballs, 19th-century tourists included literary giants of their era, among them Sir Walter Scott, Thomas Carlyle, Robert Louis Stevenson and locally born writer James Hogg, who was dubbed the Ettrick Shepherd and is remembered by a statue overlooking Loch of the Lowes.

After a tortuous day, all now seemed right with the world. The loch was still, the air quiet. 'This is the life,' I declared aloud, before snuggling into my sleeping bag. I had got the hang of this camping lark.

DAY 61 – LOCH OF THE LOWES TO KENDOON: 66 MILES
White Coomb (Dumfriesshire): 821m

It was the calm before the storm. At four o'clock I was woken by the wind roaring through my little tent. Instantly, I knew the outer sheet had been ripped from the ground and swept away. Pulling the bag tightly around my neck, I unzipped the inner sheet and poked my head outside. The first glimmer of dawn creeping across the sky illuminated a foreboding blackness enveloping the mountains. Peaceful Loch of the Lowes had been transformed into a raging ocean of sloshing waves, furiously lapping my once-idyllic beach. The wind flicked froth off the surface of the water like blossom falling from a tree. I stared fearfully at the loch, half-expecting a terrible monster to rise up and pluck me into the depths.

The outer sheet had not swirled into the night sky, never to be seen again, as I had feared. I retrieved it, tangled but not ripped, from the spiky branches of a tree close to the road bridge dividing Loch of the Lowes and St Mary's Loch. I gathered up half a dozen pegs, which had been tugged out of the ground by the ferocity of the wind, and did my best to re-pitch the outer sheet, adding a ring of rocks to prevent it happening a second time.

What a strange sight this scene would have presented to an onlooker. A dawn loon jumping around in a sleeping bag like an overgrown caterpillar, chasing parts of a tent across a field, before attempting to hammer pegs into the ground using the sole of a trainer.

Sleep was out of the question. Surrounded by the deafening furore, I felt helpless and insignificant. I thought of Fiona Russell's ominous words in the *Sunday Herald*. 'Let's hope he hasn't underestimated the magnitude of Scotland's hills and mountains.' I had been cursed. I had underestimated Scotland and now this country was testing my will, my lack of respect.

Perspective is the best antidote to dread, so I opened *The Worst Journey in the World* to page 281. My heroes, Cherry-Garrard, Edward Wilson and Birdie Bowers, had set off on a Winter Journey to capture eggs belonging to the Emperor penguins. Their world was one of permanent darkness and frighteningly cold temperatures. Now the adventurers were caught in a storm, not a wee Scottish one, but an Antarctic rip-roarer. Like me, Cherry-Garrard had also been roused from slumber by its call.

> I do not know what time it was when I woke up. It was calm, with that absolute silence which can be so soothing or so terrible as circumstances dictate. Then there came a sob of wind, and all was still again. Ten minutes and it was blowing as though the world was

having a fit of hysterics. The earth was torn in
pieces: the indescribable fury and roar of it all
cannot be imagined.

Catching my reflection in the window of the Glen Café, I
fancied I had the look of a polar explorer. My face was
tanned with an untidy beard creeping across my chin and
cheeks. My eyes were wild, almost animal-like, while my
hair was straggly and blond after weeks of exposure to
the sun. Evolution was going into reverse. I was
becoming a caveman. Perusing the menu, I pre-selected a
feast for breakfast – egg, beans, bacon, potato scones,
haggis, William Wallace sausage and toast.

The café didn't open for another five minutes, so I
dashed to the public toilets next door to smarten myself
up, which in reality, meant washing my hands, brushing
my teeth and running my fingers through my hair. When
I emerged from the gents, I saw to my horror that around
30 pensioners were queuing at the door of the café. There
were still others joining the back of the line and I barged
in front of them, convinced this was an appropriate
moment for violence, however old they were.

A hungry and frustrating ten minutes slipped by
before I neared the front of the file to order. It was
Margaret and Maud's turn, then me.

'Ooh, shall I have a cake?' wondered Maud aloud.

'Why not?' Margaret encouraged her. 'You're on holiday.'

Chop chop, Maud, I wanted to say. And get out of my
bloody way.

'Ooh, but I shouldn't.'

'Why not?'

'Ooh, I shouldn't really.'

'Go on.'

'If you insist. Now what shall I have? Date slice or coffee and walnut cake?'

'Tough one.'

'It is.'

'Tricky.'

'Hmm.'

'Decided?'

'What are you going to have?'

'Just a coffee.'

'I shouldn't really. Should I? Just this once then.'

'Date slice or coffee and walnut?'

'Ooh, I don't know. What do you think?'

I gripped the toothbrush in my right hand. If Maud deliberated for another five seconds, I was about to become the toothbrush killer.

'I've changed my mind. I'll have a scone.'

'Do you want that with blackberry jam or strawberry jam...'

Unrelenting head-on gusts – presumably the tail end of the morning hurricane – made for a hellish five-mile slog to the foot of White Coomb, where James was waiting for me. Standing outside his car, looking up at the mist-capped mountains, he wore a worried expression and pristine boots.

'We're going up there?' he enquired, pointing into the grey gloom, hoping I'd had a change of heart and would call the venture off.

Our ascent of White Coomb began from a National Trust for Scotland car park, where a rocky path curved upwards, providing a bird's eye view of a hanging valley waterfall known as the Grey Mare's Tail. Mist had settled above the 500-metre contour line and once in the thick stuff, our visibility was reduced to less than 20 yards. Instead of following a well-walked tourist track to Loch Skeen we waded across the Tail Burn, high above the 60-metre waterfall and toiled across slippery mud and rock for a mile. Even with the lights off, White Coomb was an unmistakable dome of green grass, Dumfriesshire's gentle giant.

James set off to Kendoon. He could have given me a lift but that would have meant breaking the rules. Stupid, sodding rules. Ahead were 60 miles and four hours of treacherous weather. As I pedalled to Moffat, I couldn't help but feel desperately sorry for myself. Cycling must be the most masochistic mode of transport. When the wind blew, it made every effort seem futile and meagre. Then there was the boredom. Tarmac. Road sign. Dead animal. Tarmac. Road sign. Dead animal... A film of mist had obscured any countryside or hills there might have been. I attempted to switch off my thoughts, to not obsess about arriving. Isn't the true wonder of travel the journey itself, and not arrival? Whoever came up with those words of wisdom clearly wasn't a cyclist pedalling across southern Scotland in torrential rain.

Over the A74, with Dumfries in my sights, the southwesterlies eased and I began to feel stronger, growing in confidence with every turn of the pedals. The revelation was short-lived. After bypassing Dumfries, I split the 25 miles to St John's Town of Dalry into five-mile sections in my mind. I was suffering. When I finally reached the hostel, another five miles north of Dalry in Kendoon, I barely had the energy to dismount my bicycle. I staggered into the building, too tired to be relieved and collapsed on a bed.

DAY 62 – KENDOON TO MINNIGAFF: 29 MILES
Merrick (Kirkcudbrightshire): 843m
Kirriereoch (Ayrshire): 781m

When I opened my eyes I was a quarter of a century old. It was 13 July – my 25th birthday. How should someone celebrate such a milestone? Sup a few beers with friends? A summer barbecue? Dance the night away in a club? Or cycle nearly 30 miles and walk another ten?

Had I needed motivation to climb Merrick, the highest mountain in southern Scotland, I had chosen the right starting point. Three miles east of Glentrool village, I came to Loch Trool, a slender band of water glistening in a valley patriotically known as Scotland's 'cradle of independence'. Overlooking the lake is Bruce's Stone – a memorial laid in 1929 marking 600 years since the death of Robert the Bruce. The words etched on a plaque were enough to stir even the soul of a hardened Sassenach.

In loyal remembrance of Robert the Bruce, King of Scots, whose victory in this glen over an English force opened the campaign of independence which he brought to a decisive close at Bannockburn on June 24, 1314.

Viewed from the air, the mountains among which James and I were climbing are known as the Range of the Awful Hand, because they resemble the shape of a right hand with outspread fingers. Benyellary is the thumb; Merrick the index finger; the second and third fingers are Kirriereoch and Tarfessock, and the peak of Shalloch on Minnoch, furthest to the north, is the little finger.

Ticking off the thumb, we made for the index finger along the Neive of Spit. On the summit of Merrick, I heaved my body up on to the pillar, stretching my arms into the billowing wind. James took a photograph. It was a picture that would later appear on the front page of my hometown newspaper, the *Bromsgrove Advertiser*. Continuing north, Little Spear deposited us on the soggy lower slopes of Kirriereoch. We didn't have long to wait for our second county top of the day. Ignoring Kirriereoch's highest point, we paused at a low wall of stone marking the historic county boundary of Kirkcudbrightshire and Ayrshire, as well as the modern-day administrative dividing line of Dumfries and Galloway and South Ayrshire. Here, hunkering on the northwest shoulder of Kirriereoch, we found Ayrshire's county top.

DAY 63 – MINNIGAFF TO MINNIGAFF: 29 MILES
Craigarie Fell (Wigtownshire): 320m

Why can't all hills be like Craigarie Fell? After cycling a little under 15 miles, some of it on the dusty tracks of the Southern Upland Way, I was within 400 yards of the summit. The reward for a short burst of exertion to the top was a splendid view of Merrick, a vast presence to the east.

At midday, James and I convened in the Minnigaff hostel car park. After reluctantly leaving my bicycle in a shed adjoining the building, I sunk into the passenger seat of his Mini. It had taken 46 days of cycling and walking to travel between Bromsgrove and Minnigaff. The return journey took six hours.

DAY 64 TO 66: MINNIGAFF TO MINNIGAFF, VIA BROMSGROVE, SALISBURY AND PETERBOROUGH

I took three days off for three reasons. Firstly, to see Fi who was working at a summer school in Salisbury. Secondly, to attend an interview for a reporter's job at the *Evening Telegraph* newspaper in Peterborough. And thirdly, for a little recuperation – the last chance I would have before Ben Nevis. If I wanted to complete this expedition in 92 days, there would be no more breaks.

I haven't mentioned Fi for some time, have I? Well, we were getting on – just. We had a rather awkward reconciliation in Salisbury, tiptoeing around one another, her resisting the urge to holler 'You're a selfish bastard' and me unwilling to counter with 'You're an unsupportive cow.' In the end, I was relieved to drop her off at the summer school that she was working at and wave goodbye. An hour longer and one of us would have exploded. I knew that in Fi's head our meeting was all too brief, rendering it pointless. We kissed and she promised to meet me on Ben Nevis in a month's time.

I knew little of Peterborough, except that any sentence using the word 'Peterborough' is usually followed by the question, 'Where's Peterborough'? Approaching from the west, simply follow the drone of the A1 and look out for the yellow neon light of a McDonald's. You are now in Peterborough, possibly the flattest place on Earth. Find a hill here and the city council will hand you the keys to the town hall.

Peterborough depressed me. Not because it was Peterborough, you understand – although that didn't help. I was depressed because Peterborough provided a glaring reality check. Being here symbolised the next chapter in my life. A chapter when the summer would be no more, my journey would be over and – worst of all – there wouldn't be another hill or mountain to climb. Days of pulling on a suit and making small talk at the water cooler no longer felt as far away as they had in Bodmin 66 days earlier.

ELEVEN

MIDGES – SURVIVING THE SPERRINS – 'PLEASE, PLEASE, PLEASE, LET THIS BE THE LAST' – THE ERODED HEART OF AN EXTINCT VOLCANO – FAIRYTALES – SLIEVE DONARD – 'ARE YOU MAD?' – A TRIBUTE TO CARL STEPHENSON – 'DON'T YOU KNOW WHO I AM?' – PROCRASTINATION

DAY 67 – MINNIGAFF TO CAIRNRYAN: 28 MILES

Scotland in summer. Think midges. Great clouds of the wee beasties. And no, midges are not a Scottish ruse to scare off the namby-pamby English. They are as bad as every horror story, and worse. Just writing these words sends me into a frenzy of itching. My first encounter with these dreadful insects came as a surprise. I had reached the port of Cairnryan, perched on Scotland's southwestern coast, at 10pm – six hours before the early morning ferry departed for Northern Ireland. At the suggestion of the ferry terminal's staff, I rolled my sleeping bag onto a luxurious mattress – the plastic surface of a children's indoor soft play area. It was a little public, perhaps, but more comfortable than the car park. Wriggling into my bag, I looked up at the ceiling. It was then that I saw them – black dots zipping across the room. Midges.

With a wingspan of just one to two millimetres, midges

are true mini-monsters. I should not have been surprised to see them, as the shores of Loch Ryan ticked all the boxes for midges. The conditions were damp and humid; there was no wind; the sun had long gone. It made the ferry terminal a midge's lair – an insect's version of the Costa del Sol. At first they crawled in my hair, then down my neck and arms, before invading my bag and investigating my crotch. I slapped, cursed and scratched till I bled. Nothing seemed to help. For six hours, I slipped in and out of sleep, as what seemed like a thousand pinpricks penetrated my skin. To add to my discomfort, the terminal building had retained the day's searing heat, making me sweat profusely. Every now and again, I had to peel my clammy skin from the play area, and shuffle a little to the right or left to find a dry spot. When my alarm sounded at four o'clock, rarely had I been so relieved to get up.

DAY 68 – CAIRNRYAN TO DUNGIVEN: 76 MILES
Trostan (Antrim): 551m

As our ship bounced across the Irish Sea, an orange sun climbed over a smaller and smaller Scotland. I was the only tourist on board. The other passengers were long-distance lorry drivers, who huddled on the deck in twos and threes, smoking cigarettes and flicking unwanted butts into the grey water. Cravings answered, they wandered into the lounge, leaving me alone in the sharp morning air to watch the sunrise.

Larne marked the start of my mini-Irish adventure, an

anti-clockwise loop around the country, visiting Antrim, Londonderry, Tyrone, Fermanagh, Armagh and Down in turn. Because Londonderry and Tyrone shared a county top, the round route would take five days.

The road clung to the shoreline, slipping through Ballygalley and Glenarm, where there were few humans and even fewer cars. With little to distract me, I pressed on to the unremarkable 551-metre Trostan, a no-nonsense hike from the gently rising road pass linking Cushendall and Ballymena. Within half an hour, I was standing on the sandy tabletop of Antrim, gazing north to Trostan's marginally lower neighbours, Slieveanorra and Knocklayd. On a clear day, I would have glimpsed the Sperrin Mountains to the west, but a heat haze meant the view barely stretched to the sea less than five miles away.

Today was 19 July, the day when the UK's weather was predicted to go bonkers. National newspapers concurred that it was going to be the hottest 24 hours on record. Although the weather refused to live up to the hype, 19 July did prove to be the hottest July day ever chronicled. Charlwood, in Surrey, took the accolade, cooking in 36C heat, a temperature almost as hot as the blood pumping through our veins. In Leeds, roads melted. Drinking water had to be handed out in Nottinghamshire. Across England, there were National Grid blackouts as air-conditioning systems went into overdrive.

In Antrim, the mercury tipped 28C. An astonishing 1,000 hits of lightning were recorded, and a forest fire burned on the slopes of Armagh's Slieve Gullion, a hill I would be climbing in three days time. The hundred firefighters battling the inferno were unable to save 40 acres of land from ruin. Across the rest of Northern Ireland, the *Tyrone Herald* reported temperatures had edged above 30C, making it the province's hottest July day since the 1930s. It was hotter even than Crete, Rome and Sydney, the newspaper boasted. Even if Australia was in the depths of winter, the *Herald* didn't want to miss an opportunity to gloat.

Me? I was sweltering, sweating faster than I could drink, roasting like a joint in the oven. Eggs would have fried on my forehead. The last thing I needed was the steady climb over the 300-metre Glenshane Pass. I was panting hard and without sunglasses my eyes throbbed in the glare. Passing Northern Ireland's highest pub, the Ponderosa, I knew it was downhill to Dungiven. Even with a breath of wind in my hair, I was too shattered to entertain the idea of camping. I booked into the 17th-century Dungiven Castle, which had been converted into cheap sleeping quarters.

DAY 69 – DUNGIVEN TO ENNISKILLEN: 66 MILES
Sawel (Derry & Tyrone): 678m

After I'd announced I was bound for the Sperrins, the warden launched into the kind of tale only a local who'd spent a lifetime in the shadows of these hills could know. It was 1943 and Northern Ireland was at war. A damaged aeroplane was spiralling to earth, its only possible landing strip the steep-sided slopes of the high Sperrins. Miraculously the two airmen survived the impact, emerging from the wreckage with only broken bones. So imagine their horror when no one came to rescue them. Either the crash went unnoticed or rescuers couldn't find the aircraft's resting-place. Exposed to the elements, the pair struggled over the hillside in search of safety. For three days and three nights they dragged themselves across rock, peat hag, streams and gorse, until they finally came to civilisation. It was a truly inspiring story of human endeavour and courage.

The warden paused.

'And then what happened?' I enquired eagerly.

'They died.'

The Sperrins stretch for 18 miles along the Londonderry and Tyrone county border, from Draperstown in the east to Plumbridge in the west. They are not the prettiest of hills, nor do they look terribly terrifying. But when potential English settlers visited Ulster in the 17th century, the then Lord Deputy of Ireland ordered their guide to avoid the bleak moors of the Sperrins in case they scared them off. As the OAPs of the hill world, the Sperrins can be forgiven for looking a little jaded. Sawel itself is more than 600 million years old, formed from an ancient ocean bed of sand and mud. A continental collision did the rest.

I cycled along the eastern flank of Sawel until – at its highest point – the road was broken by a cattle grid, the county boundary. Turning my back to County Rock, a boulder dumped by moving ice 13,000 years ago, I made my way across the spongy slopes of Sawel. A little uphill effort later, I was standing on the summit, where a previous visitor named Raicheal Oisin had spelt out her name in fist-sized white granite boulders.

The Sperrin Heritage Centre, in Glenelly Valley, was empty, save for a skeleton staff manning the café and museum. I perused a rack of brochures about the Sperrins. All the tourist information one could wish for was here: where to walk, where to cycle, where to drive, where to eat, where to stay. There was one problem. Where were the tourists? It was mid-July, the school holidays had started and the sun had got his hat on, yet the roads, towns and hills were deserted.

I ordered tea and a toasted cheese sandwich, sat down and daydreamed for a minute, before suddenly realising I didn't have enough money to pay for the meal. Searching the crevices of my bag, I scraped together 14p and explained my embarrassing dilemma to the slender freckle-faced girl who was already toasting the sandwich. 'It's not a problem,' she said, in a knee-buckling Irish lilt. 'I'll make up the difference.' Bless her.

Another display of Irish etiquette came three miles north of Omagh. While I fixed a puncture on the roadside, a man driving a Porsche pulled over and offered to help. I looked at him as if he were a paedophile asking me to stroke his dog. What did he want? 'Or I can give you a lift to Omagh,' he added. The man, it seemed, just wanted to help.

Fermanagh was the scene of my 3,000th mile and I headed south to the county's capital, Enniskillen. At midnight, 40 or so teenage Italians were still frolicking along the hostel corridors, giggling, flirting and playing music. I didn't mind. I was still young enough to remember when it was me causing a nuisance. But one resident had come to the end of his tether. A bellow roared along the corridors. 'Shut the fuck up! Now!!' The

Italians didn't need a phrasebook to understand this command. There was a scurry of feet and a dampening of hormones before the hostel fell silent.

DAY 70 – ENNISKILLEN TO ARMAGH: 71 MILES
Cuilcagh (Fermanagh): 665m

Standing on the national boundary between the UK and the Republic of Ireland, Cuilcagh is the highest point in both counties Fermanagh and Cavan. Cuilcagh Mountain Park and the nearby Marble Arch Caves became a UNESCO European Geopark in 2001, and earned UNESCO Geopark Global recognition three years later. It's all thanks to Fermanagh District Council's efforts to play its part in restoring the UK's rapidly diminishing bog habitat. Over decades, the natural hydrology of boggy areas has been disturbed by peat extraction, drainage works, overgrazing, burning the surface vegetation and rampaging 4x4 vehicles.

The Legnabrocky Trail followed a wide gravel track before twisting upwards to Cuilcagh's hard gritstone top. A towering Neolithic burial mound of rock marked the summit. From this elevated point, the view can stretch to the Atlantic Ocean in the west and the Irish Sea in the east. However, fine days are a rarity, with cloud cover far more likely; around 2,000mm of rain is dumped on these mountains every year.

I shook hands with another walker who had reached the summit moments before me. Simon was a member of a walking group called Meath Trekkers and was checking out a route for a guided walk he was leading in three days' time. 'It looks like Table Mountain in South Africa as you come up,' he said. 'Pretty impressive.' Simon told me he was meeting a 'gal' in Londonderry that evening after chatting her up in a Belfast bar the previous weekend. 'I don't want to have to drive all the way from Londonderry to Meath, then back here. Hopefully I'll get lucky,' he grinned. 'Then I won't need to go home.'

Once I was back on the bicycle, my route now led west to the town of Armagh. Near Rosslea, I came across a shrine of 20 bouquets on the roadside, next to a car-sized hole in a hedge. Yellow police markings were still on the road marking the final moments of a life. One note said: 'Please, please, please, let this be the last.' Five miles up the road, there was another clutch of flowers, this time for 'Chris'. It saddened me and reminded me of my own vulnerability on the road.

DAY 71 – ARMAGH TO NEWCASTLE: 61 MILES
Slieve Gullion (Armagh): 575m
Slieve Donard (Down): 850m

Setting out from Armagh, I mentally rehearsed the day ahead. A short ride south to Meigh, a swift ascent of Slieve Gullion, a sprint between Newry and Newcastle, and a leisurely stroll up Slieve Donard. By now, my tenth week on the road, I should have known better. Iffy weather, misjudging the length of a hill or taking a wrong turn meant a 'short ride' becoming a mission. All three factors came together between Armagh and Slieve

Gullion Forest Park: a long drag out of the town, a chilly wind and a bad decision at a junction.

A series of brutal switchbacks climbed through the forest until the cover of trees came to an abrupt end. The acrid stench of stale smoke now wafted up my nostrils. Ahead were the charcoal consequences of the fire that had ripped through these woods only three days earlier. Over a vast area, bare branches, spindly stems and scorched earth were all that remained.

Slieve Gullion – a Gaelic name that translates simply as mountain of the steep slope – is the eroded heart of an extinct volcano, standing at the centre of a circle of hills known as the Ring of Gullion. As at Cuilcagh, a Neolithic burial chamber marked the highest point. The chamber is known as the House of Calliagh Berra, a wicked witch who is said to have tricked legendary Irish giant Finn McCool. Calliagh persuaded Finn to dive into the 'bottomless' crater lake, a quarter of a mile north of where I stood, to retrieve her lost ring. The giant found the ring but surfaced as an old man after falling under her spell. Eventually Calliagh undid her magic but Finn's hair stayed white. Legend says that those who bathe in the water will emerge with hair as white as snow. Curiously, the lake is also said to cure toothache.

After a 25-mile cycle to the east coast, the time had come to tackle the mountain I had been longing for, Slieve Donard, the highest peak in Northern Ireland. The seaside town of Newcastle is a depressing strip of chip shops and amusement arcades, but it's also the gateway to the Mourne Mountains, a series of majestic peaks rising from of the depths of the Irish Sea. Into this seven-mile wide Area of Outstanding Natural Beauty are crammed a dozen 600-metre plus mountains. Highest of the lot is Slieve Donard, named after Saint Domangard who built a prayer cell on its summit.

It was six o'clock when I arrived at my seafront hostel. Was there enough time to climb Slieve Donard and return before darkness? I looked up at the mountain. Mist obscured the top and showed no sign of budging. Even so, the prospect was too tempting. I had to climb Slieve Donard there and then. I walked purposefully along Newcastle's main street, passing groups of giggling women in short skirts, before a path alongside the Glen River led me into the invisible jaws of the Mournes. Mist hunkered on the saddle I was aiming for, Slieve Donard on the left and Slieve Commedagh on the right.

A pair of bedraggled walkers emerged out of the murk. As we came nearer, I could see the woman had pulled the hood of her red coat over her forehead, letting the jacket flail in the wind behind her like a cape. 'Da, da, da, da, da, da…' she sang. Fists clenched and arms thrust forward, she was bellowing the Superman theme tune. There was a joyous, almost psychotic expression across her face. Crusty hillwalkers would complain that this is the sort of person who destroys the peace and tranquillity of the mountains. They argue the wilderness should be a place for quiet reflection, not raucous behaviour. I don't agree. Like my superhero friend, mountains made me feel exultant. Being high and exposed, the wind in my face and nervousness in my stomach – that is how I want my life to be. Mountains make me want to scream until my voice is hoarse and throw my hands in the air like some crazed Evangelical.

The woman broke off from singing to ask if I was going to the top. Shaking her head as I confirmed I was, she warned me not to, telling me it had taken them an hour to walk a single mile because of the ferocity of the wind. 'Be careful – it's getting worse,' she cautioned as we went our separate ways. Howling winds greeted me as I crested the saddle, where a group of 10 or so walkers filed past, presumably on their way down. It was now after seven o'clock and they looked startled to see someone heading towards Slieve Donard at this hour. Each one wore the same bemused look, until the last one asked, 'Are you mad?'

My guide to the summit would be the Mourne Wall, which I reached a few strides later. The 90-year-old structure loops for 22 miles across 15 hilltops, and was built to separate the catchment areas for two reservoirs, Silent Valley and Ben Crom. Rearing nearly a metre over my head, not only did the wall shield me from the worst of the wind, but it made for straightforward navigation as it passed directly over the summit of Slieve Donard. With every step, visibility dropped, making adrenaline pump so furiously that I broke into a jog. The resolute wall was a source of strength, reassuring me that I was heading the right way. Soon I was on the summit, a simple pile of rocks. Standing on top of the cairn, I turned to face the wind. It was breathtaking. Waterfalls of mist rushing towards me at terrifying speeds. Fearing the wind could at any moment toss me into oblivion, I crouched on all on fours, grinning like a madman.

A few months earlier, Carl Stephenson had been breathing the same high air as I. He was also caught in the eye of a storm. Like me, Carl would have been thinking about tomorrow, dreaming up his next challenge. He would have gasped in the icy wind and been awed in the dreary loneliness. But then something happened that Carl had not anticipated – lightning. He didn't stand a chance. To be caught on a mountaintop with virtually no shelter and no lightning conductor in an electric storm; I can't even begin to imagine the fear. He lay undiscovered for two days until a group of walkers came across his snow-covered body, close to the summit's stone shelter.

There lies the thin line between life and death. As I read the simple words on Carl's memorial plaque, I shivered. Exhilaration had given way to apprehension. Carl had been 29, a sergeant in the 218 Signal Squadron based at Ballykelly barracks in county Londonderry. Originally from Withernsea, East Yorkshire, he had gained a long list of outdoor experiences, from caving and canoeing, to rock climbing and hill walking. For a man who aspired to be an outdoors instructor, clambering to the top of Slieve Donard was a doddle, the very least of his worries. On that fateful day – 8 April 2006 – he would never have expected to die. Consumed by sorrow, I now just wanted to escape this place.

DAY 72 – NEWCASTLE TO DUNURE: 96 MILES

Racing across Down and Antrim, I cursed every red light. I had a ferry to catch. If I missed the one o'clock sailing from Larne, I'd have to wait four hours until the next one. Even after a frantic surge between Belfast and Larne, it looked like I hadn't made it in time. 'I'm sorry, you're too late,' a woman at the ticket office confirmed.

Don't you know who I am? Jonny Muir, UK traveller extraordinaire. I'm on a mission. How dare you hold me up?

'Too late?' I pleaded. 'It's just me and a bicycle. No car. Please...'

She shook her head defiantly and pointed to the clock. 'You're seven minutes after the last check-in time.'

Just then a voiced boomed behind her. 'Let him on.' Her boss, I assumed. As she wrinkled her nose, I threw the money over the counter and departed with a smug smile.

A hovercraft zipped us across the Irish Sea and it was still early afternoon when we touched down on Scottish soil. I drew the line at sinking to my knees and kissing the ground, but after five days in Northern Ireland, arriving in Scotland felt like coming home. With the coast on my left shoulder and the wind at my back I pedalled north – the direction which felt natural. Revelling in the freedom of the open road, I ghosted through Ballantrae and Girvan without pausing. It wasn't until Turnberry, where preparations were in full swing for the British Senior Open golf tournament, that I began scouting for somewhere to camp for the night.

The green grass of Maidens was tempting, but I pressed on to Dunure and swung my cycle into the grounds of Kennedy Castle. It was seven o'clock and having covered 96 miles in the day, I knew it would be reckless to keep going. However, I had arrived too early.

When faced with camping wild, my head was still full of doubts. Where am I going to camp? Am I allowed to camp here? What if I'm caught? The uncertainty unnerved me.

In my world, excess time equals procrastination, and mark my words, in ten years' time procrastination will be diagnosed as a mental illness. When I could have been reading a book, strolling around the harbour or having a pint in the pub, I was doing some heavy-duty procrastinating. By dusk, I had quibbled over every blade of grass and walked across to the north side of Dunure to see if I could find a better spot to camp. I had even got back on my cycle and pedalled north to Fisherton to seek a pitch. Back in Dunure, a group of girls warned me not to camp in the grounds of Kennedy Castle, because it was apparently patrolled at night by a local man who didn't take kindly to campers.

With options fast running out, I headed down to the beach. If it had been a golden stretch of sand, I would have seized on the idea sooner. But this beach was an undistinguished one of pebbles. I picked a spot of land I hoped was unreachable by the tide, and after realising it was impossible to sink pegs into pebbles, I secured the outside of the tent with large rocks. Settled at last, I watched the sunset over Arran, silhouetting the jagged peak of Goatfell. I lay awake listening to the gently lapping sea, too excited to sleep. I was back in Scotland.

TWELVE

SEEING THE WHOLE WORLD FROM GOATFELL – BEN LOMOND, THE BEACON HILL, GLASGOW'S HILL – PEDAL OR DIE – MUNRO-BAGGING – A TELEPHONE CALL FROM THE SUN – EMBELLISHING TALES – CAMPING AT LOCH LEVEN – A CLOUD INVERSION ON WEST LOMOND – THE DREADED MOUNT BATTOCK

DAY 73 – DUNURE TO LOCHWINNOCH: 62 MILES
Goatfell (Arran): 874m

'A larger prospect no Mountaine in the world can show, pointing out three Kingdomes at one sight.' Not my words, but the utterances of William Lithgow – a 17th-century Scottish traveller and writer – after he'd climbed Goatfield Hill in 1628. Dominating the northern half of Arran, Goatfell, as it is known today, is a honeypot for walkers who clamber up its rocky approaches to glimpse the 'three Kingdomes'. Starting out from Brodick Castle, there were over-enthusiastic dads, sullen teenagers with hands in pockets and grumbling girlfriends pleading for a rest. There was even a vertigo-sufferer trying to conquer his fear on the mountain's steep eastern flank. A group of children scampered past the poor man in an impromptu fell race. One skidded on loose rocks, bloodying both knees.

'What can you see?' a mother asked her young son

as he stood wide-eyed on the summit. He spun around on one foot, absorbing the collision between mountain and ocean.

'The whole world,' he whispered.

The panorama from Goatfell was incontestably exquisite, a generous reward for the three-mile uphill foray. All around were cliffs and fearful depths, a land of sharp edges and harsh faces. To the south, the land sloped downwards until it reached Arran's kidney-bean-shaped bottom where it plunged into the deep. Across the Kilbrannan Sound, Kintyre flung a protective arm around Arran. Beyond was a world of islands: lonely Islay, mountainous Jura and tiny Gigha. Bute extended a finger into the Firth of Clyde, flanked by Great and Little Cumbrae. Ailsa Craig was a dot in the sea, rising proudly in front of the Ayrshire coast.

With lush lowlands to its south and soaring highlands to its north, Arran is known as 'Scotland in miniature'. A cliché perhaps, but an honest description. Six hours on Arran, Scotland's seventh largest island of ancient castles, sandy beaches, stone circles and whisky distilleries, wasn't long enough to explore its charms. It gave me time only to beetle up Goatfell and lick an ice cream on Brodick seafront while I waited for a Caledonian MacBrayne ferry to whisk me back to the mainland.

Once on board, I unfolded my road map of Scotland. Maps are mirrors to the world. If you have been to a place, a map will take you back. If you haven't, a map will take you there. My map was frayed around the edges and strips of sticky tape held its ageing folds together. Three years earlier, it had been my faithful guide as I cycled from John O'Groats to Carter Bar, en route to Land's End.

Instead of taking the customary fortnight to travel between Britain's northern and southern extremities, I spent that time drifting around Scotland. A line of black ink marked my casual course. In dire weather, I had pedalled west to Durness, south to Ullapool, up, over and down Bealach na Ba, before venturing onto the Isle of Skye. A dotted streak across the Sound of Sleat indicated I had caught a ferry from Armadale to Mallaig. From here, I had followed the Road to the Isles in reverse to Fort William, where I'd hiked up a snowy Ben Nevis. The line then cut through lonely Rannoch Moor and ran along the west bank of Loch Lomond, before taking an abrupt left turn to Balloch. In a pub on Balloch's main street I lived the highs and lows of the UEFA Cup final between Celtic and Porto, a thrilling game that the Glasgow side lost 3-2 after extra time. After the match I had eaten a spicy chicken pizza and a stray piece of meat was responsible for an indelible brown smudge across Glen Garry.

After visiting Stirling I had plunged south, across the shaking Forth Road Bridge, the scene of near-catastrophe as I inadvertently cycled along a two-mile stretch of motorway. I had crossed the border in Berwick-upon-Tweed, but deciding I missed Scotland too much, I returned, only to exit again a day later over Carter Bar. A 'p' marked where punctures had occurred, while a thicker mark showed where I had stopped each night. Every village and town with a youth hostel was circled and there were occasional triangles marking campsites.

Now in need of a clear plan, the map was here to help,

to formulate my thoughts. Having reached 72 highest points in 73 days, I was behind schedule. The 92-day dream was fading fast. I had to accept defeat or come up with a way of making it possible. I couldn't give up on my 92-day ambition, not yet. I'd cycle through the night if I had to. Realising it was time to grasp the nettle, I knew a phenomenal effort and an upping of mileage was required. Plotting a 500-mile course from Renfrewshire to Moray, I set myself an ambitious target of reaching Inverness in nine days, which would mean climbing 13 mountains, six of them Munros, in that period. There would then be seven mountains remaining, with 10 days to conquer them.

Between Largs and Lochwinnoch, I saw countless places to wild camp, from the slopes of Irish Law to the sides of Camphill reservoir. I scorned all options until it was dark and I was desperate. It was best that way. No chance of procrastination. It was 10 o'clock when I finally decided to camp on a playing field in Lochwinnoch. Faced with having to lug my loaded bicycle over a metal fence to get into the field, I hoisted the machine on to my shoulder. A pannier wedged itself between the fence and bicycle frame, exploding a carton of apple juice inside the bag, drenching my sleeping bag and tent. I didn't care. I hadn't showered for nearly three days. I hadn't even bothered to brush my teeth. Camping alone in a random field in a far-flung corner of Scotland – when would I be doing this again? I smelled a little, but who was here to sniff? I was within touching distance of my next summit, Renfrewshire's Hill of Stake. That was all that mattered.

DAY 74 – LOCHWINNOCH TO ROWARDENNAN: 52 MILES
Hill of Stake (Renfrewshire): 522m
Ben Lomond (Stirlingshire): 974m

When I told the assistant at the Clyde Muirshiel Park visitor centre about my wanderings, she handed me a wad of paper and cuttings. 'You'll be needing these.'

I had spent two hours trudging up and down the loneliest countryside I had come across, over sphagnum moss, gurgling morasses and gorse, to stand on Hill of Stake. The walk had thoroughly bored me. The hills, I thought, were dull and lifeless. Leafing through the bundle, I realised my ignorance. From mining to mass hunting, the Renfrewshire hills have sung with life for centuries, and the area is reputed to be Scotland's Bermuda triangle, a sinister graveyard of wartime aircraft.

There were a number of *Paisley Daily Express* articles written by Derek Parker, a former Muirshiel ranger, on the subject. One in particular captivated me.

> All alone in that aviational ghostly graveyard strewn with blitzed Beauforts, splattered Seafires and trashed Typhoons, you freeze in terror when you remember the tale of the hollow-eyed, white-robed woman with the deathly pallor driving a pony and trap through the mist to one haunted crash site.

The white-robed woman was met by Quentin McKellar, a farmer and member of the Home Guard, whose gruesome task it was to recover the bodies of dead airmen. The woman, perhaps a tragic airman's sweetheart, asked to be shown the way to Queenside Hill, where a pilot had died on 24 January 1943. McKellar gave the direction and she disappeared into the fog. Years after, the couple were said to roam the moor: 'one was an elfin woman in a long white dress and the other was a handsome hero wearing a RAF uniform.'

The park shared its name with Muirshiel House, a property built in the mid-1800s as a grouse-shooting estate. By the 1930s, the sound of gunfire was ringing out across the moor as thousands of grouse, rabbits, hares, partridges, woodcock, black game and snipe met their maker. The demand was so great that a five-mile railway line was laid to ferry hunters into the inner reaches of the hills and Edward VIII is said to have been among the visitors.

Meanwhile, the crumbling remains of a mine I had idly wandered past once saw the excavation of a mineral called barium sulphate. The mineral was used as a lubricant in oil drilling and it is also the stuff patients once gulped before having an X-ray. When work ceased in 1969, it was Scotland's last barytes mine.

The Erskine Bridge over the Clyde took me from south to mid-Scotland – straight onto the roaring dual carriageway linking Glasgow and Dumbarton. Unable to keep pace with 70mph traffic, there was nothing for it. I had to resort to a dreaded cycle path. Within 100 yards I came to a gate, which as far as I could fathom, had no reason to exist. Oh yes, I know the reason – to really get on my nerves. I stopped, dismounted, opened the gate, pushed the bicycle through, propped the bicycle up, closed the gate, remounted and cycled away... only for a second gate to appear moments later. What's the point of a cycle path, if you can't cycle on it? I had an evening date with Ben Lomond and didn't need these delays. Pedalling to Balloch, I vowed never to set rubber on a cycle path again, even if it meant risking life and limb on a dual carriageway.

On this comely summer's day, it seemed half of Glasgow had descended on Loch Lomond. Traffic had come to a grinding halt in Balmaha, creating a cocktail of petrol fumes in the air, accompanied by a soundtrack of pipping horns. I weaved to the front of the melee and came across the cause of the jam. A motorist was attempting to reverse his car and boat down a narrow lane. He was stuck fast, car and boat straddling both sides of the main road and plugging the lane. No amount of revving or cursing helped. Dying of humiliation, the man's face was red and seething. After five minutes of to-ing and fro-ing, not very well received advice from passers-by and a little more profanity, car and boat were prised free, and a little cheer went up from the gathered audience. All the while, an oblivious baby slept in the back seat.

'What's the best route up Ben Lomond?' I asked the hostel warden upon reaching Rowardennan.

'The Ptarmigan path,' he replied instantly. 'It's shorter, steeper, has better views of the loch and prettier flowers.'

I wanted to saviour Ben Lomond, to embrace the first Munro of my adventure, to be mesmerised by the revered view of Loch Lomond and surrounding hills and mountains from the summit. In a bookshop three months beforehand, I had scrawled down a paragraph from Cameron McNeish's *The Munros*, which I re-read now.

> Ben Lomond, the beacon hill. Glasgow's hill. This, the most southerly of all the Munros, has indeed been a beacon to a generation of Clydesiders, summoning them from the urban sprawl of Scotland's biggest conurbation to the gateway that it represents on the very edge of that geological fault, the Highland Boundary.

They were motivating words, making it abundantly clear Ben Lomond was more than a mountain. This was a place of pilgrimage and escape, of beauty and awe, as well as representing a geographical watershed.

In light of all that, I shouldn't have opted to climb Ben Lomond in that day's late afternoon haze. In my current mood, I simply couldn't appreciate the mountain. Tackling Ben Lomond the next morning, with fresher legs and a brighter mindset, was a far more tantalising prospect, but a one I stubbornly refused to admit to. As it was, I was hot and bothered. The midges were getting to me. I hadn't drunk enough water. And apart from the epic crossing of the Clyde, the day had been monotonous and frustrating. There was one reason I climbed Ben Lomond: to finish in 92 days. A target that had begun life as a sketchy ambition had become a noose around my neck, a pointless obsession that meant nothing to anyone except the person who had turned this random number into the centre of their universe. I walked for the sake of walking, for the sake of reaching the summit of Stirlingshire, for the sake of crossing another name off a list, for the sake of edging a little closer to a 92-day journey.

Light-headed and breathing hard, I leaned against the summit pillar and raised my eyes. The view from this lofty spot was indisputably beautiful, a vista of mountains and lochs. The country below didn't have the brazen, jagged and wild looks as seen from Goatfell or Scafell Pike; it had a flowing, graceful elegance and a calming loveliness. If views were women, I was gazing at Keira Knightley, not a Page 3 Girl.

DAY 75 – ROWARDENNAN TO KILLIN: 73 MILES
Ben Vorlich (Dunbartonshire): 943m

I was the odd one out. Every other guest was preparing for another day on the West Highland Way, a 95-mile footpath running from Milngavie, near Glasgow, to the foot of Ben Nevis, in Fort William. If walkers were following the advice of their guidebooks – which they must have been, for almost all had appeared stunned into silence by the books the previous evening – this would be day three out of seven.

I looked longingly across Loch Lomond. Mist hung over the millpond waters and gathered on the western shore. That shore, less than half a mile away, was where I needed to be. From there, a short cycle would take me to the foot of my next mountain, Ben Vorlich. All I needed to do was catch the little Rowardennan ferry across to

Inverbeg. It would cut 35 miles, nearly three hours, off my journey. It was tempting, so tempting, but I knew I would regret 'cheating'. Years would drift past, but each time I recalled this expedition, there would always be the nagging memory of the day I couldn't be bothered to go the long way round Loch Lomond. Besides, I had cycled 3,300 miles so far and another 35 wouldn't hurt.

After doing yesterday's journey in reverse, through Balmaha, Drymen and Balloch, I reached the far from bonnie banks of Loch Lomond's west shore. The A82 was not designed for the amount of traffic that was pounding along it today. Heavy juggernauts, coaches filled with white-haired grannies, cars towing boats and caravans, cumbersome motorhomes, growling motorcycles and doddering cyclists. 'Pedal or die,' a West Highland Way walker had remarked when I told him I was destined for the A82. Frightening for a cyclist, irksome for a motorist – there simply was not enough room for all of us. But what are the highways authorities meant to do? Fill in Loch Lomond? Build a dual carriageway?

Between the villages of Inveruglas and Ardlui, I left my cycle and followed a track on foot around Stuckendroin Farm. As I crossed a stile, a hundred or so sheep charged towards me, assuming I was their farmer carrying some scrumptious snacks. 'Look,' I said, raising my hands above my head as I if I had been told to stick 'em up, 'I haven't got anything.' The disappointing news provoked a chorus of furious baaing and the beasts chased me out of their field.

As I emerged from the gloom of a passageway under the Ardlui to Tarbet railway line, the summit of

Dunbartonshire loomed ahead. Any suggestions why Dunbartonshire is so-spelled when its capital is Dumbarton? Even a professor of Scottish history didn't know when I asked him. The best conclusion he could come up with was that the name was misspelled and the inaccuracy stuck. But which one was misspelled? The county or the town?

Ben Vorlich looked enormous. After 74 days of climbing vertically challenged hills, these Munros were giants in comparison. The tops seemed so high that they must be out of reach, but by a little toil and determined effort I knew I would defeat them. Ben Vorlich was a real mountain with few trodden paths, and standing on the summit, I felt immersed in wild Scotland. Were I to hand a child a crayon and ask him to draw mountains, they would sketch the view from Ben Vorlich. In every direction there are humps and lumps poking between bumps. And they would draw a big yellow blob in the sky, birds that resemble an upside down 'w' and a stick man at the top. That was Ben Vorlich. Simply perfect.

Those who notch up Munros are known as Munro-baggers. Phil, a fellow guest at the hostel in Killin, was an archetypal Munro-bagger, a man with a nerdy disposition and a brain brimming with mountain knowledge. Ploughing through a trough of pasta, Phil ran through the history of his Munro-bagging, from starting on the Cairnwell in 1990, to his last, Ben More, a colossal mountain I had passed beneath shortly after leaving Crianlarich.

'I must be the slowest Munro-bagger in history,' he joked. 'Sixteen years and I still haven't finished them.'

'How many have you done?'

'About 228.'

The conversation turned to the potential dangers that lurk on Scotland's oft-misunderstood mountains. One experience stuck in Phil's mind. He was climbing a snow-sprinkled Ben Vane when a jittery French couple approached him, asking for directions to the Five Sisters.

'I said I'd show them on a map. The man pulled out a road atlas, which I told him was no use on a mountain. It was all they had. I laughed at first. We all did. But then I was concerned. It was cold. The visibility was dropping. It would have been dark in a couple of hours. Who knows what happened to them? I feared for their lives. Folk from European countries look at the heights of Scottish mountains and assume they are a doddle compared to the Alps or Pyrenees. But Scottish mountains are complicated landscapes and with their northerly latitude, the weather can change in an instant, from good to bad. I can't reiterate it enough, these mountains are dangerous places. They take lives. Be careful on the rest of your journey.'

As he rounded off his speech, my phone rang. It was John, a friend who lived in London. After exchanging the usual pleasantries, he said: 'I hope you don't mind mate, but I've emailed the *Sun* about what you're doing.'

'The *Sun* newspaper?'

'Yes. And they want to do a story on you.'

DAY 76 – KILLIN TO STIRLING: 52 MILES
Ben Lawers (Perthshire): 1,214m

Ben Lawers, the seventh highest mountain in Scotland, is a victim of its own success. Rising 10 miles east of Killin, Perthshire's summit is just too popular. While much of the area around Ben Lawers is a National Nature Reserve because of the arctic and alpine plants that survive there, conservation has failed badly when it comes to controlling footfall. The footpaths leading up Ben Lawers and its neighbour Beinn Ghlas were awfully eroded, with some tracks up to ten yards wide.

The Sole Trading campaign was attempting to stem footpath erosion on the 74,000 hectares of land owned by the National Trust for Scotland, including Ben Lawers, Ben Lomond and Goatfell. In the previous 15 years, £2million had been spent out on improvements. Another £4million of investment was needed by 2011, the cost of repairs to a single yard of path being a staggering £35. What were they doing? Lining it with gold? I was baffled. It was obvious that the sheer number of walkers had taken their toll and there are some serious erosion problems, but I can't help but feel that the National Trust for Scotland has been indirectly and unintentionally responsible.

The organisation had built a visitor centre, toilets and car park within spitting distance of Ben Lawers. As I started up the mountain, I counted 30 cars and two vans in the car park. Without the luxury of this car park these walkers would have chosen a variety of different – and arguably superior – routes up the mountain. The convenience of the car park meant they all converged on the same place and piled up the same path. So, National Trust of Scotland, I've got a simple solution. Shut the car park. Shut the visitor centre. Don't waste your money. Scottish mountains have stood for millions of years. Given time to heal, they will recover.

Seeing as I was in William Wallace country, it seemed appropriate to stay in the Willie Wallace hostel in the centre of Stirling. Desperately tired after three Munros and 175 miles in the past three days, I could have fallen asleep standing up. The dark-skinned, dark-eyed beauty on reception perked me up a little. I don't think her lustful stare was directed at me – unless she had a Lycra fetish. She was a tease. Leading me up a flight of stairs to my dormitory, the top of a lacy red thong rose seductively above the waist of her jeans.

The Willie Wallace was an independent hostel, a different breed to the chain of Youth Hostel Association lodgings I was used to staying in. The YHA tends to be the domain of middle-aged groups, confident independent travellers and well-spoken children on a Duke of Edinburgh trip. Men and women sleep in separate dormitories and everyone goes to bed before 11 o'clock. Needless to say, no one at Willie Wallace had come to Stirling to trot up hills. This crowd were genuine globetrotters. They were Americans and Canadians, with the odd Japanese thrown in, who were 'chilling out', calling each other 'dude' and sending emails home reliving the previous night's whisky-fuelled revelry. At 11 o'clock, I was yawning but no one else seemed ready to go to bed. Eventually I gave in and lay down in my bunk, one of 12 in a tiny room. It was a sweat pit, where the buzz of flies was drowned out only by the thumping beat of a nearby nightclub.

DAY 77 – STIRLING TO KINROSS: 32 MILES
Ben Cleuch (Clackmannanshire): 721m
Innerdouny Hill (Kinross): 497m

On Ben Cleuch, the highest mountain in Scotland's smallest county (Clackmannanshire), it struck me that no one from the *Sun* had called. John had emailed the newsdesk with my story and someone had promptly replied, promising to ring me. Now, three days after he had pressed send on the message, I doubted it was ever going to happen. So, as I negotiated the streets of Yetts o'Muckart, it was a surprise when the call came and a journalist with a serious name like Rebecca or Virginia introduced herself. As I explained carefully what I was doing and why, she ummed and aahed at appropriate moments, seeming impressed on a personal level but disappointed on a professional one.

'Has it been dangerous?' she quizzed.

'Sort of. Actually, not really,' I admitted. What was I saying? Did I want to be in the newspaper or not? I did what all good journalists do: embellish. Changing approach, I said: 'I had to cross a MoD firing zone in Yorkshire. Bang, bang, bang. I could hear the guns going off. It was terrifying. I kept imagining a platoon of soldiers or a tank would appear over the horizon.'

'Go on,' she said. This was more like it. Music to the ears of a journalist.

'And I was petrified because I'd heard stories about unexploded shells blowing walkers' feet off.'

'Did that happen?'

'What?'

'Did you step on a shell?'

'No.'

'Oh.'

There was an awkward pause of silence, before she sighed and asked: 'So has anything interesting happened?'

My mind went blank, 77 days on the road and I couldn't think of a thing to say.

My second summit in the Ochil Hills was the Forestry Commission-managed Innerdouny Hill, a marvellous perch from which to savour a view of sparkling Loch Leven. In a few hours, I had grown fond of these hills, which, despite their proximity to four major urban hubs (Dundee, Edinburgh, Perth and Stirling), seemed secretive and deserted. Perhaps it is little wonder the Ochil Hills are under-appreciated. The Scottish are spoilt for options. When faced with the alternatives of the nearby Cairngorms or Grampians, the Ochils are bound to be a bridesmaid.

Following three consecutive nights in hostels, I was feeling the pinch. Needing to save pennies, it was back to wild, free camping. After choosing undisturbed pitches in Dunure and Lochwinnoch, my confidence was high and I picked a spot a yard from the western edge of Loch Leven, in a public park a short way out of Kinross. It was a poor selection. Public park. Saturday night. What had I been thinking?

It was midnight when I was woken by the words

'tramp' and 'tent'. I lay still in my bag, dreading what might come next. Three men were close by, their voices slurred by alcohol. Alone and defenceless, I was a sitting duck. Their attention switched from the 'tramp' when a fourth man turned up, complaining about a bust-up with his girlfriend. Their conversation went on for what seemed like an hour, at moments aggressive and threatening, and at other times inaudible. At last, they smoked their last cigarette and swigged the dregs from their last can of lager. Four car doors slammed. As an engine roared into life, one of them bellowed a final insult before I was left alone.

DAY 78 – KINROSS TO GLEN ESK: 80 MILES
West Lomond (Fife): 522m

From low to high. Nine hours earlier I had been a tramp. Now I was standing on the 522-metre West Lomond gazing down on a cloud inversion – a wonder of nature when valleys fill with cloud. Below me was a fluffy white blanket, which only West Lomond and East Lomond were tall enough to punch through. In spite of the show, West Lomond had a sorrowful air. On the summit, I found a metal plaque propped against the triangulation pillar, simply reading Susan C Mackay, 3-11-82 – 18-8-95. Presumably it was a memorial to a 12-year-old girl whose life had ended too early, only the plaque had come adrift from its original site.

On the way down, I ducked into a cave known as Maiden Bower, the legendary meeting place of two local lovers from rival families. On the way to meet his sweetheart one evening, the man was ambushed by his lover's father and killed. Seeing the murder, the heartbroken woman refused to return to her family and spent the rest of her days living a hermit's existence in the cave. Far from being shunned, the woman became known as a local saint who people visited to share their sorrows. Legend says that for those pure of heart, a wish made in this dank hole will be granted. Today the cave was tinged with the melancholy of our modern age, for fizzy drink bottles, yoghurt tubs and sheep droppings were strewn across the floor.

After a second breakfast of tattie scones and haggis in Perth, my spirits plummeted on the 35-mile ride to Brechin. Monotonous countryside, ceaseless winds, overwhelming boredom. A wrong turn or red light would send me flying into a rage. The final straw came in Forfar in a public toilet. On the wall, graffiti said, 'I want big cock' and 'Meet me in the toilets in Arbroath on Monday'. Disgusted, I walked out and relieved myself all over Angus instead.

DAY 79 – GLEN ESK TO SPITTAL OF GLENSHEE: 58 MILES
Mount Battock (Kincardineshire): 778m

Ever since I had compiled a list of the county tops, I had dreaded Mount Battock, and over the past 78 days I had developed an irrational hatred of the mountain. On paper, it seemed too far and too dull – a point I had to reach for the sake of ticking it off a list. I just wanted to get to the splendid Cairngorms, not waste time in the second-class mountains of the Mounth.

In the end, I reached the summit of Mount Battock in 90 breezy minutes, following a wide track bordered by a carpet of purple heather. On top were two other people – a man with a bald pate and a woman in untypical hill wear of red hotpants. The man pointed from north to south, identifying every visible landmark; the most easterly Munro Mount Keen, the soaring cliffs of Lochnagar, Aberdeen's skyscrapers and the curve of Montrose Basin.

'You know,' I said to the couple, 'I thought I'd hate this hill.'

'Rather be in the Cairngorms, would you?' he said, laughing.

'A few hours ago I thought so, now I'm not sure.'

'That's the magic of the Mounth.' He pointed again at Mount Keen. 'Queen Victoria has been up there, carried to the top on the back of a pony. And Lochnagar – Prince Charles loves that mountain. He even named his children's book *The Old Man of Lochnagar*. If it's good enough for the Royal Family, it's good enough for me.'

Cycling north on the A93 to Braemar, I opted to save the Cairngorms for tomorrow, calling it a day in Spittal of Glenshee. For £3, I camped on a patch of springy grass behind the Spittal of Glenshee Hotel, but biting midges soon forced me into the bar. Inside a musician was playing an accordion and four Rochdale ladies on a coach holiday line-danced to Tony Christie's 'Is This the Way to Amarillo'. It was marginally better than being attacked by midges.

THIRTEEN

**THE CAIRNGORMS – WALKING INTO THE WILDERNESS –
MIDGE-FRIENDLY MIDGE REPELLENT – CORROUR
BOTHY – AM FEAR LIATH MÒR – MIGHTY MACDUI – THE
COLDEST PLACE IN THE UK – A FANTASY HOME**

DAY 80 – SPITTAL OF GLENSHEE TO CORROUR BOTHY: 25 MILES
Glas Maol (Angus): 1,068m

Aged ten and standing at the Linn of Dee, I was transfixed by a rough track wending a way towards the high mountains of the Cairngorms. To walk along that path was to walk into the wilderness, to throw off the shackles of civilisation and to live among the hills, lochs and streams. To a little boy from Bromsgrove, it was a thrilling but daunting prospect. As I grew up, the Cairngorms never lost their tantalising allure. They would always be perfect. And as the onslaught of 'real life' arrived – passing exams, earning a living, forging relationships and paying bills – I longed to pick up the track and just walk away, leaving everything behind.

In the time I had been away, the Cairngorms had become Britain's newest, biggest and arguably best National Park. The Cairngorms are 40 per cent larger than the Lake District and double the size of Loch Lomond and the Trossachs. Containing four of the UK's five highest peaks and 52 summits over 900 metres, they offer a veritable playground for hillwalkers, mountaineers and climbers. Meanwhile, because 68 per cent of Cairngorms land is higher than 600 metres, it is the most extensive area of Arctic mountain landscape in the UK. And in 1895, the Cairngorms became the coldest place in the country, when a Braemar thermometer recorded a temperature of minus 27.2C. For my purposes, the National Park was also home to the five county tops of Aberdeenshire, Angus, Banffshire, Moray and Nairnshire.

The A93 climbed to the 670-metre reach of the Cairnwell Pass, the highest motorable road in the UK. This tarmac summit – on the border of Aberdeenshire and Angus – heralds the southern reach of the Cairngorms National Park. Surrounded by vast, empty car parks, it is an inauspicious start. Skiers rule the roost here, not walkers. The result is an untidy jumble of wooden fences, swaying ski lifts and tatty huts. Ski resorts without snow just aren't ski resorts. They are unpretty, ghostly places, of which prominent walkers have been damning in their criticism. In Chris Townsend's *The Munros and Tops*, an account of the first continuous journey across Scotland's 277 Munros and 240 Tops, the author, in a rare outburst of genuine emotion, can barely contain his anger at the damage he believes has been wreaked.

> The Cairnwell and Carn Aosda are the most ugly, depressing summits in the Highlands.

248

That's not because of the hills themselves but rather because what has been done to them. They've been stripped bare, gouged raw and totally desecrated in the name of mass industrial tourism in the form of alpine skiing. This is often considered a mountain pursuit. It's not. It's a mountain destroying pursuit.

Skiing has only existed on these slopes since 1957, when Dundee Ski Club set up the first tow on Meall Odhar. Townsend is right to grumble, but humans were devouring mountains long before someone came up with the idea of strapping a plank of wood to each foot. How about the strict management of hundreds of square miles of moor and mountainside so that a financially privileged few can blast the living daylights out of Britain's wildlife in the name of sport? Then there are pylons, quarries, railways, reservoirs, roads, transmitters and turbines.

To the east of the road pass stood Glas Maol, the Gaelic words for green/grey bare hill. The Munro required a two-mile stretch of the legs, first under and around a mass of skiing paraphernalia, stretching almost to the top of Meall Odhar, then a short scramble up to a plateau, the flat roof of Angus. Surrounded by a wall of mist in every direction, I had little concept of the altitude I had gained, even though at 1,068 metres, Glas Maol was the third highest mountain I had accomplished in 80 days.

Some 15 years after my first visit, I was standing at the Linn of Dee again. Tonight I was to venture down that path and spend the night among the Cairngorms. A stream of walkers were leaving the hills as I cycled to

Derry Lodge, where I secured my bicycle, before continuing on foot, carrying a rucksack brimming with provisions. I was smug. My fellow walkers were going home, while I was destined for the Corrour bothy, a mountain hut next to the embryonic River Dee. Tomorrow I would climb Ben Macdui, the UK's second highest mountain, before triumphantly walking out of the wilderness.

As always, the weather was determined to follow an alternative script. Threatening clouds hung low over the mountains to the west, beginning a steady march towards Derry Lodge. It started to spit. Spit turned to light rain. Light rain turned to heavy rain. And then the heavens opened, cascading great torrential drops. Still two miles from the Corrour bothy, I looked around frantically. There were no trees and there was nowhere to hide. Rarely had I experienced such helplessness. Feeling humiliated, a tiny speck in this endless scenery of towering peaks, I threw up my tent. After 20 frenzied seconds, I was huddled inside, water dripping off the end of my nose.

To say the tent was 'up' is a misleading description. Pegs were indeed in the ground and the canvas stretched over the structure, but the tent had taken on a haphazard shape the manufacturer could never have envisaged. There was worse. In my haste, I had snapped one of the two poles, the shorter one responsible for keeping the bottom half of the tent upright. Without it, the outer sheet rubbed against the inner sheet, allowing the rainwater to get in, very quickly. Everything I carried was wet: spare clothes, food, sleeping bag – all saturated. The sheets were now clinging to my bare legs like a sodden blanket.

The thought of spending the night here, trying to sleep in a puddle of brown water was intolerable.

After 30 miserable minutes of downpours, the rain relinquished, becoming a gentle pitter-patter. I poked my head out. Midges. The little bastards were lying in wait, zillions of them, swarming around my refuge. I zipped the inner sheet shut. This time they weren't going to get the better of me. I had a secret weapon. Midge repellent. 'Shake bottle and spray or dab on exposed skin,' was the advice on the bottle. My advice: 'Don't apply midge repellent when confined in a very small space.' The brown concoction smelled vile, reminding me of a vulgar cough medicine. Spluttering, I leaped out of the tent.

A flying black ball was on me in a flash – biting, gnawing, chewing. 'Come on boys, dinner is served,' they screamed. 'Get stuck in!'

I turned the spray on them. 'Take that, you bastards!' I roared. 'Die, die, die!'

They loved it.

'Rosemary – our favourite,' they chuckled, backstroking through the spray. 'Is that a touch of lavender? And... mmm... witchhazel. Right, give us your blood.'

I swung my arms around like a windmill, effing and blinding at the critters. They were everywhere. Buzzing in my ears, crawling through my hair, wandering up my shorts. It was hideous, like lying in a pit of snakes or being trapped in a hole of rats. As maniacally as I put the tent up, I ripped it from the ground, stuffing pegs, poles, sheets, food, maps and clothes anywhere they would go. I did the only thing I could to escape the monsters. Run.

An hour later, I rounded the slopes of Carn a'Mhaim

and glimpsed the glinting roof of the Corrour bothy. Positioned on the legendary cross-Cairngorms path Lairig Ghru, the building looked minuscule, dwarfed by the 1,004-metre giant known as Devil's Point rising behind. Flustered, wet and itching all over, I burst through the door, gatecrashing the gathering inside. A vicar (I really wished my first words on entering hadn't been 'Jesus Christ'), his wife and two Scottish lads sat around the small wooden-floored room, drinking, eating and generally having a better time of it than I was. They glanced at me uncomfortably, possibly because of the Jesus Christ comment, but probably because I smelled – according to the ingredients listed on the bottle of repellent – of *hamamelis virginiana* and *lavandula augustifolia*. More like a camel's rear end. Not that I cared. I had found heaven – a warm and dry retreat, without a midge in sight.

After the vicar and his wife had retreated to a blue tent pitched on ground outside the bothy, a bottle of rum was passed around, and one of the men, Hamish, managed to fix my tent pole with plaster and a nail. Apart from the glow of a head torch and the flicker of a candle, the valley was now plunged in darkness. While the lads had a smoke outside the hut, another bedraggled walker, Paul, struggled in the door. As soon as he had brewed up, he handed me a mug of coffee and we swapped midge horror stories. After a final swig of rum, the lads disappeared into the night, leaving Paul and I alone in the bothy. He settled on a bunk, while I laid out my damp sleeping bag on the floor. After a minute of silence, Paul murmured through the darkness.

'What I was reading in the bothy book was right.'

'What's that?' I asked.

'About the mouse that lives here.'

'A mouse? Where?'

'I just heard its feet scampering across the floor. Sleep well.'

I pulled my bag tightly around my neck. No mouse was getting in here.

DAY 81 – CORROUR BOTHY TO TOMINTOUL: 42 MILES

Ben Macdui (Aberdeenshire & Banffshire): 1,309m

Eight hours had fluttered away in what seemed like eight minutes when a shaft of sunlight streaming through a bothy window stirred me from dreamless sleep. Despite the blue skies, Ben Macdui was shy this morning, firmly holding a blanket of mist around its upper reaches. Too impatient to wait for the inclement cloak to lift, I waded across the shallow Dee and marched north along the Lairig Ghru.

Somewhere along the path I missed the right fork that last night I had assigned as my way up the mountain. Realising I had gone too far north, and rather than turning back, I climbed directly up Ben Macdui's steep western flank, confident I'd meet another track on this well-walked mountain. Grass soon gave way to an eerie mist-smothered field of boulders that seemed to extend endlessly in every direction. They shifted under my feet like a slowly moving conveyer belt, convincing me the whole lot could tumble in an avalanche of boulders, with me riding the wave.

For 15 long minutes my ears were pricked, as I waited for the terrifying 'crunch, crunch' of Am Fear Liath Mòr, the Grey Man of Macdui. The Grey Man is the Cairngorms' answer to the Abominable Snowman or Bigfoot, a giant figure that is said to roam the mountain sending petrified climbers and walkers running for their lives. The supposed existence of this hairy monster was first chronicled in 1925 by university professor Norman Collie – 34 years after he allegedly heard 'a crunch and then another crunch, as if someone was walking after me but taking three or four steps the length of my own'.

The mysterious Grey Man must have been having a lie-in, for I heard no 'crunch'. As the conveyer belt ended, dull featureless rises lay ahead. In a world of shadows, the cairn marking the summit of Ben Macdui was indiscernible until I almost came face to face with the low wall of stones. Shortly before nine o'clock, on the mistiest of August mornings, I stood on the summit of the UK's second highest mountain, Aberdeenshire on one side, Banffshire on the other.

Aesthetically, mountain summits aren't unique places, particularly at misty moments. Whether they sit on top of a flat plateau or a soaring peak, there is likely to be a wind-blasted triangulation pillar, a pile of rocks, a stone shelter and an ancient collection of orange peel and banana skins. If it happens to be winter, they will all be covered in a layer of snow.

Emotionally, however, no two summits could possibly be the same. There seemed to be something in the high air of this particular mountain, something sombre and sorrowful. It wasn't the solitude, or the envelope of gloom. Nor was it the nagging fear of the Grey Man's presence. Like a graveyard, Ben Macdui is a melancholy place where one should stand in memory and respect, rather than in celebration of reaching this high place. Others had been less fortunate than I. In August 1942, an Avro Anson aircraft from RAF Kinloss crashed on the mountain, killing all five crew on board. In November 1971, five children and an instructor perished in a Ben Macdui blizzard. In March 2001, a pair of United States F15 single-seater fighter jets crashed close to the summit, killing both pilots and scattering debris across the mountainside.

Four hours later, I was in Braemar, munching my way through haggis pie and chips, lost in reflection. I had walked down that path, closing a decade and a half of childish dreams. For once, those dreams had lived up to expectations. Thunder and lightning, a mountain bothy, a misty summit, clouds of midges and the Scottish Yeti: now that is an adventure.

The A939 from Ballater to Nairn is one of Scotland's finest road journeys, rising and falling, twisting and turning like a fairground ride. From Royal Deeside the road ploughs a course through remote moorland, climbs giddy heights and bridges great rivers before reaching the Moray Firth coast. At the road's summit, it rises over the 637-metre Lecht, the second highest road pass in the UK, but arguably a greater challenge than the Cairnwell.

At Cock Bridge, the tarmac lurched upwards in a series of viciously steep hairpins. Turning a final sharp corner, the road straightened, running over a series of whalebacks destined for the summit. The wind couldn't make up its mind. One moment it would swing behind me, like an invisible arm on my back. Then it would attack me from the side. As I gained altitude, the gale assaulted me head on, an icy blast interspersed with hailstones. The weather at the top was bitter and so bitingly cold it wouldn't have been a surprise to see the Lecht's slopes caked in snow. As it was, the ski runs – like those around the Cairnwell – were painfully bare, making the car park redundant. I sat alone in a deserted café, cradling a hot mug and desperately trying to get some life back into my shivering body.

At a hostel in Tomintoul, I threw my clothes into a washing machine, washed off the whiff of midge repellent and headed to the pub. No sooner had I sprinted through puddles and ordered a pint than a local collared me at the bar.

'English?' he demanded, his rasping Scottish accent making me stand to attention, as if I was being told off. 'Well, laddie, what do ye know about Tomintoul?'

Before I could open my mouth, he had interrupted. 'Well, I'll tell ye something about Tomintoul. It is the coldest place in Britain.'

'Oh, really?' I said, surprised. 'I thought it was Braemar.'

'Braemar?' he exclaimed with disgust, rolling the 'r' and emphasising the 'mar'. I might as well have called his mother a whore.

'Braemar?' he repeated in an appalled tone, shaking his head. 'Nay. Tomintoul. Right here in this village. I recorded it on my thermometer. Colder than Braemar it was. I wrote to the Met Office, but they said they couldn't verify it. Silly buggers. But I tell ye laddie, Tomintoul is the coldest place in Britain.'

I didn't question him again.

DAY 82 – TOMINTOUL TO CARRBRIDGE: 38 MILES
Carn a'Ghille Chearr (Moray): 710m
Carn Glas-Choire (Nairnshire): 659m

All night rain fell on Tomintoul, repeatedly waking me up as heavy drops lashed the windows. Thank goodness I wasn't camping. The deluge continued into the morning, sending rivulets of water running down the road. The prospect of climbing Carn a'Ghille Chearr, a mysterious name I had wrapped around my head months earlier, now seemed as appealing as walking naked through a swarm of midges. I was going to get wet today. I just had to grit my teeth and get on with it.

Carn a'Ghille Chearr rises from the central ridge of the Cromdale Hills, between the villages of Knock and Cromdale. Starting from the frothy banks of the River Avon, it was another wet trudge up a mist-shrouded slope to a forlorn and wind-battered trig point. All the while I was serenaded with the sound of gunshots as a local farmer slaughtered the abundant rabbits on his land.

The lower Carn Glas-Choire, standing four miles north of Carrbridge, was another two hours away. According to a map, a number of tracks led up to the mountain, all originating from the B9007 mountain road, which – apart from times of heavy snow – connects Carrbridge and Forres. Arriving at the first track, I was faced with a stiff sign nailed to a gate: 'Cawdor Estate. Private grouse moor.' The name Cawdor sounded terribly grand and I didn't want to bump into a gamekeeper, especially with the start of the shooting season just ten days away. I pedalled another half-mile up the road, abandoned my bicycle and tiptoed across a field of sheep. I could see a building in the distance, probably the home of the gamekeeper. I had been doing an admirable job of not drawing attention to myself when a flock of birds swooped low over the field, spooking the sheep, sending them sprinting up a bank in a frenzy of baaing.

My cover blown, I half-expected a gun-wielding keeper to give me a good clip around the ear, so I sprinted off through the gorse until the house was out of sight. Fortunately, there were no signs of life. A 4x4 track zigzagged into the bowels of Carn Glas-Choire, petering out on the hill's northwest slope, with the final few steps across a spongy field of sphagnum moss.

Carrbridge is renowned for its old packhorse bridge, which still forms a perfect arch across the River Dulnain. Finished in 1717, under the orders of Brigadier-General Sir Alexander Grant, the bridge was built to ensure floods did not delay funeral corteges. Rather morbidly, the structure was dubbed 'coffin bridge'. It was nearing seven o'clock when I stopped on the present road bridge and rang around hostels in Inverness in search of a bed for the night. I rang five numbers. All were full: a total of 345 beds completely booked up.

Five minutes later, I was standing outside a wood-panelled cabin, ringing the bell of Carrbridge Bunkhouse. A smiling Scot with a West Highland terrier under her arm ushered me in. She didn't introduce herself, but told me the dog was called Lilly. Walking across the threshold was like coming home. Not my real home, but a fantasy home – somewhere I felt instantly warm, safe and at ease. There was a snug kitchen complete with a wood-burning stove and a shelf of food inviting me to help myself, and a big bedroom with wooden floors had triple bunks to the ceiling.

Already arrived was a family from Elgin who had a barbecue on the go, and the youngest daughter was practising the chanter, a mini-version of the bagpipes. The older girl sketched the great deer antlers strung from the walls and ceiling. Soon afterwards, a Cornish family, who had spent 16 hours on a coach to get to the Cairngorms, turned up. A plane from Heathrow will get you to Thailand in that time. Still, they were in high spirits and had spent the day around Loch Ness. There was also a teacher from southeast England who was scouting for a house in the mountains. So the nine of us sat on plump cushions around the kitchen table, toasted by the stove. One of the Cornish daughters pulled a quiz book from the bookshelf and we stayed up until the wee small hours, trying to remember the *Coronation Street* cast from the 1980s, who won the 1993 Cup Final and what was Abba's first UK number one.

The Cairngorms had been cruel to me. The mountains had displayed their merciless side, bringing wicked weather and biting bugs. It had been a journey within a journey, testing me and – in truth – finding me out. But in the 72 hours I had spent among the Cairngorms, I had learned a valuable lesson. While I obsessed about my journey and craved the loneliness of the mountains, it was the companionship of others – what I had found in Corrour bothy and Carrbridge bunkhouse – that had brought true comfort.

FOURTEEN

DIANA ROSS – 'IS THIS MAN CRAZY?' – GERMANS –
LOST ON BEN MORE ASSYNT – BRITAIN'S NORTHWEST
TIP – RESORTING TO ALCOHOL – RESTLESS SOULS –
OVER THE SEA TO SHETLAND – THE 60TH PARALLEL –
STARTING OUT ON THE LONG ROAD SOUTH –
BURSTING BUBBLES – OBSESSION

DAY 83 – CARRBRIDGE TO ULLAPOOL: 93 MILES

'There ain't no mountain high enough. Ain't no river wide enough. Ain't no valley low enough. To keep me from you...'

The radio presenter spoke over Diana Ross. 'We are going mountain climbing. A north Worcestershire adventurer is nearing the end of what is believed to be a unique challenge. Jonny Muir has cycled to and is going up the highest point in all the counties of the UK. Is this man crazy?'

I was about to be interviewed live on BBC Hereford and Worcester's breakfast show. Midway through that haggis pie in Braemar two days ago, I had mumbled answers to a questioning producer, assuring him I would be in Inverness where there would be clear reception on my mobile phone. Instead I was in Carrbridge, deep in the Cairngorms, where the reception bar on my phone danced up and down. I listened to the pre-recorded preamble.

'Ninety-two counties, 92 mountains, 92 days. Actually a lot of them aren't exactly mountains, but they are still the equivalent of climbing seven Everests. And Jonny says it's been pretty eventful so far.' The hyperactive voice changed to the pre-recorded tones of weary traveller. 'One of my tent poles broke during a storm, which meant I couldn't put it up. It rained non-stop for the first two weeks. I've had all sorts of weather, you name it – heatwaves, sunstroke, downpours. I've had to go through a MoD live firing zone and deal with swarms of biting midges.'

I was on.

'So Jonny, where are you this morning?'

'Carr...'

Beep, beep, beep.

The phone went dead. And there ended my glorious broadcasting career.

It was a new month and I was nearing the end of my long journey. In ten days' time I hoped to be clambering up the slopes of Ben Nevis, my last mountain. There were seven summits remaining, four of them Munros, all of them remote. First my route lay to the northwest and the lonely territory of Sutherland. From Ullapool, I would pedal up the west coast to Durness, before following the line of the north coast to Caithness. At Scrabster, I would catch a ferry across the Pentland Firth to Orkney, followed by a further six-hour ferry trip to Shetland, where – after 87 days of bearing north – I would head south.

Cycle tracks along what was at one time the main road between Aviemore and Inverness led me over the 406-metre Slochd summit, from where I was able to freewheel downhill towards Tomatin. I was making rapid progress, until close to Loch Moy misfortune struck. A Tuxford moment. Only this time there was no clunk or crunch. One moment I was pedalling easily with 24 gears to choose from. The next, all but three were gone and I was off the saddle pushing. Ruefully, I scrapped plans of reaching Sutherland's Ben More Assynt that day and limped to Inverness. There was no sense in getting annoyed. I was fortunate that the bicycle had capitulated close to the last major settlement on my route.

After two unsuccessful attempts, I found a shop where a mechanic agreed to patch up my bicycle within the hour. With time to kill, I ventured into Inverness and took up a seat overlooking the sweep of the River Ness to eat lunch. A seagull strutted towards me, feigning disinterest. As I lifted a sandwich to my mouth, the bird soared into the sky and swooped at the food, sending bread, bacon and chicken flying into the air. Before the contents had even landed, a pack of seagulls were brawling over the remains. Feeling like a little boy who had just dropped his ice cream on the floor, I traipsed back to the bicycle shop.

A mechanic led me through to the workshop with a grimace. 'I've got some bad news,' he said, in a tone that made me feel I was being prepared to hear about the death of a relative. In the workshop, my mud and grease-spattered bicycle was suspended in mid-air by a clamp. 'There's nothing wrong with the gear cable,' he explained. 'Something has gone wrong inside the gear lever and without taking it to pieces I don't know what. You'll need a new one, or you won't be able to carry on.'

I stared at the bike, letting this news sink in. I won't be able to carry on. 'Is there anything you can do?' I pleaded.

There was. An hour of emergency surgery later, I was pedalling across Kessock Bridge with an extra gear lever on my handlebars. It didn't look pretty, but this makeshift lever had rescued my journey.

The A9 was grim: swaying lorries and a cruel wind. I bridged the Cromarty Firth and escaped onto a quieter road to Dingwall, still 47 miles from Ullapool. Between Garve and Braemore, the A835 nosed through a silent backdrop of mountain, moor and loch. Ben Wyvis, the biggest mountain in the area, was at my back and only the Inchbae Lodge Hotel and Aultguish Inn hinted at any life in 20 miles of nothingness. The wide skies and lonely country epitomised postcard Scotland, but it was a fragile beauty. A roadside banner with the slogan 'Highlands Before Pylons' indicated that change was afoot. Giant climbing frames of steel, 50 metres high and sited at 300-metre intervals, were the threat to this untouched land. There were plans for overhead power lines to take energy from Western Isles wind farms to the mainland grid. The electricity would come ashore at Ardmair, two miles north of Ullapool, and pylons would carry it to Garve and on to a substation in Beauly.

Ullapool grew up in the herring boom of the 1780s and is now deluged by summertime visitors en route to the Western Isles. The port juts out into Loch Broom and I made the packed campsite on the town's western tip my home for the night. As I pegged out my tent, a luminous orange coach pulled up and 40 Germans trooped off. Springing into action, they pulled out benches and tables from their magician's hat of a coach. A curtain was pulled back to reveal an onboard kitchen, which started dispensing food. They even slept on the thing. I watched for some time, mesmerised by German efficiency. Two young women returned my stares and beckoned me over, clearly impressed by my English minimalism.

'Your tent is so small. Where are you sleeping tonight?' one giggled.

I'm in here. Play my cards right and I'm in for a night of German loving. It was rather forward of her, but a no-nonsense approach. I liked it. I needed to explain that if anything were to happen, it simply wasn't the British way to go about it sober. We would have to go to the pub first, get so pissed that we would forget each other's name and vomit over the harbour wall. Then we would be just about ready. I was about to utter some devastatingly witty one-liner when she slipped her arm around her long-haired boyfriend next to her, who from a distance I had taken to be a woman.

They were from Frankfurt and had travelled along the Garve to Ullapool road today. 'I just loved it,' she said. 'Nowhere in Germany is so wild. How do you say it? There is just nothing. I do not mean to cause offence,' she hastily added. 'Nothing is so beautiful I mean. No human interference, just mountains and lakes. Have you seen the film *Braveheart*?'

Never mind nouveau cuisine, fish and chips was the culinary choice of visitors to Ullapool. Dozens of folk were sitting by the lapping harbour waters using wooden forks to shovel down fish, chips and mushy peas. There were two chip shops in the town and fish wars had broken out.

First up, Seafresh Foods. Winning awards since 1999, it boasted. Even celebrity chef Rick Stein had revered its fish and chips. A hundred steps away was The Chippy. It had scooped the coveted title of Best UK Chippy, awarded by BBC Radio 4. Who should I put my faith in? Rick Stein or Radio 4 listeners? It was no contest. Rick Stein won hands down and I marched into Seafresh Foods and ordered cod and chips. I'm no food critic but the chips were better than the fish and I could have done with more. With a hole in my stomach I ran back to my bed to escape the gathering midges.

DAY 84 – ULLAPOOL TO DURNESS: 68 MILES
Ben More Assynt (Sutherland): 998m

Next morning I packed up hurriedly, gave my *Braveheart*-loving German friend a wave and made haste before the warden could collar me for the £9 site fee. I sat on the sea wall, eating breakfast, wondering whether the knot in my stomach was caused by a pang of guilt for not paying or tingling excitement for the day ahead.

Stretching from Dornoch to Durness, Sutherland is a vast county of black lochs and thrusting peaks. Perhaps the fact it is home to an army of super-midges explains why it has the lowest population density in Western Europe.

Tiny Inchnadamph, a 25-mile bicycle ride northwest of Ullapool, is made up of a hotel, hostel and handful of houses, and this hamlet became base camp for my ascent of Ben More Assynt. This 998-metre mountain, together with its neighbour Conival, is a gigantic dome of shattered quartzite – a daunting prospect, especially when I didn't have a map and thick mist smothered both summits. On my last four mountains, when their tops had been enveloped in cloud, I had found the way thanks to my GPS. Today it refused to work. I was effectively blindfolded. In Inverness, I had studied a map of Ben More Assynt, and as well as attempting to recall the contours, markings and potential hazards, I tried to empty my brain about everything I had ever read about the mountain.

I knew Conival stood 11 metres lower than Ben More Assynt and that a narrow ridge joined the two. But which direction was the ridge? East or south? Confused and unable to see more than 20 yards, I followed a series of steep zigzags across scree until I reached a pinnacle. This must be a summit I reasoned, because there was a small stone shelter and a smooth slab of rock, which had once been the base of a triangulation pillar. I had reached Conival.

A path led along a narrow ridge, which dropped away from Conival before rising gradually again, hopefully to Ben More Assynt. To my right, steep cliffs were too close for comfort. I couldn't make out what lay to the left. It was probably best I didn't know. It had been 45 minutes since I'd left Conival and I began to feel I was walking to nowhere, destined to roam forever, never finding the summit of Ben More Assynt. I turned the GPS on again. It still wouldn't work. How could it fail me now?

Wind-blown, cold and fearful, I contemplated turning back for the first time in my adventure. I had walked a mile, maybe two. Surely the summits were not this far apart? I must have taken the wrong ridge. I sat on a rock and hammered the ground with my fist. The summit of Ben More Assynt could be ten yards away or ten miles: I had no way of telling. How stupid I had been. Technology could only take me so far. To venture up a mountain in this weather without a map was lunacy. I couldn't bear the prospect of Ben More Assynt eluding me, especially when I only had myself to blame. As if pitying me, at that moment the GPS sprung into life, telling me I was a mere 300 yards from the summit of Sutherland. I made for one of the two rocky outcrops considered the equal highest points. My one was unmarked, just a pile of rocks, not even a cairn – a gloomy, petrifying place.

It was wonderful to be back in the warm valley, clear of the mist, cycling on a breathtaking stretch of road to Durness. I took it easy. The five-hour walk had jangled my nerves and made my body cry out for rest. It was a reasonable request. Since resuming my journey in Minnigaff, I had cycled and walked for 18 consecutive days, covered more than 1,000 miles and clambered to 21 county tops. Each morning, after sleeping uncomfortably and cold in my tent, I had woken feeling a little worse. Days followed the same pattern. Waking suddenly, usually cold, legs heavy like lead. The first few miles were hard, but cycling didn't feel like exercise any more. My body was used to it. It had become a way of life: spinning the pedals felt the most natural thing to do. Walking was the problem, and the 11-mile trip up and down Ben More Assynt seemed to have tipped me over the edge. I had worn shorts, so from my knees down the skin was red raw with countless midge bites, while my ankles were covered in painful, swelling cuts. The worst cut was on the ball of my right ankle, a wound that seeped blood all day, turning a sock red.

That night I resorted to a centuries-old painkiller: alcohol. I only needed two pints of Tennent's before I was in la-la land, flirting with the barmaid, chatting to the Japanese tourists and singing rather loudly on the way back to my tent.

DAY 85 – DURNESS TO STROMNESS: 78 MILES

Blue seas, clear skies and brooding mountains heralded an exhilarating day. Home to only 320 people and cast away on the remotest extremity of the British mainland, Durness represents the end of the road, 56 miles from the nearest train station in Lairg, but a million miles from the hectic pace of life in the fast lane. Down at Balnakeil Bay, I indulged in a little early morning theatre. Nature's theatre. A two-mile stretch of Caribbean-coloured sand stretched out to Faraid Head, where dolphins, porpoises and seals frolicked in the surf. The northwest tip of the British mainland – Cape Wrath – lay some 15 miles to the west, not far from Clo Mor, where cliffs stand 281 metres above thrashing seas. South and east of Cape Wrath is the Parph peninsula, a lonely place of hills, lochs and streams, but because of its remote location it is a favourite training base for the armed forces.

Back in Durness, even though a fine mist hid the hills behind the village, brilliant sunshine turned the water a shade that accentuated its Caribbean credentials. Were I an artist, I'd have pulled out a canvas and easel to paint the scene. Instead, I pointed my nose towards John O'Groats, pedalling east through an ever-changing vista of sandy beaches, high cliffs and rugged moorland.

As I skirted the perimeter of Loch Eriboll, the deepest sea loch in the UK and the surrender point for North Atlantic U-boats in 1945, I passed two cyclists with bulging panniers. A tent, roll mats, sleeping bags, pots and pans were mounted on top of their bags. Being one myself, I always wondered what long-distance cyclists were carrying and why they chose to make life even tougher for themselves. Every pound of weight makes each mile slower, each climb longer and each day more exhausting.

A slowly winding procession of floats – led by a pair of bagpipers – blocked the road in Bettyhill. The floats were destined for nearby playing fields where a summer fete was in full swing. A tractor pulled the first float, carrying children dressed as pirates. 'Pirates of the Caribbean' had been written across the top of the float, with Caribbean crossed out and replaced by the word Naver, a nod to the river that flows through Bettyhill. A second float was daubed with the slogan 'nuns on the runs', and half a dozen writhing 'nuns' waved their hands between the bars of a metal cage. It wasn't Notting Hill, but they were clearly having a good time. As I cycled away from the village, I could hear two girls murdering 'Flower of Scotland'.

I was drawn to the harbour in Scrabster by the sound of a lone piper. In a romantic scene, a couple were getting married on a lifeboat moored in the dock. They stood on deck with the minister, while their guests huddled on the pier, the piper playing in the background.

I was one of five cyclists crossing to Orkney. Three of them were a mum, dad and daughter from Hampshire, who were spending a week riding and island-hopping. The 11-year-old girl, who was also a keen hillwalker, told me she had already climbed 180 Wainwrights, and had been hoping to be the youngest person to climb all 214. To her disappointment, a girl from Keswick had pipped her to the accolade, achieving the feat prior to her 12th birthday.

'It would have been easier if we lived in the Lake District,' her mum remarked.

'You'll just have to settle for me being the youngest in Hampshire, won't you, Mummy?' the daughter piped up cheerfully.

The other cyclist was an interesting fellow, a Swede I think. Travelling cyclists have limited space and tend to cut down on frivolous items, but they will still make room for so-called luxury items, such as a selection of books or a video camera maybe. His luxury? A guitar. A full-sized guitar. Not the easiest thing to carry on a bicycle, so he'd brought along a trailer that he loaded his instrument into. He needed a lesson in English minimalism from the master.

Skuas and puffins soared overhead as *Hamnavoe* sailed close to the cliffs of Hoy, Orkney's second largest island. We were close to the dramatic Old Man of Hoy sea stack, first climbed live on TV by Chris Bonington in the 1960s, when the ship slowed until the engines stopped.

The deck fell silent as everyone had the same thought – what's going on? It clearly wasn't a plot by Scotland's tourist board to show off the Old Man. Speculation spread around the deck. The engines had failed and we were drifting in open water. Someone had jumped overboard and a rescue boat was being launched.

Expecting drama, the crowd was not to be disappointed. An orange life raft with three men on board was hoisted over the side and slowly lowered into the waves. The engine revved and it was off at a rate of knots, bumping across the water. It was not until we reached port in Stromness that we were told that two sea-kayakers had been caught in strong tidal currents off Hoy. They were well equipped but had become exhausted fighting the relentless buffeting of waves and alerted the coastguard. They were rescued safely, arriving in Stromness with a story to tell.

That night, four restless souls – two wanderers from Israel, a teacher from Cumbria and a north Worcestershire adventurer – relived their travelling tales and travails. The Israeli pair sought solitude and wilderness, cravings they said couldn't be answered in their home country. Unfortunately, they were having difficulty finding it in Scotland. The West Highland Way had been busy, Ben Nevis heaving and the Great Glen Way chock-a-block. They had put their faith in Orkney, where they planned to visit the islands in a series of day trips.

Romany was a philosophy teacher from Ivegill, near Penrith. Her contract had run out in April, so she'd decided to travel north. After driving through Dumfries and Galloway, she'd worked her way up the west coast and climbed Ben Hope, before motoring across the north coast and catching the boat to Orkney. She was booked on the same ferry to Shetland as I was, only her journey was continuing to Norway and the Arctic Circle. With a day to kill, she agreed to keep me company on Ward Hill.

DAY 86 – STROMNESS TO KIRKWALL: 22 MILES
Ward Hill (Orkney): 479m

The majority of Orkney's 70 islands and skerries are low-lying and gently sloping. The exception is Hoy, where the island's northwest is dominated by Lakeland look-a-like hills. The highest of them all, Ward Hill, rises to a modest 479 metres, but as our boat phut-phutted from Orkney's mainland to Hoy's Moness pier, the hill appeared twice that height, promising a momentous challenge.

Clutching cans of lager and rolling spliffs, the Israelis made off along the path towards Rackwick and the Old Man, while Romany and I followed close behind. The path cut a route between Hoy's two tallest peaks, Ward Hill to the east and Cuilags to the west. Tracks rose up the steep slopes of Cuilags, but nothing appeared to venture towards Ward Hill, so on reaching the southern edge of Sandy Loch, we began an exhausting tramp through knee-deep gorse.

Romany found it tough going. It was one thing walking along a straightforward path on Ben Hope and quite another battling thick gorse. Such a task required an almighty effort, for each foot had to be pulled clear of the undergrowth before being plunged back in, invariably landing on an uneven, ankle-twisting surface. Our pace quickened as vegetation gave way to glaciated sandstone slabs, allowing us to claw ourselves onto the summit of Orkney. The view was mesmerising, stretching across the Orkney archipelago of aquamarine seas, golden beaches and a patchwork of multi-coloured fields.

It was nearly midnight when the ferry slipped out of Kirkwall. As it was an overnight crossing, many passengers had had the foresight to book sleeping bunks. For the remainder, it was a mass stampede to find a comfortable spot to bed down for the night on the sofas and chairs scattered around the ship. By the time I boarded, for some reason last, there was scarcely a speck of floor remaining, let alone anything with a degree of comfort. Even then I chose badly, selecting a spot close to the bar and next to an exit to the deck.

I could put up with the inevitable noise emanating from the bar. The problem came when the late-night drinkers wanted a cigarette. Forbidden from smoking inside, they had to answer their nicotine craving on the outside deck, which meant walking through the door a yard from my head. To make matters worse, the chunky metal door seemed to close only after three or more meaty slams. It meant that every few minutes, not only was I woken by a chorus of bangs, but I was also blasted by a gust of chilly North Atlantic air. By three o'clock, I was too cold to sleep and took a walk around the ship. Passengers lay sprawled across restaurant seats; one man lay on a blow-up sleeping mat; many others had brought sleeping bags, duvets and pillows from their cars. All I had was what I stood up in.

Returning to my 'bed', I thought of Shetland. I had ten hours on the island – ten hours to cycle 35 miles north, climb Ronas Hill and cycle 35 miles back in time for the return ferry. Folk in Orkney had taken great delight in telling me Shetland horror stories, usually based around the infamous wind that buffets the islands. 'You could get two cyclists heading along the same road in opposite directions and the wind will be blowing in both their faces' was the best – and most ominous.

DAY 87 – KIRKWALL TO KIRKWALL (VIA NORTH COLLAFIRTH): 72 MILES
Ronas Hill (Shetland): 450m

Shetland lies at the extreme northern tip of the UK, a place where puffins outnumber humans 20 to one and in summer it is light for 19 hours a day. It is a treeless land where Scottish and Norwegian cultures collide and Bergen is closer than Edinburgh. Ever since Harold Haarfagr, the first king of a united Norway, sailed across the North Sea to conquer Shetland 1,000 years ago, the islands have retained a strong Scandinavian flavour. It wasn't until the reign of James III, in 1468, that the islands were eventually returned to Scottish rule. Today the names Haggersta, Hamnavoe, Hegliblister and Veensgarth scream Scandinavia. Meanwhile, the inhabitants of remote Foula, an island pitched to the west of Shetland's mainland, spoke Norse until the 19th century. Even the voes, or bays, that puncture the islands resemble the Norwegian fjords.

The 60-degrees line of latitude slices through Shetland. Following this line around a model globe I got a sense of Shetland's northerly latitude. Heading east across the North Sea it ploughs a course through the Norwegian coast and its capital Oslo. It then continues along the Gulf of Finland to St Petersburg and across the Central Siberian Plateau to Magadan on Russia's remote east coast. Across the Bering Strait, it continues through Alaska, Canada's Baffin Island and the southern tip of Greenland. A 2,000-mile hop across the Atlantic brings it back to Scotland. The line is invisible, unmarked and uncelebrated, but it marked the very limit of my journey.

As the ferry doors clanged onto Shetland soil I was first off the boat, charging up a hill and away from Lerwick, the island's capital. As the road turned north I braced myself for the wind. Shetland's relatively flat geography and lack of trees make the land very exposed. It was blowing hard, but to my relief it gusted across me, so angling my bike at a slant I pedalled along unchallenged. Nevertheless, the wind was whipping straight off the Atlantic, sharp and icy, making me curse the fact I had refused a lift.

Romany had tested my will to its limits. 'I'm going towards Ronas Hill,' she had said. 'Would you accept a lift off me if I offered? What if you couldn't carry on? What if the wind was too strong or the road flooded? Will you carry on until it kills you?'

I tried to explain. Our every day lives are governed by guidelines we set in our own head, things that no law or regulation can say is right or wrong, only a person's conscience. In my mind, I knew that taking a lift now would wipe out everything I had already achieved.

The road carried me due north across desolate moorland until I reached Mavis Grind, where only a narrow causeway attaches Shetland's mainland to the northern region known as Northmavine. Here the Atlantic Ocean and North Sea come within 100 yards of one another and signs warn road-users to watch out for otters flitting between the seas.

I had not seen Romany go past, so I was surprised to see her sun-bleached red Fiat parked up in the village of North Collafirth, the nearest settlement to the imposing red dome of Ronas Hill. Happy not to be alone again, we followed a steep, curving road to a row of radio masts atop Collafirth Hill. The road then petered out into peat hag and barren moorland, over which lay Ronas Hill.

'You will be climbing into an Arctic world, the southern edge of the frozen north,' an information sign told us. Romany opted to stay behind and I set forth on the 45-minute walk over the empty slopes of Shetland's 335-million-year-old highest point. The summit, surrounded by a protective wall of stones, was situated close to a burial chamber. I was standing at the most northerly point of my journey. A wooden box propped inside the cairn contained a visitor's book, something I had never seen on a hill or mountain. It had been left by Alan Ratter on 9 May 2006.

I was the first visitor to record my presence in 48 hours and only the fifth that month. I had joined an exclusive club – one of only 200 names in the book. As it was the

UK's least accessible county top, the majority of visitors were islanders. But there were others from the Scottish mainland, northern England, Cambridge, Gloucester, Wolverhampton and London. Then there were Swiss, Germans, Dutch, Norwegians, Japanese, Swedish and New Zealanders.

Many of the observations included the words 'thick mist', 'very windy', 'wet' and 'miserable'. But others remarked they could see the entire stretch of Shetland, from Muckle Flugga in the north to Fair Isle far away in the south. At last blessed with clear skies, it was the most wonderful view of the last 87 days. White horses crashed on the western shores. The sea around Sullom Voe oil terminal glinted in the sunlight. Foula rose majestically from the ocean. Beyond Muckle Flugga there was only the icy wastelands of the Arctic Circle. A walker from Lerwick simply wrote: 'Crackin' view,' while a Dutch visitor noted: 'This is what I came for. The top of Shetland.'

The views from Ben Lomond, Helvellyn or Goatfell have stirred the soul, inspired poetic words and life-changing emotions. But sometimes it is not simply what you see, but how what you see makes you feel. Standing utterly alone, in the brutal jaws of the Atlantic wind, nothing could match this. I attempted to draw every moment into my brain. I wanted to remember the ferocious wind, the overwhelming sense of satisfaction and purpose. I wanted to bottle this feeling and put it in a cupboard, so I could feel it again and again.

There was no sign of Romany when I reached Collafirth Hill, even though her car was where she had left it three hours earlier. I waited for 10 minutes and cycled along the road to see if she had ventured into the village. Wary of passing time and the ferry leaving me behind, I slipped a note under a windscreen wiper thanking a kindred soul for her company, and began the long cycle south.

Make no mistake, I was immersed in a bubble – and bubbles always burst. The bubble was my journey, dictating my every action, consuming my waking thoughts and haunting my dreams. Nothing else mattered. I lived for today, but there would always be a tomorrow. A tomorrow where I would turn a new corner, climb a new mountain and meet a new horizon. I knew it had to end, but the bubble popped with such vengeance it brought a deep gloom. I had already ignored my phone twice, letting it vibrate silently in my bag. I knew who it was. It was Rebecca Stephens, then editor of the *Evening Telegraph*, and she was going to offer me a job. It rang again. I picked up.

'Your interview went really well... I'd like to offer you a job... When do you finish?'

DAY 88 – KIRKWALL TO DUNBEATH: 47 MILES

Somewhere between the summit of Ward Hill and a hostel in Kirkwall, via Ronas Hill and four ferries – I had lost my camera. I was devastated. All 200 photographs from Minnigaff to Orkney – including proof I had reached each county top – were gone. The last place I could remember seeing the camera was Moness pier, but Kirkwall police officers searched the area without success. Before boarding the ferry back to Scrabster, I called the island's weekly newspaper, *The Orcadian*, and pleaded with a reporter to put an appeal in the next edition. The whole affair rather ruined my last few hours on Orkney.

Back in Caithness the sprinklers had been left on. Torrential rain fell and unceasing prevailing winds blew. Mulling over Rebecca's job offer, I pedalled the 27 miles between Thurso and Dunbeath at a miserably slow speed. In these desperate three hours, my world of self-immersion slowly collapsed around me. I admitted defeat.

It was Tuesday and I had to be in Fort William by Saturday morning. Ben Nevis was a distant 250 miles away. In between were four unclimbed county tops, each positioned in remote territory. Up to yesterday, I had been on schedule. But today's planned ascent of Morven had been aborted and looking ahead, the forecast for the coming days – more heavy rain and high winds – was atrocious. Cycling would be bad enough, but walking in gale-force winds on mist-shrouded summits would be ill advised. Was it really worth putting my life in danger for the sake of not being a day late? The thing is, it probably was. That's the problem with obsession.

FIFTEEN

**LONELY MORVEN – A STRANGER'S KINDNESS –
CARN EIGE – THE GLORIOUS GLEN AFFRIC – CYCLISTS,
MOTORISTS AND THE A82 – CELEBRATING IN THE
CLAICHAIG – WHAT HAVE I ACTUALLY ACHIEVED? –
BRITISH HEROES ON BEN NEVIS – THE END
OF THE ROAD**

DAY 89 – DUNBEATH TO BALINTRAID: 73 MILES
Morven (Caithness): 706m

An intimidating, slate-grey sky dawned over Caithness. Listening to the wind billow through the tent's outer sheet and rain thump on the roof, I tried to stoke my enthusiasm for the day ahead: an ascent of Morven, followed by a long cycle south into the teeth of a storm. All I could muster were feelings of dread.

As horrid as the seven-mile, rain- and wind-lashed ride to Braemore ultimately proved, it was a fitting prelude to the spectacular Morven. Apart from Ben Nevis, few other county tops dominate their surroundings so convincingly. Morven's conical dome was a constant presence in Caithness, unfriendly yet alluring. Adding to the mystique, I reckoned it would be the least walked peak out of the 92 summits. It may not be as distant from roads as Ben Macdui, but the number of walkers who come here was a stark contrast. While the paths in the Cairngorms can be like Inverness city centre on a Saturday afternoon, Morven would be deserted.

The road ended a short way after Braemore, where a sign warned: 'During August to January deer culling using rifles is in progress.' The sign instructed walkers to contact the estate stalker before setting off into the hills. Fearing a Mickle Fell situation, I knocked on the door of a house in the grounds of Braemore Lodge, but a man inside gave me a thumbs-up before I even had chance to speak.

Although I was standing only three miles away, for almost the first time since returning to the mainland I couldn't see Morven, for its cone was concealed by the distinctive nipple-shaped outline of Maiden Pap. As I made progress along a stalker's track, Morven reared up to the sky, its head in the clouds, with defences so steep they seemed impenetrable. After reaching the base of the cone, for 30 minutes I cautiously moved upwards, often on hands and knees, sliding on loose rock and wet moss. There were holes everywhere, big enough to swallow a foot or arm. Repeatedly, I fell into the invisible crevices, my heart beating faster as I feared the next slip would cause a twist or break. This was not the time or place to be injured.

Hauling myself to the summit, I took in the view. Commentators often talk about the UK's perceived wilderness areas, when in truth the UK does not have any. Morven was the closest I came to wilderness, a view more or less untouched by man. The mountains seemed to puff their chests out, some smooth green humps, others steep pinnacles. Brown veins of water drained off these high points into the grey ribbon of Berriedale Braes. Framing it all was a brilliant rainbow.

After trudging back to Braemore, I realised that like many parts of the Highlands, this 'wilderness' was fighting for its life. A campaign poster said it all.

> You are here to enjoy the pristine wilderness of this area. There is a proposal to establish a massive windfarm straddling the public road into Braemore. You will have noticed an anemometer mast on the way and the top of this mast will be the height of the central hub of the proposed turbines, some 400ft (130 metres) overall. Try to imagine how this will affect the amenity of the area.

The controversial plan was to erect 520 wind turbines across Caithness, and visitors were urged to sign a petition to prevent 'mass industrialisation of the Highlands through indiscriminate windfarm development'. Recalling my sentiments in the Lammermuir Hills, I signed.

After returning to Dunbeath and turning southwest, the first two miles along the A9 were the hardest (and slowest) of my entire journey. The wind was frenzied and merciless, thrashing me with 40mph blasts. Memories of wind-blasted days in Derbyshire, Wiltshire and the Southern Uplands seemed laughably incomparable to this. Testing my will with cruel hit after hit, the weather urged me to retreat to Dunbeath, to admit the gusts it sent forth were too powerful. Only once did nature win the battle, sending me flying off my bicycle and into roadside bushes.

Grimly I pressed on, riding through Ramscraig, Borgue and Newport, concentrating on staying upright. As I laboured up an endless slope south of Berriedale, half a dozen cyclists whizzed past, powered by the storm-strength wind at their backs – presumably on the last leg of a Land's End to John O'Groats tour. One shouted 'Good luck!', assuming I was just starting out. I hated them. To them I must have looked utterly pathetic, a gasping, helpless wreck, not an esteemed cyclist who had pedalled 4,000 miles.

As I paused for breath in Brora, a lean, tanned figure sitting cross-legged on a bench casually remarked he had walked there from Land's End. 'This is my 51st day,' he announced proudly. 'Three more and I'll be in John O'Groats.'

The weather – as it tends to be in the UK – was the day's conversation piece, and as two long-distance travellers we attempted to outdo each other with wild weather stories. 'I was in the Pennines, crossing Bleaklow, when a storm came down,' he said. 'Thunder, lightning, torrential rain. I had to lie flat on the ground for an hour-and-a-half or the wind would have blown me away'.

After I'd concocted some similarly outlandish story about being attacked by a swarm of killer wasps in the Cotswolds or having my left foot amputated after suffering frostbite on Helvellyn, my friend warned that the wind was even stronger in Golspie, six miles down the coast.

'Knock it on the head for today if I were you. The

forecast is better tomorrow and you'll make twice the distance in half the time.'

I shrugged, but knew there was no chance of me knocking today on the head. I had been heading southwest into the full force of the wind since Dunbeath, but I knew my task would become easier when I reached the shores of Loch Fleet. Here, as the A9 turned due south, crosswinds made life remarkably easier, resulting in a late-evening surge across the Dornoch Firth to Tain, before I finally pulled off the road in Balintraid.

A home overlooking the Cromarty Firth had been converted into a hostel, but when I arrived at nine o'clock all the rooms were full. Taking pity on me, the manager said I could pitch my tent in her garden. When she heard about my 73 miles of torture, she dashed upstairs and returned with her son's duvet. 'I can't offer you a bed,' she said. 'But hopefully this will make you a little more comfortable.'

Lying in the dark, I contemplated the last three days of my journey. There were three Munros to climb: Carn Eige, Bidean Nam Bian and Ben Nevis – numbers 12, 23 and one respectively on a list of the UK's highest mountains. Of the three, Ben Nevis was the only one I had prior experience of. Poor weather on Bidean Nam Bian, and particularly Carn Eige, the most remote of the trio, would end my chances of finishing on Saturday. However, at least today's dogged effort in reaching Balintraid – which had seemed an impossibility as late as four o'clock, had given me a glimmer of hope.

DAY 90 – BALINTRAID TO CANNICH: 65 MILES
Carn Eige (Ross and Cromarty): 1,183m

There were few days when my enthusiasm failed. But on this day, the 90th of 92, body and mind were bruised. Even so, it wasn't that I didn't want to climb Carn Eige, a colossal mountain that rises north of Glen Affric. Rather I didn't think I had the capability to climb it. The previous day's surge from Dunbeath to Balintraid sapped what little strength in my legs had remained, making the cycle along the Cromarty Firth and then through Dingwall, Muir of Ord, Beauly and Cannich, en route to Glen Affric, a frustrating slog.

A party of five Germans, who were walking west to the youth hostel deep in the glen, wished me well as I set out on the long track to the summit of Ross and Cromarty. But as my feet became drenched by the flooded path and midges swarmed around my head, I was overcome by a disturbing sense of unease about this mountain. Smothered in mist, which sat as low as 500 metres, Carn Eige was an unattractive prospect, where I knew conditions up high would be grim. Unease became dread as thunder rumbled overhead.

I walked as slowly as I can ever remember walking and rain began to fall heavily, great fat drops. It seemed to take an eternity to reach the misty bealach beneath Mam Sodhail, a Munro just two metres lower than Carn Eige. With a furious wind at my back, I half-walked and was half-blown along the ridge to the county top. There was no view, for I was surrounded on all sides by grey walls of impenetrable mist. I crouched behind the wall of the summit cairn to shelter from the wind, wishing I was anywhere other than here.

Beginning my descent, I followed a route between two distinctive boulders that I had passed a short time earlier on the way up, which would ensure I was going the right way down. I wasn't. Call it what you will. Simple confusion, tiredness or chastise me for neglecting to take a bearing from the summit. It was, however, a foolish error. Inexplicably, I was heading north, along a ridge that I later learned would have eventually led to 1,005-metre Beinn Fhionnlaidh. It was only after 15 minutes of wandering across terrain unrecognisable from the ascent that I realised my error. Even the fact that the wind was still on my back, when it should have on my face, didn't awaken me from my navigational ineptitude. I took the most sensible course of action in the circumstances, retreating along the same way I had come and mercifully re-emerged on Carn Eige's gloomy summit a short while later. This time I took a bearing and stumbled into the thrashing wind towards Mam Sodhail.

Time drifted by, but I was making steady progress, so much so that reaching the giant stone cairn on Mam Sodhail took me by surprise. In my relief, concentration waned again. Instead of returning to the saddle between Ciste Dhubh and Mam Sodhail, I turned east too soon, leaving me again walking across foreign soil. I plodded on, sometimes uphill, sometimes downhill. Occasionally, I would find a faint path, only for it end as abruptly as it had appeared, or I would lose any sense of direction and unwittingly wander in circles. In the darkness, everything looked the same: each rock, each clump of grass, each rise, each fall. Despite being lost, I had gone too far to turn back. Pride forced me onward, refusing to let me acknowledge another mistake.

Far from panicking about my predicament, I was overcome by a queer feeling of contentment. I no longer felt sorry for myself, to the point of being quite giddy and giggly. I unfolded a map, laughing hysterically, the laugh of a man gripped by heights of madness. As if I knew where I was any more. What use was this map now? I tossed it into the wind, watching it unfold and rise upwards like a kite, before disappearing into the grey void. A few steps later, I glimpsed a sharp drop to my left. My brain may have been befuddled and my body exhausted, but a shred of instinct remained intact. As a windy battering ram threatened to lift me off the mountain, I threw myself to the ground – digging my nails into grass, mud and rock – anything that was securely bolted down to the Earth.

It was then that I started singing the National Anthem, over and over again, taking care to say 'the Queen', not 'our Queen' in the last line. I don't know how long it went on for, but as quickly as it left my head, another patriotic song entered. I was bellowing the Flower of Scotland - in a ridiculous Scottish accent - louder and louder, until my vocal cords croaked. Now perched on a rock, facing the wind, I belted out the words to an invisible audience, orchestrating theatrically with both hands.

I was abruptly brought to my senses by the sound most feared by mountaineers – thunder. There were two claps, then a third louder one, which seemed to make the surrounding mountains tremble. I have never been so scared.

It is hard to explain the level of confusion and disorientation in my mind. The simplest analogy is to imagine your home with the lights off. Home may be so familiar a place, the centre of your universe, but in the dark it can feel like an alien environment. You stub your big toe on the skirting board, bang your head on a door, walk into the kitchen table, while fingers fumble along walls searching for a light switch you are sure exists. Now imagine being 1,000 metres up in the air with the lights off. There is no on switch here. The wind is howling. A suicidal drop could be a step away. You are scared and alone. You have no ardour left, for your energy source has seemingly been unplugged. No food. No water. No map. No hope? The only escape will be by virtue of good fortune, because eventually one of these paths will lead down into a valley. The only problem is finding that path. When you don't, panic sets in. Panic causes haste, forcing mountain wanderers to make rash, even life-ending, decisions.

And then I saw him. A dazzling flash of red and blue – another walker, the first person I had seen in four hours. Just 20 yards away, a man was walking slowly but strongly, a large sack on his shoulders. As I jumped to my feet, he waved. I saw him cup his hands around his mouth and shout in my direction. 'Are you OK?' he was probably asking, but the words were lost on the wind. I did the only British thing possible. I gave him the thumbs-up. 'What are you doing?' my common sense screamed. You will die on this mountain without help!

As the last red fleck of fleece disappeared into the mist, I ran. Finding a burst of energy from a crevice of my being, I ran like never before. Running for my life. Tumbling and tripping, I picked myself up each time, until I was breathlessly alongside him. There was a moment of awkward silence as I tried to mask my desperation. After a minute of pleasantries and bluster, I came out with it.

'I'm lost.'

He pulled out a map, running a bony index finger from west to east along a fin of high ground. 'We are in the middle of a wide ridge connecting Mam Sodhail and Sgurr na Lapaich,' he explained. 'The ridge slopes gently down, before rising again to the summit of Sgurr na Lapaich. From there, every way down is steep, but head to the southeast and you'll soon find a path. The mist is thick, but it's lifting. Once you reach 800 metres, it will be gone.'

As I write, I wonder if I did meet another walker on this mountainside? Was this chance meeting a figment of my imagination? Nevertheless, I followed the advice, and just as it seemed the world could get no darker, the mist rose, as if some higher force had intervened. The respite lasted only a few seconds, but in those precious moments, I could see the world had been spared. I felt the glow of the sun, watched my shadow return to the ground and ahead I saw the final rise of Sgurr na Lapaich.

I was dropping quickly now, the way ahead steep but not perilous. Still the mist wrapped itself around me. As I lost a little more height, in an instant the shroud was gone, this time for good. There was the most beautiful sight. Seven hours after it vanished, Glen Affric returned, a vision – not a mirage – of magnificence.

It was dusk when I reached the floor of the glen, where I sat for a while by the loch, half shell-shocked, half-elated, letting the midges swarm around me. Thank God it was over.

DAY 91 – CANNICH TO GLENCOE: 87 MILES
Bidean Nam Bean (Argyll): 1,150m

It wasn't until I glanced at a rack of newspapers in a Drumnadrochit newsagent that I realised 8 August 2006 would be a day written into the annals of our island's history. A plot to blow up ten trans-Atlantic planes, committing 'mass murder on an unimaginable scale' had been sensationally foiled. The story of alleged terrorists who planned to detonate liquid explosives hidden in Lucozade bottles was carried on the front page of every newspaper. Gatwick and Heathrow were closed, and there was major disruption at Belfast, Bristol, Cardiff, Edinburgh, Luton, Manchester and Stansted airports. The UK was suddenly put on 'critical' terrorist alert. So while I had been battling lethargy and thick mist on Carn Eige the country had come to a scared standstill, with an unprecedented disaster narrowly averted. It brought a timely sense of perspective to my adventures.

Questions about the worst moment or moments of my journey tended to be more popular than enquiries about the best. No surprise there. Our tabloid nation wants grisly tales of bear attacks, severed testicles and eating live wallaby. Who cares if everything is plain sailing? We want drama and guts. We want to be titillated and repulsed. So when asked the question, I would sigh, roll my eyes and give a thoroughly disappointing answer. Yes, I would recall histrionics in Okehampton, the putrid Mr Twit, burning thighs on Hardknott, midges in the Cairngorms, the Caithness hurricane and those seven dreadful hours on Carn Eige. Then I would admit that without doubt the most hideous, godforsaken time was the five hours I spent pedalling along the A82 to Glencoe.

On a map, the A82 – which clings to the banks of lochs Ness, Oich, Lochy, Linnhe and Leven in turn – has the appearance of a jolly cycling excursion, with much of the road following the diagonal line of the Great Glen. However, apart from twists, turns and low speed limits in Invermoriston, Fort Augustus, Invergarry, Spean Bridge and Fort William, the road is generally straight. Straight means fast, and straight, fast, single-carriageway roads are the nemesis of touring cyclists.

The previous 4,300 miles had not prepared me for this. In fact, cycling on three continents and in 11 countries had not prepared me for this. The A82 is a petrifying place for a cyclist. It made me wonder. Do motorists hate me because I'm riding a bicycle? It's not like I'm flashing at cars from the bushes or dropping tacks on the road. I may cause you to slow down, delaying your precious journey for all of 10 seconds. I appreciate how that can be mildly irritating. But, never forget Mr Motorist, you are commanding a monster, a killing machine. One clip from your vehicle and I'm as good as dead. That fatal clip never came closer than on the A82. Time and time again, cars flew past my right ear, charging at 70mph or coming so close my nervous breath would have steamed the windows. Was I invisible? Or are motorists prepared to live with the death of a cyclist on their conscience?

After 80 miles of head-down effort, I pitched my tent in the Red Squirrel campsite, a mile north of Glencoe village, and pedalled up the Glen of Weeping, so-named after the massacre of the McDonald clan in 1692. The clan had not sworn allegiance to King William by the due date and one February night his agents, the Campbell clan, had attacked them – after accepting their hospitality. Those who escaped the massacre died a miserable death on the snowy slopes of the Bidean range.

Dubbed the 'spiritual home of mountaineering' by Cameron McNeish, Glen Coe is a land of gigantic hills and mountains, separating Rannoch Moor from the banks of Loch Leven. On either side of the A82, the trunk road that slices through the valley, there are names that thrill the longing dreams of climbers and mountaineers, even humble hillwalkers. Buachaille Etive Mor, Sgor na h-Ulaidh and the Three Sisters line up on the south side, glaring northwards across the road to the Devil's Staircase, the formidable Aonach Eagach ridge and the Pap of Glencoe.

Bidean Nam Bian – the Gaelic name for the Peak of the Mountains – lay to the south, towering high above the truncated spears of the Three Sisters. My route crossed a wooden bridge over the River Coe, before leaping up a ravine to the summit of Stob Coire nan Lochan. At first the rocky way ahead dropped before rising again, climaxing on the pinnacle of mist-veiled Bidean Nam Bian, the meeting place of four converging ridges.

The grey cloak had dampened my zest for the climb, but as I returned to Stob Coire nan Lochan, the mist vanished, sweeping off the high land as swiftly as it had dropped. In every direction, mountains extended into the distance. Cars on the A82 were like insects scurrying across a nest. As the mist had lifted, so had the tremendous weight of my journey. I need not obsess any longer. It was done. I had succeeded. Only Ben Nevis remained. Halting at the heavenly top of Stob Coire nan Lochan, it would have been right to fling my arms in the air and dance a jig of delight. Instead, I pulled out my journal, put a cross through the words Bidean Nam Bian, and began the descent to Glen Coe, consumed by a quiet but joyous sense of satisfaction.

An hour later, as I bathed throbbing toes in the cooling water of the River Coe, nature seemed more wondrous than ever. The air was soft and still. A fiery red glow illuminated the sky. A curlew cried a loud 'coor-li'. The outlines of the mountains were as sharp as I could recall seeing them. If only I could always look upon the world with these eyes.

Those eyes were soon bleary, staring down at the bottom of a pint glass in the Clachaig Inn. As an impromptu ceilidh broke out, my mind replayed the last 91 days, my thoughts turning increasingly nostalgic with every beverage. Three months ago I had set off with the simple aim – to see the summit of the UK's 92 counties. What had I learned? That Boring Field really is a boring field. That it's a good idea to take a map up Ben More

Assynt. That midges are rather partial to my blood. But in all seriousness, what had I learned? After all, I hadn't discovered a new route to the South Pole, conquered an unclimbed Himalayan peak or rowed across the Pacific. That was precisely the point. What I had learned was something that couldn't be measured, proving – in the words of Sir Edmund Hillary – that 'adventuring can be for the ordinary person with ordinary qualities'.

In 91 days, I could have died three times, by stench, by Saab and by sustained stupidity. I had collided with a cow, crossed a military firing zone and walked in the footsteps of Alfred Wainwright. After 5,000 miles of bonking, cursing and changing nationality – with the occasional cycling and walking stint thrown in – my body was shattered, my clothes and shoes in tatters and my bicycle knackered. All courtesy of England, Northern Ireland, Scotland and Wales. Alas, I hadn't grown a beard to rival Messner. Nevertheless, I raised my glass to toast every mile of road, every summit, hill and mountaintop, every breath of wind, every drop of rain, every blessed ray of sunshine, even every damn midge.

DAY 92 – GLENCOE TO FORT WILLIAM: 23 MILES
Ben Nevis (Inverness-shire): 1,344m

I was standing on the rocky roof of the United Kingdom, the 1,344-metre summit of Ben Nevis. I could go no higher. Not that I could see much through the swirling mist. From time to time, shadows emerged out of the gloom. They were slow-moving figures who had slogged uphill for hours just to stand on this miserable plateau, where the year-round temperature barely breaks above freezing and the sun rarely shines. Walkers queued patiently for their turn to touch the litter-strewn triangulation pillar and – for a precious, unforgettable moment – stand on our nation's summit.

Where do I start with Ben Nevis? The ruined observatory on the summit? Its long history of ascents? The heroic meteorologist Clement Wragge, who climbed the mountain every day in the early 1880s to make weather reports? The insane mountain fell race? The Ford Model T that was driven to the summit by Henry Alexander in 1911? Or the sorry catalogue of death and tragedy? It has all been written before. Indeed, entire books have been devoted to the subjects.

I would prefer to pay tribute to the estimated 100,000 people who climb Ben Nevis each year, for no other mountain sums up our island race quite like this one. It is a symbol of the people who live in the UK, making it a fitting place to end a homeland adventure.

Three hours earlier, I had been basking in sunshine-soaked Glen Nevis, looking up at the procession of walkers who were striding up the tourist track. They were day-trippers with a trio of grumbling children in tow, a woman hobbling in stilettos, a gaggle of teenage girls in flip-flops, a man wearing only a nappy, and sweat-stained charity walkers who told me they had never climbed a mountain. Naïve optimism – two words that could have summed up my 92-day journey – means that we have mastered the art of under-preparation. 'It'll be fine,' we say. 'Look, it's not very far.'

It's true. Ben Nevis doesn't look very far. But even before I had reached the loch marking half way, bodies were scattered on either side of the path, their dry mouths asking if they were nearly there. They were nowhere near. There were miles and hours left. Still they climbed. The higher they went, the more agitated they became, the more they gasped for air and shivered from cold. Turn back? Never. Somehow, mustering the dogged spirit of Dunkirk, they drag themselves to the summit. Their knees are bleeding. They are reaching for the inhaler. They are bent double. All that effort, time and toil. And for what? To conquer Ben Nevis, to stand on our great nation's summit, to breath this high air, to realise anything is possible.

Back in Glen Nevis, I paused by a message board in the mountain visitor centre, where walkers revealed what Ben Nevis meant to them. Eleven-year-old Ryan had scribbled: 'Was brilliant. Took six hours up and down. Was my biggest achievement yet.' Sophie and Darren had climbed to the summit and back in seven-and-a-half hours, which was 'very good considering Sophie is asthmatic'. And one for the romantics: 'Ken and John. Climbed Ben Nevis – 22/7. Got engaged on the top.'

I added my own. 'Ben Nevis. The end of a 5,000-mile journey.'

In Fort William, I ignored the Grand Hotel, where Dad had booked us rooms for the night. Instead I cycled south towards Onich, unable to accept the end, unable to contemplate the last turn of the pedals. While I was elated to have finished, I was devastated it was over. Accepting there had to be an end, I returned to Fort William, spinning the pedals on my bicycle for the final time. As I halted outside the Grand, there was a scamper of feet behind me.

'You went the wrong way,' Fi said, throwing her arms around my waist. 'I thought you'd never get here.'

Nor did I.

EPILOGUE

JANUARY 2009

It could reasonably be argued that there are precious few adventures left to challenge us. We've circumnavigated the globe, conquered the poles, scaled the highest mountains, swum the coldest seas and crossed the widest oceans. We've skateboarded across Australia, heaved a fridge around Ireland, swum a 3,274-mile stretch of the Amazon, carried an ironing board halfway up Everest and cycled around the world in 195 days. Armageddon may as well come tomorrow. The achievements of our forefathers have left us idle, forcing mankind to live out an existence ensconced in front of computer and television screens, growing ever weaker of will and limb.

In a world obsessed with extremes – the fastest, the hardest, the longest, the shortest, the most audacious, the most ludicrous – we have seemingly lost an old-fashioned sense of adventure, when escapades were born out of Famous Five-style curiosity and George Mallory 'because it's there' purpose. No longer do children disappear on a day-long bicycle ride or spend their formative years messing about on a river. They are more likely to use a den to smoke their first cannabis joint and gulp from a bottle of cider than make notes on the surrounding flora and fauna.

The 21st-century notion of 'adventure' is confused. From humble beginnings, our so-called adventures have become a fortnight trek in the Himalayan foothills, a helicopter ride over Iguazu Falls or watching lions and tigers from the safety of a jeep in the Serengeti. Adventure has lost its innocence, its simplicity. Too often, it is adventure with a small 'a' – controlled, claustrophobic and costing several thousands of pounds, with any hint of danger squeezed out by the rules governing our health and safety era. These package adventures, with their meal-by-meal, day-by-day itineraries, epitomise our fast-food planet, heralding the death of adventures actually being adventurous.

Various dictionary definitions tell us that an adventure is 'a bold undertaking, in which hazards are to be encountered', 'an exciting or very unusual experience' or 'to run the risk of, to dare'. They are appropriate enough, but, in my mind, do not capture the essence of what is adventure. For that I look to Christopher McCandless – or Alexander Supertramp, as he liked to call himself – the young American who died trying to live off the land in Alaska in 1992. In a letter penned four months before his death, McCandless wrote: 'The very basic core of a man's living spirit is his passion for adventure. The joy of life comes from our encounters with new experiences, and hence there is no greater joy than to have an endlessly changing horizon, for each day to have a new and different sun.'

Crossing into the 'danger zone' on Mickle Fell. Fending off biting midges in the Cairngorms. Watching Atlantic Ocean waves break on a Shetland shore. Cycling Derbyshire's Snake Pass in driving rain. Seeing the 'whole world' from the summit of Goatfell. Those are what I call adventures – moments that made me thankful to be alive. I reckon Blyton, Mallory and McCandless would approve of that.

Who knows what the future holds? I could venture along the Silk Road between the Mediterranean and China, the hallowed Route 66 across the USA or the Road of Bones from Magadan to Yakutsk, but I don't believe I could find a truer adventure. What other journey could combine the frustrations of rush-hour Corby and a Lincolnshire cabbage patch, with the isolated splendour of Orkney and wondrous heights of the Lake District? Where else on our planet could a day's perambulations embrace city, coast, fen, moor, mountain and village, torrential rain lashing the left cheek, sunshine scorching the right? Of course, I'm biased. And so I should be. This is my homeland; nowhere could possibly be so infuriating, yet so enthralling, so extraordinary, so satisfying.

Still today – almost three years after I rode those first few tentative yet exhilarating miles east of Bodmin – I revel in the absurdity of a journey that catapulted me to the extremities of the United Kingdom, from Cornwall to Shetland via the limits of Norfolk and the coattails of

Anglesey. Will I ever have reason to visit the likes of Brechin, Enniskillen, Lampeter or Market Rasen again? I'm glad I've seen them – and a thousand other places, be they remarkable or unremarkable – at least once in my lifetime.

Then there was the danger. The UK's mountains are potentially fearful places, claiming many lives each year. I shudder as I relive reckless exploits on Ben More Assynt and Conival, or the confusion on Carn Eige that could have turned me into a statistic. But then isn't the fickle nature of these high places and the uncertainty they can bring the very reason we choose to go there?

As for the Specialised Allez bicycle that transported me 4,400 miles, I'd like to say it was stowed away, preserved for eternity in some safe place. Unfortunately not. In March 2007, I flew to Marrakech with the intention of spending a week cycling the high roads that criss-cross the Atlas mountains. It was in Marrakech that I discovered that the cycle's front forks had been snapped in transit from London. The forks could not be fixed – at least not in Marrakech – and such was my determination to cycle, I traded in the Specialised for a 12-gear mule of a racing bicycle that I immediately christened The Beast. Somehow this cumbersome, heavy and infuriating contraption and I got to Imlil, a village 1,700 metres up in the Atlas mountains and the starting point for the climb to Jbel Toubkal. It was a Herculean effort, but it did not stop me selling The Beast on my return and replacing it with a fancy yellow Ribble racer.

A month after journey's end, I began a job in Peterborough. Normality was resumed. My career progressed steadily, from a senior journalist to a political specialist, often putting me on a collision course with the local authority. By day, I made small talk at the water cooler, before returning to my desk to daydream about lofty summits and open roads. By night, I ran – a diversion that plugged the physical void left by 92 days of perpetual motion.

Each morning and evening, I embarked on the same half-mile trudge along Peterborough's London Road – a four-lane highway clogged with traffic and the seemingly unceasing paraphernalia of roadworks. The horizon never changed. To think the view was once of rolling hills, gorse-smothered moorland and skyscraping mountains. The thrill of uncertainty had been replaced by the dullness of conformity. How I missed waking up to a new dawn and not knowing what the day would bring.

During that period, I tried to keep a promise to myself, a promise made as I beheld a postcard panorama – a flaming sun, the serrated edge of Aonach Eagach and an unending march of mountains – while descending my penultimate summit, Bidean Nam Bian. So as I sauntered along London Road for the umpteenth time, a fine rain falling and the traffic building, I reminded myself to look upon the world with the eyes that captured those moments of perfection.

Fi and I reconciled. After two years spent in different towns, we lived in neighbouring streets in Peterborough for a short time while she trained as a teacher. Drawn to London, she took a job at a secondary school in Tooting. Repeatedly, I assured her I'd move to London 'soon'. Repeatedly, I reneged on that assurance, unwilling to surrender to the lure of the capital. Then, in August 2008, I finally took the plunge, swapping Peterborough for London.

With no home, which meant relying on the good will of friends, and no job, the following month was miserable. At the end of September, the inevitable happened – after three-and-a-half years together Fi and I broke up. The sting of rejection was balanced by the realisation that I was no longer on the relationship treadmill, or to use a terrible cliché: the world was my oyster. For a week, confusion reigned in my head. Did I try to win Fi back or did I accept that it was not meant to be? I could not decide, but there was one thing I was certain of – I didn't want to be in London. The decision was made. If I wasn't going to be in London, then I wasn't going to be with Fi. I accepted a job in Inverness, 600 miles away, and within a month I was living in the Highlands, a free spirit again.

There will be other grand adventures I'm sure. For now I'm happy to satisfy my yearnings with short-term fixes: dashing up Munros, pedalling along Scotland's west coast and exploring untouched beaches. But that Linn of Dee urge – the desire to walk away from it all again – still consumes my fantasies. There will come a point when I won't be able to resist it any longer.